T5-ARZ-685

THE ERRANT ARK

Man's Relationship with Animals

Books by Philippe Diolé

THE UNDERSEA ADVENTURE

4000 YEARS UNDER THE SEA

THE GATES OF THE SEA

SAHARA ADVENTURE

OKAPI FEVER

with Jacques-Yves Cousteau

LIFE AND DEATH IN A CORAL SEA

DIVING FOR SUNKEN TREASURE

WHALE, MIGHTY MONARCH OF THE SEA

OCTOPUS AND SQUID

THREE ADVENTURES

THE ERRANT ARK

MAN'S RELATIONSHIP WITH ANIMALS

by Philippe Diolé

Translated from the French by J. F. Bernard

G. P. PUTNAM'S SONS
NEW YORK

Translated from the French by J. F. Bernard

Published simultaneously in Canada by Longman Canada Limited, Toronto.
SBN: 399-11379-7

Library of Congress Catalog Card Number: 74-79644

PRINTED IN THE UNITED STATES OF AMERICA

Contents

Foreword 7
1. The World Is Not Enough 13
2. The Cruelty of Paradise 36
3. No Extra Charge for Lions 69
4. The Hercules Complex 98
5. The Secrets of the Cave 130
6. From the Minotaur to Mickey Mouse 147
7. The Blood of Sacrifice 168
8. The Synthetic Animal 188
9. The Horse with Five Lives 207
10. To Each His Own (Animal) 221
11. Return to Asia 234
12. At the Service of the Heart 249
13. The Prehistoric Era Is Still With Us 272
14. A Meaning to One's Life 297

Foreword

by Jacques-Yves Cousteau

THIS BOOK treats of one of the great problems of the twentieth century: the future of animal life on earth. It is a subject which is as inseparable from the future of man as it is from his past.

For 2 or 3 million years man depended on animals to feed him and clothe him, to sharpen his abilities, and to develop his intelligence. Today it is the animal which depends on man. To all appearances, animals no longer serve a useful function in human life. There is some doubt that there will even be room for animals on the earth of the future.

It is Philippe Diolé's thesis in this book that appearances are deceiving, that man still has an essential need for animals. And here is why he reaches that conclusion: In thirty years, there will be 7 to 8 billion human beings on this planet. The rivers will be polluted, the forests devastated, the seas poisoned, the air unbreathable. Man will be doomed. Doomed, that is, unless he has the will to allow animals to survive, free, in their natural state, in their primitive purity. For to preserve animal life is to preserve the environment; and to preserve the environment is to preserve mankind.

An animal is not merely flesh and bone, or fins and

scales. An animal is a unique composite which requires, above all, oxygen, carbon, and nitrogen. But it is also a being which is bound up in a system of relationships with its environment. Every creature is irreplaceable and every creature has need of nature as a whole. That is why species cannot survive unless the earth is free of pesticides, unless the waters are sufficiently clean for fish to multiply, unless the air is sufficiently pure for the birds to sing.

To begin with, we must understand our terms and our intentions. No one is against animals. Everyone wants to "save the animals." Many people work at it in one way or another. And everybody hopes that "something" will be done. This particular road to hell, like so many others, is paved with good intentions. We've put lions into cages, okapis into zoos, and black rhinoceroses into preserves. We take "wild beasts" and make captives of them; or, at best, we grant them supervised freedom. And thus, we turn them into miserable creatures, psychological cripples, sexual freaks, and, sometimes, into clowns.

We are all for saving the animals, but we do not know quite which animals to save. Wild animals? Tame animals? Trained animals? Domestic animals? Household animals?

The quality of human life requires that animals be free, just as it requires that man himself be free. Obviously, this is a moral point, belonging to the new morality of life which we have learned from the sea. We now know that animals too have rights. This is something we learned when we first dreamed of breaking through the surface of the sea in order to discover what lay beneath that obstacle to human vision, beyond that wall which blocked human destiny. In the depths of the oceans we found life existing in a profusion and a wealth of forms which man had never suspected. Thus, in the middle of the twentieth century, we found ourselves in a prehistoric situation. We were permitted to observe an animal environment as yet untouched by man.

Thirty years have passed since that time. Now, the first stage of man's experience in the sea, that of the slaughter of animals, is drawing to a close. All the films shot in the sea by *Calypso*'s team and by myself preach a single message: that of respect for life.

During his life on dry land, man, for many centuries, killed in order to eat. In the sea, face to face with a tame grouper, with fractious triggerfish, with an almost-human dolphin, and even with the yawning jaws of a shark, we sense the shame of killing; indeed, the impossibility of killing. Yet, it is an ancient belief that animals exist to be killed. It is not even necessary that an animal be edible to be slaughtered. The relationship between men and animals seemed always to end in the same way: with the death of the animals.

Now, we prefer to make friends of marine animals instead of killing them. Friends, I said; and not servants. Which means that this new relationship must not be developed for profit, for the sake of training animals to perform in a circus, and still less to take part in man's wars. It disturbs me greatly when I see or hear of dolphins being taught to leap through flaming hoops or to lay underwater mines. To my mind, these are violations of the freedom which is the right of our companions on the highway of evolution.

Philippe Diolé's book is inspired by a principle which is very real both to him and to me; a principle which is illustrated every day in the sea: the principle of respect for the personality of an animal, with all that this implies of wonder at the fact of life and of mistrust at man's interference in that life.

JACQUES-YVES COUSTEAU

THE ERRANT ARK

Man's Relationship with Animals

CHAPTER ONE

The World Is Not Enough

After all, is it not less necessary to reach an understanding of ourselves and to situate ourselves within a nature that we have created than to do so within a nature which has created us?
—SERGE MOSCOVICI, *La Société contre nature*

ANIMALS, like men, have a history, but it is a history which has been only partially written. Historians have traced the stages of domestication, the progress of zoology, biology, and genetics. It still remains to investigate the evolution of the mythical, superstitious, religious, emotional, arational sentiments by which man and animal are united.

Once, animals were feared; then, they were used. And now they are an encumbrance because there is not enough room for them. Food and living space is now as much a problem for animals as for men.

Ironically, it is at this stage that man, who has slaughtered and displaced animals and destroyed their habitats, now has developed a new affection for them. Many of us feel a common bond with animals, a bond based on a common precarious hold on life. What can the future hold for animals in a world which seems no longer suitable either for animals or for men? That is the question which this book attempts to explore. Man is now brought face to face with his former companions in creation—companions which man has rendered useless, has deformed, has imprisoned, has turned into neurotics; companions which man, as their master, can bring himself neither to kill, nor to set free, nor to reject.

Twenty-five years ago I visited a paradise on earth. There were no tourists, no great white hunters. This paradise was in Africa, at a bend in the Niger between Gao, Timbuktu, and Bamako. Lions, antelope, and ostriches abounded. The river flowed, slow and dark, past verdant banks, giving and receiving life. Hippopotamuses wallowed in the mud and crocodiles basked in the sun. The horses, in order to protect themselves from the flies and gadflies, submerged themselves in the river with only their nostrils protruding. Buffalo wandered slowly through meadows which, in the dry season, were covered with tall grass the color of gold or of wheat. Along the river there were tiny African gardens, villages of dried mud, ancient mosques.

Only those who have never visited Africa can persuade themselves that this river, these banks and reeds, these walls and gardens, have no past. It was there, along the Niger, that I first glimpsed some of the age-old secrets of that land to which I have felt myself bound ever since; that ancient Africa which, within the past twenty-five years, has become heir to the modern world, to technology, tourists, diesel trucks, and political and emotional confusion. For, like a vast arch stretching across the desert, the Niger turns northward to meet the first winds, the first voyagers, and the first ideas to come from Europe.

A quarter of a century ago, when one crossed the Sahara by the means available at the time, it was at Gao and Bourem that one first encountered Black Africa in all its sweetness and cruelty. It was there that one saw stately Sonrhai women wearing jewelry of gold, and there that the beat of the drums drifted hypnotically from the campfire into the surrounding countryside.

I was truly a stranger in that paradise along the Niger. I carried a gun; a big Mauser, noisy, effective. I used it very little. Nonetheless, I was at that time, I admit it, a killer of animals. Today I can think of nothing that I would take in exchange for the life of an animal. There is nothing that could make me look upon the corpse of some magnificent being stretched out on the ground, its reddish hide glistening in the sun, its white underside moving in a final tremor; nothing that could compel me to see it and say to myself, "I have done this. I am responsible for this irremediable disaster."

If there is one thing I remember with pride it is the hardship entailed in living in the brush in those days. I slept in the open air, or else in a hut made of red clay the openings of which were stuffed with thorny branches by my African companions to discourage curious lions. The Africans kept fires burning throughout the night. Beyond the red and yellow glare of the flames, in the darkness as impenetrable as black water, animals stirred, breathed, chewed on bones, and made our very pots and pans tremble noisily in the mess tent.

On those moonless nights, the earth seemed large enough to contain an animal kingdom as formidable as that of prehistoric times. Africa itself seemed too vast for us humans. The blackness of the night seemed to thrust us back, like the waves of some mighty sea, until we huddled on our island of dried mud, within our magic circle of fire.

When dawn broke, the savanna before us seemed incredibly bare and, so far as we could see, empty. There was only a limitless stretch of sand and yellow grass, punctuated occasionally by thorny shrubs. There was no road; only a path. We loaded our gear into a dilapidated truck and we were off—usually on foot

—across the savanna in the fresh dawn air. As the morning wore on, warmth seemed to rise from the ground itself, and by ten o'clock, the heat was already uncomfortable.

N'golo, who marched at the head of the line, was the first to see the scimitar horns, the powerful neck, the tawny hide, the black head with its two white crescents, the mane of the antelope.

The sunlight blazed down on us and the air shimmered in the heat. I was already picking my way cautiously through the grass, silently, careful to avoid the dead grass whose crackle would give me away. The antelope now stood motionless. N'golo was close beside me. I could smell the strong odor of his sweat. It seemed an eternity of waiting, yet it was but a few seconds. The Mauser roared, destroying both the silence and the peace of the savanna.

The antelope did not fall. Instead, it seemed that its head was raised higher, in proud defiance. I ran forward, ready to deliver the *coup de grâce.* I saw the bright eyes, the damp muzzle, the horns sketching a splendid curve against the sky. The animal began to buckle. Then it saw me and panic drew it erect again. It trembled, turned its head, and stiffened its legs to bound away from the alien creature before it. It was not the look of death which was upon it, but that of horrified astonishment. We stood under that sky, the antelope and I, in the middle of that boundless savanna, and it seemed that the universe was but a circle of which we were the center.

I knew that I had wounded the animal, though I saw no blood. I would have to finish the job, and quickly. I had aimed at the shoulder, and I knew that the antelope would surely die. I raised the Mauser to fire again. I aimed, this time with great care. My finger began to tighten on the trigger. And N'golo threw himself upon me and knocked the weapon upward.

"What are you doing?" I shouted angrily. "Are you crazy?"

In the silence my voice echoed eerily. Above all, I was afraid for N'golo himself. I knew what the horn of a large antelope, even a dying antelope, could do to a man. But N'golo was already upon the animal, his knife drawn. I saw the blade flash in the sun and bury itself in the animal's neck. Dark blood ran from the wound and a thick pool formed on the sand.

N'golo's voice was deep, solemn when, in anticipation of death, he pronounced the ritual words: *"Bism' Illah"*—"In the name of Allah."

The antelope, its eyes clouded, sank forward and then fell slowly to the ground.

N'golo had braved the horns sharp as swords, he had thrown himself in front of me because it was necessary that the throat of the antelope be cut before it died and that the sacred words be spoken.

My victim and I had not been alone in the universe as I thought. A god had interposed himself between us; a very ancient god, the God of the Semites. The same God who had commanded, in the Bible—and no doubt well before that—that no animal could be eaten which had not been slaughtered ritually. The death of an animal was not a matter of indifference to that God, for it brought into play the whole order of the universe. Under the African sky, in that apparent solitude, the sacred had intruded, and with it more than 4,000 years of religious history. If blood had not flowed from that open throat, if God had not been invoked, the antelope meat would necessarily have been left to the vultures; and the death of the animal would have been an absurdity.

The death of that great antelope marked the beginning of a stage in my life. It was then that I first sensed the importance of the religious ties which bind together man and animal; ties which, on that occasion, were evident with the coming of death. But death alone is not enough to conjure up one of the dominant and most ancient themes of human history. There must also be space. On that occasion, it was the almost deserted savanna, the domain of free animals, and that narrow circle in the center of it, the site of a confrontation which only death was competent to resolve.

Space, as I knew it then, has become quite rare today, even in Africa. To an urban civilization, to the finely honed Cartesian intellects of our day, the ritual and religious link between man and animal seems to belong to a distant historical past. It seems an outdated concept, a tradition long since abandoned. There are no longer temples on the altars of which bloody sacrifice is offered. There are only slaughterhouses, and we moderns prefer not to know what happens there. We are certain beyond a doubt that our attitude toward animals is unequivocal and quite honorable. We feel pity, occasionally, and even affection—the affection which a civilized man must have with respect to an inferior being, a sentiment characterized more by condescension than by sympathy.

It is easy enough to demonstrate that our reasonable and civilized attitudes are but a cover for passions and emotions which render the relations between man and animal enormously complex, ambiguous, and even unintelligible. Twentieth-century man, whether he is conscious of it or not, is heir to attitudes which go back to prehistoric times. Along with a vocabulary he has inherited fear, and respect; and these are factors which are the most powerful precisely because they reside in the human subconscious, unrecognized but nonetheless decisive.

Our essential error is to believe that our past is very distant and that it becomes more distant with every new generation. It is true that we now live in houses and travel in automobiles over splendid highways; but it is also true that we are still frightened wayfarers and superstitious hunters who have need of meat, and of fur—and, yes, even of witch doctors. We still seek the shelter of the cave. We are still afraid and we still require the cover of the trees to kill our deer, cut its throat, and thus encounter our gods. We still possess the patience, the skills, and the urge to kill; and we still experience the need to make reparation after we have killed. We can no more rid ourselves of these things than we can of the salts of all the seas which are in our blood. And these are the reasons why the amount of space which our civilization can make available to animals is one of the most important problems of our age.

It is a recent problem. The demographic explosion of the past few decades has suddenly reduced the amount of space available on the planet. Even a quarter of a century ago, the earth was still large. Africa, for instance, was a vast expanse, given over for the most part to animals. There they were free to live their lives in accordance with the territorial requirements of their respective species. They were free, not only in their movement, but also in their pride, their fear, and their secrets. They were still wary of the unknown and they still fled from what was not familiar—which was their means of assuring the survival of their species. In other words, they lived as they had always lived, as nature had intended them to live.

Now, only twenty-five years later, the animals of the great forests and savannas have been gathered into preserves and parks. This is for their own good, we say. It's to save them. Otherwise, the hunters would wipe them out. The land speculators would let them starve. The automobiles would run them over. After all, we say, man must progress. And, at the same time, we are moved by motives the nature of which we ignore, to feel that we do not wish to be the only species on the face of the earth. Therefore we take our animals and enclose them in zoos and aquariums and preserves. Then we go to stare at them. We look through the bars and into the tanks and we feel that we have accomplished something. We congratulate ourselves on having discovered a means of deriving pleasure and, at the same time, of soothing our consciences.

The confining of animals for purposes of display is not the beginning of closeness between man and animal. Instead, it is the beginning of a separation between them. And, even now, it is possible to divine what catastrophic consequences that separation will have for the future. There will no doubt come a time when man will live as a prisoner in his cities, and his green spaces and his outings will be confined to occasional forays onto his highways. And of the animal kingdom there will remain only animals which have been either domesticated or imprisoned (at best, in preserves), subjugated, perverted by captivity, obsessed by sexuality, dulled by inactivity, and changed by controlled reproduction. At that time the efforts of our society to divide the world between men and animals in order to make it livable for all will be seen for what it is: a trap or a hoax. Already we sense that we are losing ground; and we know, however vaguely, that it is ground that we will never recover.

Our remote ancestors owed their survival and their development to the animals around them—animals which were more numerous than they. The animals battled with them for space and were a constant threat to their very lives; yet they also represented food, and life itself.

The survival of the human species in prehistoric times depended wholly on man's ability to stalk animals, take them unaware, and kill them. The order of the day was not, "You shall earn your bread in the sweat of your brow." It was, "Kill, or die."

Man's ability to kill was probably an unconscious discovery. Man at the end of the Tertiary era and at the beginning of the Quaternary era (Anthropian, Zinjanthropus, Australanthropus) was already fashioning tools and going out to hunt. The Omo digs, in the southwestern part of Ethiopia, have uncovered tools dating back 6 million years. But it is by no means clear that at some point he had concluded that if he picked up a rock and used it to strike an animal with sufficient force, the animal would die. Tools were born in the human hand and of the hand, "like claws," as Leroi-Gourhan says.* It was as though the tool were part of the human body. Thus, there was born between man and his stone an affinity which still exists,† just as there is an affinity between man and animal. Or perhaps it would be more accurate to say that man, stone, and animal were all united in the work of death. This union endured for ages and it was modified only when human intelligence blazed forth. Until then, this union of man, stone, and animal was what conferred on man the mastery of nature. "The mind forms the hand," says Henri Focillon, "and the hand forms the mind."**

Man has lived his life in the midst of a world of animals. At the time that his mind was being formed, he was bound to animals in an ambiguous relationship of dependence. And he has never gotten over it. He was both the tributary of the animals and their executioner. And that is why it is not possible for man today to stand aloof from animals. Animals were an integral part of man's early life, of his basic psychological life.

Man's development through animal contact can be designated as neither primitive nor archaic. It has occupied almost the entire span of human evolution

*André Leroi-Gourhan, *Le Geste et la parole.*

†"A man who works with stone loves stone; and his love of a rock is no less than his love of a woman." Gaston Bachelard.

**And Immanuel Kant wrote, "The hand is man's external brain."

—hundreds of thousands of years as compared to an "age of science" which has occupied barely a century of man's existence. In order to be able to imagine what man's life must have been like in that state of nature, one must have spent a night alongside a water hole in Africa or Asia.

Today many of the larger animals are free to roam only during the hours of darkness. However, many of these same animals—the lion, for instance—must drink three times in a twenty-four hour period. Obviously it is impossible for them to do so when they must remain in hiding during the daylight hours. So it is that in present-day Africa more animals die of thirst than from the hunters' bullets. Every watering place, therefore, is a center of life, and there are many such, all of them different.

In Angola there is a pool of pure water. On its surface, water lilies float. I spent a night there, well hidden, downwind; the most memorable night of all those I spent in Africa. The animals came from all directions. I remember my astonishment at how many of them there were. Where did they all come from? I wondered. And where did they live? They approached slowly, very careful of their entrances, like actors on a stage. If a group of animals came together, one of them came ahead to sniff the wind, and the others followed shortly thereafter. Their muzzles dipped into the water and ripples spread over the surface.

Animals drink whenever they are thirsty, at any time of the day or night, so long as water is near and nothing frightens them. The horse-antelope of Angola makes it a practice to remain near water and drinks two or three times a day. Waterbucks, which give off a strong odor of musk, drink more frequently. The Derby eland, the largest of all the antelope, feeds at night or early in the morning, and it is late afternoon before it comes to drink. It is then that the pool is busiest, when the sky is blue, gold, and red in the setting sun. But darkness comes quickly in the tropics, and the water is soon dark and seems deeper than it is.

Drinking is always a hazardous undertaking for wild animals. With their heads held low and their attention occupied in inhaling or lapping water, they cannot be on the lookout for enemies. And that is a dangerous moment, a time during which they may be attacked. Though their guard is somewhat relaxed, it is never truly down. Their heads may be lowered, but they do not look at the water. Their eyes are always on the brush around the water and on the tall grass of the savanna. Nor is it only the timid gazelle which is constantly vigilant. The lion and the panther are as cautious at these moments as their less fearsome associates.

Of all the animals that come to drink, the giraffe is perhaps the one most exposed to danger. It cannot reach the water without an awkward spreading of its legs. It is unsteady in this position and it takes several seconds for the giraffe to right itself when it is through drinking and to move away with that disjointed stride which is called the amble. Giraffes never drink all at once. One of them remains on guard, turning its upright ears in all directions and moving its eyes from side to side.

Some animals do not leave immediately after drinking, but remain to play or otherwise entertain themselves. Antelope butt one another with their horns, and some of the males take advantage of the occasion to approach females. Waterbuck wade out into the water until it reaches their necks. A number of animals roll in the mud in order to rid themselves of insects and parasites.

Then, when darkness comes, they all withdraw—unless there is a moon.

Such nights are times of great excitement. And in Angola, on that particular night, there was a full moon in the sky at eleven o'clock. The water hole was in the shadows, so that I could not see clearly. But I could hear the animals in the darkness, sniffing, breathing, lapping.

At about midnight the lions began calling to one another. I heard their great voices in the distance, on both sides of the pool. They were hunting and they had no doubt caught their prey. But their roars were not frightening. Rather, they were pathetic, sorrowful. I knew that having made their kill, they would come to drink at dawn.

I saw the silhouette of a great eland standing motionless against the water. There were two females with him, or at least two smaller antelope. There was also a flesh-eater of some kind; not a lion, I knew, but perhaps a panther. A bird of prey passed directly over my hiding place. There was the sucking sound of a great paw being drawn out of the mud—a buffalo, or a rhinoceros. Then I heard nothing more. I must have fallen asleep.

When I opened my eyes the eastern sky was green. A gray brightness seemed to rise from the earth. Nearby, a dove cooed sleepily. I looked around. A lion was there, not thirty feet away from me—a very large lion, busily eating grass like a dog. His lean flanks seemed lighter in color than the rest of him. I could make out the musculature of his hind legs in the morning light. There was an animal smell about him, discernible even at that distance. He was an altogether magnificent specimen. As he moved toward the water, his hind quarters swaying, every muscle came into play. I could see the silhouettes of other animals at the pool: antelope standing in the water, a family of warthogs, an eland. They all raised their heads for a moment and then continued to wade about and to drink. The newcomer did not condescend to return their glance. He drank for what seemed a very long time. A lion requires fifteen minutes to quench its thirst. Like all cats it laps water; it does not inhale it as horses and antelope do.

The reason that the other animals do not scatter when one of the great predators arrives to drink is that there exists a sort of perennial, but precarious, armistice at the water hole, based on the fact that even predators of the jungle do not kill except when they are hungry. If a lion has eaten or if it is not actively engaged in hunting, the other animals are safe. When the other animals see that a lion is making no attempt to conceal itself they do not flee—though they do watch him very closely. Their vigilance is never abandoned, for they live in constant fear. Fear is their milieu, as water is that of a fish. This fear is at once a heavy burden and the basis of that intensity of life which develops their reflexes and their speed—that is, it accounts for their continued existence. I remember thinking of the time when man was also subject to that fear, and when he came to drink at the water hole with the animals. Like the animals, man once depended on a water hole or a stream for his life. For there was a time—and it lasted for many thousands of years—when man lapped his water or drank it from his cupped hand as gorillas still do.

Man has now emerged from the animal milieu which surrounded him for almost all of his existence on earth. But it was not very long ago that the rupture finally occurred. Until then we lived and drank at the banks of the same rivers.

We can only imagine what man's struggle must have been during that period, with the limited means at his disposal, to survive in the midst of a world of animals. Man's life expectancy was very low. Fifty-five percent of the Neanderthals died before the age of twenty and the large majority died before forty. Certainly, every human knew exactly what to do with an animal: kill it, eat its meat, use its hide for clothing and tents, use its bones and horns as weapons or tools. There came a time when man also began to make use of wool from the animals, and of milk; when he hitched the buffalo, the donkey, and the horse to his plow and chariot. But these accomplishments were more compromises than they were victories. They were accommodations, undertaken only with prayers, rites, and ceremonies designed to legitimate man's new power over animals. The gods had already begun to interpose themselves between man and animal; they conferred greater power on man, but they narrowed his contact with animals and they increased his dependence on them. Thenceforth, man—whether he was to be a shepherd in Mesopotamia, a charioteer under the walls of Troy, a Mongol horseman, a mason, or a builder of cathedrals—would never rid himself of his need for animals. He would have to accommodate his style of life, his forms of his civilizations, and his religious beliefs, to cattle, to sheep, and to horses. He would become less a master and more a servant.

Alexander and Napoleon, if they had been deprived of their cavalry, would have been deprived equally of their genius. Europe without oxen might well be a Europe without palaces and cathedrals. (The oxen who carried the stones to build the cathedral of Laon have been memorialized by carved images on the walls of that edifice.) And what would our Western civilization have been like in the nineteenth century if there had been no horses?

Now, within a few decades, the animal has lost its place and function in human society. It has become a vestige of things past, a witness to a bygone civilization. It is an anachronism, replaced by the internal combustion engine and by industrial technology.

Let us try to recall what a farm was like in the 1930's or even in 1950. Essentially it was a place of human effort performed within the framework of animal labor. Today it is a mechanized, electrified enterprise. What farm animals remain have been transformed into machines producing milk, meat, and eggs. Animals have been depersonalized, devalued. This represents a revolutionary development, and one which has come upon us almost unnoticed. Animals, when they were man's servants, imposed on man a servitude of their own, in that man depended on them for his own livelihood. Now, for the first time, man is free of that dependence. There are few farmers today who know how to care for horses. But all farmers must know how to maintain an engine, adjust a reaper, and repair a tractor.

In principle, this revolution should have had the result of freeing a great deal of land, land which had been devoted to raising feed for horses. Yet, the amount of available land has greatly diminished since the passing of the horse, and its production has become increasingly inadequate. Although farm production itself has risen, there are between 300 and 500 million people in the world today who do not have enough to eat—more than there were ten years ago. It is not that farm production has decreased. It is that the human population has increased at a much faster rate. So much so that despite the enormous amount of new land under cultivation in Asia and Africa there is never enough production to feed the millions of humans who live in the teeming urban centers of those continents.

The present crisis is not solely demographic, geographic, and social in nature. It is also a zoological crisis. As the domestic animals are being bred industrially, the wild animals are being crushed by trucks and bulldozers and threatened by pollution of the air and the water. Everywhere in the world they are decreasing in numbers; and, in some cases, they have disappeared altogether or will soon do so.

All this has happened in the past twenty years. And it has been in the last twenty years, as we have already noted, that man has suddenly become aware of a new affection for animals. This is no accident. We "love" animals more because we know them less. The prospect of being without animals seems intolerable to us, but we would tolerate even less the burden we would have to assume in order to keep them as they are. What we are attempting to do, in essence, is to reconcile our refusal to kill animals with our refusal to allow them to live in freedom.

It is only superficially paradoxical that animals have never been so abused, physically, as today, at a time when the whole world seems preoccupied with "defending" animal life. The explanation is simple enough: Man protects animals not for the animals' sake, but for his own. He needs animals to bear the brunt of his own hostilities and frustrations. He needs animals as a means of compensation for his weaknesses and failings. He needs animals as victims for the violence and rage which his inhibitions prevent him from unleashing at their proper targets. Any animal, whether wild or domestic, is able to fill that role, and it matters little what the consequences are to the animal itself. It is not rare that parents, by precisely the same means, destroy their own children emotionally, turn them into neurotics and psychopaths. And yet, children are protected by the force of tradition and law from such aggressions, as well as by the supposedly natural instincts of their parents. Animals, who have no such protection, fare infinitely worse.

Along the banks of the Ubangi, I once knew a young woman who was married to a European colonial administrator. There were serious difficulties between the woman and her husband, and these difficulties were manifested externally in a form which, at the time, seemed bizarre. Almost every evening, the woman attacked her parrot, slapping it with great violence. There was a great storm of feathers and much screeching from both woman and parrot. Then, when the ceremony was over, the woman would kiss and fondle the bird. It was not hard to guess that the treatment to which the woman subjected her parrot was that which she would have liked to visit on her husband, and that poor Polly was the husband's substitute.

The principle of an animal substitute is not uncommon in human history. There was a time when it played a religious role in that the animal took man's place as a sacrificial victim. The role of the animal substitute today is not entirely different. It represents in its owner's mind a person either loved or hated—or one loved and hated simultaneously. It is the target of human frustration and unsatisfied emotions. We may snicker at the idea of a parrot-husband; but the role of the hapless parrot was essentially the same as that of the ram sacrificed in the place and stead of Isaac.

Certainly, we do not feed, groom, and lavish attention on our pets merely in order to have something to beat. Animals have other functions in modern society. A pet, for example, is a sovereign remedy against feelings of inferiority or rejection. We tell ourselves: "I can't be all that bad, since my dog loves me." And, "I am certainly not stupid, since I've figured out how to communicate with my cat." We look upon these household animals as a means of strengthening ourselves in our good opinion of ourselves and of rejecting anything which would lessen our value in our own eyes. In other words animals represent security, and the more we provide them with this commodity, the more they render the same service to us. So we are constantly enlarging the scope of our protection. We now care not only for domestic animals but also for baby seals, beavers, screech owls, and possibly-rabid foxes. They are our security; our psychological defense against women who reject us, employers who do not appreciate us, our competitors and our enemies in the office.

At the other end of the scale there are men who need dogs in order to convince themselves that they are figures of authority. They either exercise a tyranny over dogs which they are unable to inflict on other human beings in their own families or in their professions, or they establish a reign of terror which, according to their own way of thinking, should impress those around them with the need for respect and obedience.

Conversely, there are some dogs who are assigned the role of giving courage to the timid, of serving as a pretext for contact with the exterior world. One has only to watch dog-walkers in any park to conclude that this is far from being an unusual phenomenon. In the same category are watchdogs and guard dogs, which serve to allay the fears, unfounded or not, of their owners. Dogs as conversation pieces and as protectors against the outside world are at the service not of the human heart, but of human anguish.

Man no longer requires bloody sacrifices of his age-old companions. All he asks is the animal's presence, the pleasure of its touch or its look, and, above all, total and constant submissiveness. Animals have become the antidote to all the evils of urban life; they embody the modicum of nature that can still be tolerated in our streets and houses.

We are creatures who love to touch, and our sense of touch is often frustrated. It is bound up with our erotic drive, and it is therefore circumscribed by customs and taboos. We cannot stroke someone's flesh or hair whenever we wish to do so. Here, too, dogs, cats, and other animals serve as substitutes. They not only allow us to caress them, but even respond in ways which seem to convey affection and therefore increase our pleasure.

Another important aspect of the animal's role today is its ability to confer a personality on its master who, like his contemporaries, is rapidly becoming less and less an individual. Everyone reads the same newspapers and magazines, watches the same television shows, goes to the same places. But when a person owns an animal, he or she is the only person who exists for the animal. In practical terms this means that the master of a dog owns a living being which is constantly at *his* disposal and no one else's; that he has an authority over the dog greater than that which he would be allowed to exercise over any child; and, best of all, he can be fairly certain that the dog will never run away. It will remain, as a witness to and as a measure of its master's awareness of his own identity. "I exist," the master tells himself, "because he recognizes me, and because, better than humans, he knows my scent."

The Dayaks are very aware of the extent to which an animal can confer personality on an individual. They designate a particular man or woman to be the "father" or "mother" of a particular dog, according to the needs of the man or woman.*

If animals have come to play an increasingly important part in the inner life of man, while their strictly utilitarian role has decreased to the point of nonexistence, it is because they have become more and more a source of gratification to humans. The proximity of an animal, its utilization for emotional or psychological ends, are the logical consequences of the long association between man and animal. Even so it is apparent that a new stage in that association has now been reached. I mean that, in our present society, with its constantly increasing restrictions on the individual, the animal has become an intermediary—as it was an intermediary for so many thousands of years between man and nature.

Its new function is therefore a continuation of the old. The old function of the animal was to provide a means of contact between man and the world. The new

*Cf. Claude Lévi-Strauss, *La Pensée sauvage.*

one is to become a key to a compromise between man and the material world, between a man and his fellow men, between successful adaptation and unhealthy, fearful isolation.

But the animal can also provide a means of escape from the world. Through it man can create a parallel world for himself, a world in which he can move and act without danger and without responsibility. A man who has been unable to adapt to his environment can take refuge in another environment: that of the animal. There he can live in accordance with his exigencies, his fears, and his pretensions. And there, deprived of the human contact which he has rejected, he discovers a universe which is only partially unreal, since it can be justified historically and socially through the presence of living beings which depend on him for everything and on which he himself depends for so much. Animals lend themselves to this game with varying degrees of intelligence and sensitivity.

Things may even go farther. Instead of simply possessing an animal in order to make of it an object of distraction or affection, some people incorporate it into every aspect of their daily lives. They pretend to enter into an animal world of their own invention, and there they find a refuge from their own world of grief and frustration. This, however, is not a flight into "nature." It is rather an escape into an imaginary world for which an animal furnishes a pretext and an occasion. This was the universe of Paul Léautaud, the French writer, who in his lifetime was the proud owner of three hundred cats. "The best thing about animals," Léautaud observed, "is that they can't say a single word." But since it is an imaginary universe created by man, it is the man rather than the animal who benefits; it is the man who attains what he wishes and who reaches a state of contentment.

But who can say whether, when a man faces death, a

parrot or a monkey might not be more useful than drugs or alcohol? No one has counted the number of goldfish, nightingales, canaries—to say nothing of cats and dogs—who have saved their masters from the agony of solitude or despair.

Even the most unlikely and apparently alien animals can play a fraternal role in man's life. Paul Pellisson, a seventeenth-century French writer, made his years in the Bastille bearable by taming a spider which shared his cell. And I have known many persons who love snakes. Patrick T. L. Putnam, in his camp at Epulu, always kept several of them under his bed.

Lovers of birds, of course, are legion. There is a bar in Hong Kong to which Chinese gentlemen come daily in great numbers, all carrying covered canary cages. Their one goal in life seems to be to possess the most accomplished singer, the greatest virtuoso of the species.

Finally, there are people to whom *all* animals are a source of joy. It is useless to ask such people why they derive such pleasure from animals or what they derive from the presence of animals. In this area we are dealing with an instinct which is the manifestation of that vague attachment that our society has preserved with respect to the creatures with whom it has broken off all utilitarian contact, but from whom, nevertheless, it continues to derive pleasure.

There is nothing simple and nothing truly objective in the present relationship between man and the animal in a world which has become too small. Animals, after all, were once sacred, divinized, offered in sacrifice. They are an integral part of our most ancient anguish, of our racial memories. I wonder whether tourists, when they buy their tickets to Kenya to "go see the lions," know that they have been inspired to do so by a long line of gods and heroes dating from dim mists of antiquity? We carry within ourselves a mythology; a religious awareness of the distinction between pure and impure; a perpetual fable of the wolf and the lamb which, unknown to us at the conscious level, dictates our preferences and compiles a twentieth-century bestiary which is in no respect less fantastic than those which have preceded it.

The great misfortune in all this is that it is this arbitrary sentimentality which dictates our choice of those animals which must be sacrificed and those which must be preserved aboard our crowded planet. There are no longer animals which are regarded as limbs of Satan. But we still make a distinction between "good" and "bad" animals. Thus, public sympathy is now extended to animals; but only to some animals. Gazelles are favorites, as are deer and roe. But frogs, spiders, hyenas, and wolves are among the species still viewed with indifference, if not with hostility.

What is new about all this is man's imperialistic desire to extend his protection, his sympathy, and even his affection to wild animals. Yet, it is because of man and his all-pervading presence on earth that these same animals are threatened with extinction. Nonetheless, man does not wish them to become extinct. Stimulated by newspapers and magazines, by radio and television, people are concerned over oil-covered sea gulls and salmon dying of love in the mating lakes of Alaska. They are demanding that laws be passed; that there be regulations and sanctions. But that is not enough. They also want to see the animals, to photograph them, and even—sometimes at the risk of their lives—to touch and caress them.

Man regards it as an act of generosity if he allows the animals to make use of a few preserves and parks. In so doing he does not recognize an essential fact: that animals cannot adapt to *any* space. They need a particular space, a space consonant with their special needs and their special place in the order of life. Animals are dependent on the lives of other animals to a degree which man cannot imagine.

Man shares that dependency, but he has forgotten it. He no longer understands the need which makes him dream of jungles and wild animals when he pets his cats and dogs. This need is a prehistoric vestige, one of many such which are rooted in man and which, although he does not know it, influence his attitudes and acts.

Man, as he prepares to take over the entire planet, is eager to lay claim to a nature specifically different from that of the animal. And yet, he still depends on animals to carry the emotional burden which they have borne for 200,000 years—a burden which is no longer justified by the atrophy of religious belief or ritual requirements.

It is time for a new contract between man and animal; a contract which will take into account the respect which is due to an age-old companion, a companion which was for so long man's superior in strength, numbers, and courage. This, obviously, is a moral problem. Man must either make room on earth for these creatures which he regards as his inferiors, but which he also regards as indispensable, or he must reconcile himself to their disappearance from the face of the earth.

CHAPTER TWO

The Cruelty of Paradise

To create a paradise—that is not an easy job.
—DANIEL ROPS

SOME 3,000 tons of live animals arrive each year at the airports of Orly and Le Bourget, near Paris. They are then distributed among the zoos, private preserves, and menageries of France. The animal business is thriving. Public interest in wild animals has grown considerably over the past fifteen years, not only in France but throughout the world. It is, however, an interest which combines sadism with affection.

Thus, lions are increasing in number around Paris, as are zebras in Florida and camels in Boston. But the attraction exercised by these animals over the public imagination is founded on a misunderstanding—or a hoax. The visitors who file past the captive animals believe that they are taking part in a return to nature and that they are escaping from their humdrum city lives. The truth of the matter is that the "nature" of which they dream does not, and cannot, exist in a cage. Few people can imagine the horror of existence in captivity. Few are even vaguely aware that captive animals are constant prey to psychological imbalance, sexual disorders, and a disequilibration of their entire beings.

The attempt to bring man and animal closer together could be the crowning glory of the twentieth century.

Instead, it has produced, thus far, only a superficial sympathy and a host of naïve prejudices.

The Sunday crowd files past along a dusty walk, pausing to stare into cages and enclosures. A wolf paces back and forth in his cage, going first to one barred opening, then to another, frightened by the noise, tortured by his captivity. A Derby eland cringes in the shadows of its enclosure. Lions yawn beyond the moat separating them from the spectators. The monkeys are busy picking lice off one another's bodies. From time to time they make faces at the crowd. Children squeal in delight and adults point and chatter, although no one knows what the faces mean. And, from time to time, the monkeys indulge in certain acts the significance of which is all too clear; and then the parents snatch away their children and there are muffled giggles from the very young.

This, generally, comprises the present relationship which obtains between men and animals. It is a relationship in which man, beyond doubt, is the more aggressive and the more foolish party. There is rarely a day at any major zoo that a visitor does not do something either dangerous or stupid. Despite the presence of signs everywhere asking visitors not to feed the animals, there are always some people who insist on throwing hot dogs into the hippopotamus' mouth. The hippopotamus, being a vegetarian, spits out the hot dog in disgust—and thereby sometimes exposes himself to a shower of other objects, from cigarette butts to cardboard boxes and rocks.

In *Captives of the Zoo,* Vera Hegi, a former guard at the Moscow Zoo, has some horrifying stories to tell of human cruelty. "All that is most perverse and sadistic in the dregs of any large city," she writes, "seems to gather at the zoo. Despite the strictest surveillance on the part of the guards, visitors constantly throw pieces of glass, nails, and pins into the mouths of the animals. Sometimes they spit into the animals' faces, infecting them with tuberculosis and other contagious diseases. Dozens of our monkeys die from such causes."

On the whole, it seems that the more vulnerable an animal is, the more it is exposed to attack. In the United States, the police recently apprehended several youths who, night after night, broke into a zoo solely in order to mutilate the animals. One of their victims was a fox, which had had its tail cut off. As it turned out, the youths were all the children of police officers. Who can say what resentments moved these boys to such an act?

How can we explain this compulsive cruelty, this spirit of barbarism always simmering just beneath the surface of a society which prides itself on loving animals and on expending a great amount of energy and money for protecting them? If there is an explanation it is that man's love for animals is not only ambiguous, but also ambivalent. Like all human love it oscillates between two extremes: the embrace, and slaughter. Assaults on animals in a zoo are crimes of passion in miniature.

It was not always so. Less than a hundred years ago a wild animal was an alien being, strange and fearsome, the object of awe and admiration. In 1827, when a giraffe was exhibited throughout France, the enthusiasm of the crowds was such that the army had to be called out to clear the road before it. When the giraffe reached Paris, King Charles X condescended to visit it and, with his royal hand, offer it a handful of rose petals as a snack. In that year the giraffe became, so to speak, a social lion. Its bizarre silhouette was reproduced everywhere—on ladies scarves, on posters, and even on china.

Today public curiosity about animals is not nearly so lively, except for marine animals about which, as yet, little is known. Animals no longer astonish and awe human beings. We have seen them too often in books, in movies, in magazines, and on television. But, above all, we have lost our respectful admiration for animals. In zoos, the ingenuity of the spectators is brought into play only to tease the animals and play practical jokes on them. With animals, as in so many other respects, we have succumbed to *hubris.* We have set ourselves up as judges of all things—and primarily as the arbiters of beauty, moral worth, and intelligence in animals.

The spectacle of animals in cages offers as victims to a vicious or at least misinformed public, defenseless creatures which become, in the final analysis, the victims also of a style of urban life wherein man, cut off from nature, delights in confronting, without danger to himself, the beasts of the jungle. A reflex action, perhaps also urban in nature, seems to compel city dwellers, when they are in the presence of animals, to comport themselves as though they were window-shopping at Macy's. They regard animals as objects; objects to be inspected and perhaps even studied. But objects nonetheless, incapable of eliciting empathy or understanding on the part of the customers.

Even if visitors to a zoo behaved themselves perfectly, their mere physical presence would constitute a serious trauma for the animals. The constant movement, the shouts, the children screaming and crying, the dust—and, above all, the atrocious human scent—are, each of them, psychological assaults to which some animals find it impossible to adapt. The animal, therefore, does not suffer only from the loss of its freedom. That is bad enough, since to place a free animal in an enclosure is actually to endanger its life. But it is also a threat to the animal's balance in space and time. Psychologically, the animal is demolished by being unable to flee man.

There is no zoo in the world which is not afflicted by a malady known under various names, but which can best be described as Monday sickness. It is as inevitable on Mondays as the peanut shells and the candy-wrapper litter, and it manifests itself on the part of the animals by listlessness, loss of appetite, and sometimes extraordinary hostility. These are the consequences of the human invasion, every weekend, of the prison-world of caged animals, in which the inmates are subjected to the insults, the ridicule, and sometimes the assaults, the right to which, it seems, the spectators purchase along with their entry tickets.

Certainly, it is not difficult to understand why crowds flock to zoos in their leisure time. Animals attract people because of their beauty, their strangeness, their rarity. Visitors to zoos are hardly motivated only by sadism. They come also because of scientific curiosity, sympathy, and instinctive tenderness. Yet, experts who have studied this question in depth are not optimistic. "The reactions of the public," writes H. Ellenberger, "have very little to do with zoology. They are basically irrational and express obscure motivations the study of which has only begun."

The attraction exercised by animals in zoos and preserves for twentieth-century man may perhaps also be explained by the fact that the needs of many people are not satisfied by a dog's bark or a cat's purr. A deep-rooted impulse sends them out in search of larger animals, of elephants and rhinoceroses and hippopotamuses. They would like to touch these animals; and, above all, they would like to protect them as indisputable embodiments of that wild life which they know is threatened from all sides. And the larger the animal the greater the curiosity manifested and the greater the protection offered. There seems to be a direct correlation between the size of the animal and the amount of satisfaction derived by man from his sentiments toward that animal. It is regarded as more meritorious, for example, to be interested in protecting elephants than in feeding pigeons.

Bernard Grzimek, director of the famed Frankfurt

Zoo, has made an interesting observation regarding visitors to his institution. A zoo, he says, is a theater of reciprocal exhibitionism. According to him, it is man who is the aggressive exhibitionist, who tries to attract the attention of the other party—in this case, the animal. Man, in a striking manifestation of human vanity, cannot tolerate that the animals ignore him and continue feeding or sleeping. If they do so, the human being becomes angry and quickly concludes that the hippopotamus or the crocodile is stupid. And sometimes he throws stones at the animal to remind it of the respect and admiration which it is required to show toward man. On the other hand the animals that usually beg for food—monkeys and bears, for instance—are always greatly admired by visitors.

There is a sort of primitive distinction between "good" and "bad" which seems to impel such visitors to keep their sympathy, and their gifts of hot dogs and peanuts, for animals which "deserve it." The quality in a particular animal which visitors regard as deserving is known to zoo personnel as that animal's exhibition value. There are distinct categories of animals according to this moral pecking order, and the first of these divides the animal kingdom into carnivores and herbivores, or flesh-eaters and vegetarians. Herbivores are regarded as nice; carnivores, as ferocious. The problem is that the reality of the animals often does not conform to this facile distinction, and that the ideas which people bring with them when they visit zoos are often wrong. Bears are usually regarded as good animals whereas in fact they are extremely dangerous; and wolves, which are thought of as ferocious, are quite easy to tame. By the same token, spectators are always delighted by the sight of roe deer and antelope—both of which are capable of inflicting serious injury. And they shudder before the cheetah, although the instances in which this large cat has attacked human beings are extremely rare. Occasionally, this fairy-tale approach to the character of particular animals leads to trouble. In the Opel Zoo, in Germany, a visitor climbed into the enclosure of some Cape eland to take photographs of these "nice" animals. He was no sooner within the enclosure than a large male lowered its head, as though to bow before the intruder. Then, with its horns—which were almost two feet long—it began gently to prod the photographer. A guard arrived in time to prevent the eland from reaching the next stage in its attack. "What the photographer did not know," explains Vitus B. Dröscher, who wrote an account of the incident, "is that when a Cape eland wags its tail, spreads its ears, and bows, it is not being friendly. And when this large male tapped the man's body with its horns, it was looking for the proper spot to strike—either there, between the ribs, or in the stomach."

Visitors to zoos make mistakes at the practical as well as the moral level. They take great pleasure in stuffing very young animals, which are still breast-feeding, with such things as bread, while ignoring the adult animals. As it happens, baby animals cannot digest any solid food, while the full-grown animals could digest it readily. Such mistakes sometimes have disastrous consequences. It happens not infrequently that the adult animals, the parents of the young animals who are being fed, become jealous and resentful of their offspring; and, in the case of antelope, it also happens that the parents strike them with their horns, chase them, and occasionally even kill them.

Another aspect of the mutual exhibitionism common in zoos is the sense of vicarious violence inspired in visitors by some of the great carnivores. From the safety of their own side of the bars, people are able to enjoy the bloody spectacle of a lion or tiger tearing apart a quarter of beef. For this reason zoos are compelled to feed the carnivores once a day—even those carnivores which, in their natural habitat, eat only once or twice a week. Feeding time is always an attraction and the times are often announced so as to attract the greatest possible number of people.

There are visitors to zoos who, standing before the cage of a pacing lion or tiger, can sense the true horror of life in captivity. The vast majority, however, believe—and this is the great misunderstanding—that zoos provide animals with a paradise on earth where they are fed and cared for, where they are no longer required to struggle in order to survive, and where, therefore, they are happy.

The basis of this misunderstanding lies in our very nebulous concept of what constitutes happiness for an animal. There is in fact no way to effect a reconciliation between the physical and psychological needs of animals on the one hand and the limited space and constant human presence in zoos on the other.

It has been discovered in the past twenty years that animals in captivity are not happy even if we give them more living space. And yet everyone from zoologists to the general public protests that he has only the happiness of the animals at heart. The fact is that captive animals are subject to many illnesses and not all these illnesses are physical in origin. There are numerous symptoms of psychological disease: Animals bite themselves, tear off pieces of their hides, mutilate themselves, or, more simply, sink into the torpor of melancholy and sometimes into madness. Cases of serious self-mutilation are numerous. Chimpanzees insert pieces of straw deep into their ears until they succeed in piercing their eardrums. Gorillas bite their feet. Bears spin in circles until they become dizzy, bite their claws until they bleed, and occasionally attack their keepers.

Public opinion rebels against the idea of concentration camps and it rejects those aspects of prison life which degrade the human personality. More and more it seems difficult to justify restrictions on the liberties of human beings. Yet, few people acknowledge that animal captivity is also an essentially moral problem, not only because of the extreme limitation of the animals' living space, but also and especially because of the radical change in life-style which it entails and the interior upheaval, leading to psychological disintegration, which it causes.

The chief problem has to do with the love life of the animals. In captivity a male and female are perforce mated for life, whereas in nature their union would last for only a single season. Occasionally this enforced monogamy results in the development of visible tenderness on the part of the two animals for each other; but sometimes it ends with them showing genuine hatred for each other—so much so that they must then be separated. This seems to be true especially among hippopotamuses.

The fact that the space in a zoo is so limited makes it impossible for animals to flee from one another, and this too works a drastic change in their lives. In their natural state it is rare that two males will fight to the death for possession of a female. In zoos, however, this happens quite frequently among antelope and zebras.

It is common knowledge that the human inmates of our prisons are often obsessed with sex. It is no less true of the inmates of our zoos. Isolated and inactive beings, whether they be humans or animals, are prey to the same afflictions, and one of the most unpleasant of these is that state of hypersexuality provoked by abnormal confinement. Most inmates of zoos masturbate, sometimes by the most imaginative methods. Monkeys in cages masturbate so frequently and in such strange ways—some use the tips of their prehensile tails—that the public has come to believe that this is their normal behavior. The truth is that monkeys living in freedom have never been observed to masturbate. In captivity, even elephants masturbate, using the ends of their trunks; and lions, with their paws. And, needless to say, homosexuality is as common in zoos as in human prisons.

In these circumstances, animals, like humans, often take refuge in dreams. Desmond Morris, in *The Human Zoo*, tells us that captive cats have been known to have nocturnal emissions.

The sexual life of animals is most readily observable in the spring. It is then that the urge to mate sweeps through our zoos and preserves; and it is then, too, that one can sense the embarrassment of the animals—many of them are quite modest—in courting and copulating in public. There is no help for it, of course, since no space is provided for them to withdraw and pursue their idyll in peace.

I once visited the zoo at Vincennes on a weekday. The sun was shining, the air was fresh, and spring was everywhere. There were few visitors that day, and the season, combined with the relative lack of human observers, incited the animals to follow their reproductive instinct. The sight was a moving one. The great elephants began by striking their massive foreheads gently together and intertwining their trunks. The lion tried to persuade the reluctant lioness to consent by alternating persuasive oars with angry rumbles. But the most surprising animals were the giraffes, who intertwined their incredible necks with unexpected grace and ease, momentarily assuming the appearance of monstrous figures from an antique Iranian bas-relief.

If life in a zoo does not lend itself readily to mating, it lends itself even less to the rearing of offspring. Many females are visibly troubled by having to rear their young in a cage, within sight of spectators. This is especially true of the great cats: lions, tigers, and panthers. These carnivores are often accused of being bad parents, and it is undeniable that they sometimes eat their young. The fault, however, is not that of the cats, but of their unnatural environment. In the jungle a mother lion, when she is about to give birth, goes off alone and seeks out a spot as isolated as possible in which to bring forth her young. There, she hides her cubs, nurses them, and later brings them their first meat. She is, in other words, an excellent mother. But in a cage, she must remain constantly within sight of the public. She hears human voices continually. She cannot go off alone, nor can she hide her young from humans. In a panic, she picks up the cubs in her jaws and carries them from one corner of the cage to another and back again. Occasionally, in her rage and frustration, she bites them or even devours them. And the reason for this unnatural violence is the unnatural conditions in which captive felines are compelled to live and bear their young.

It has not been many years that experts have realized that mothers must have isolation in order to bear and rear their young, and they now attempt to provide some spot where the mother cat can conceal herself and her family.

The world of animals in captivity offers us at once a prophetic glimpse and a caricature of the world in which modern man lives out his life. The animal suffers psychologically and his suffering is not unlike that of man himself, since its world is characterized by deterioration of its environment and by its own degradation. The causes are the same in both cases: the increase in the number of individuals occupying a limited amount of space and the necessity for existing in a society in conflict with nature. Just as men occasionally reject society and retreat into a misanthropic solitude which sometimes impels them to murder, so, too, animals in a zoo—baboons, for example—suffer from, and are deformed by, lack of sufficient space for them to lead a harmonious social existence. When captivity has done its work and an animal has become truly dangerous, it then becomes necessary to isolate it in a cage of its own. The effect of such an existence on an animal was recorded by Dr. Henri Hediger, director of the Zurich Zoo, who relates the story of a white bear donated to the zoo by a circus. The animal had spent all its life in a small circus cage. When it arrived at the zoo, it was placed within an enclosure, but a vast enclosure, with space for it to roam. The animal seemed unaware that it was no longer locked in a cage. It immediately began to walk in a tiny circle—a circle no larger than the cage it had inhabited in the circus. Days passed, then months, then years, and still the bear walked in its circle. By then, its feet had pounded holes into the ground, for it placed its paws in precisely the same spot on each of its rounds. Everything was tried, but it proved impossible to free the bear from the circle which had been created for it in the circus cage, and which it had later recreated for itself within the enclosure. The bear had been transformed by its existence in a cage from an animal into a robot, and a neurotic robot at that, which it was impossible to reprogram.

Obviously, this is an extreme example. Most zoo directors will affirm, quite honestly, that their animals are not unhappy. What they should say instead is that they do everything they can to assure that the animals will not be unhappy. What they cannot do, however, is to spare their animals the suffering they experience from the sight, scent, and constant presence of human beings. There are some animals, of course, less susceptible to human presence than others. Antelope, for example—which are easily domesticated—as well as cheetahs, civet cats, and weasels. The reaction of most animals, however, ranges from apathy to nostalgia, from aggressivity to a craving for affection.

The zoological garden at Colombo, Ceylon, is undoubtedly among the world's finest. It is landscaped with lovely trees bearing fragrant blossoms and with such tropical plants as bougainvillea, hibiscus and exquisitely scented red jasmine. The animals are numerous and well cared for. Yet, both my wife and I came away from the animals with the same impression of deep sadness. I think that the tigers, especially, were pitiful. It is true that they were handsome specimens, well fed, in excellent physical condition, their coats shining in the sun; but when we saw these magnificent creatures, they were lying on a concrete slab at the bottom of a pit. I know that such pits are more sanitary and easy to clean, but how profoundly sad it was to know that those great muscles and claws would never be used again, that their paws would never again feel the soft earth beneath them, that their coats would never again touch the leaves of the jungle.

There are also two splendid gorillas at the Colombo Zoo. When we saw them they had apparently reached an irreversible decision. They had turned their backs to the public and remained in that position, immobile, as though they were being punished for something they had done.

It is impossible to keep an animal in captivity and at the same time to spare it the trauma of captivity, for this trauma is a necessary concomitant of the transfer of the animal from its own world to another, completely alien world. In its natural habitat an animal is wholly subject to a form of existence which combines space and time into a single, immutable complex. The whole life of the animal is programmed, regulated. Its living space is strictly set out, but it is vastly different from the sort of space available to it in a zoo. The boundaries of the animal's living space in nature—which it defends, sometimes with its life—are established in conformity with the amount of food available in the area, with the nature of the terrain, the location of water holes, the number of streams and rivers, and with the animal's own reproductive needs. Its relations with other inhabitants of the area are regulated by an etiquette stricter than any dreamed of by the most exacting dowager at the court of Louis XIV. All these are factors which maintain the psychological balance of the animal, and all these are factors which cannot be reproduced, and for which there is no substitute in captivity.

It is not surprising, therefore, that wild animals are totally deformed by captivity. This is a fact of which some directors of zoos are cognizant, and, for this reason, some of them argue that only tame animals should be confined in zoos. Their reasoning is that animals which have been tamed tend to reproduce, within their enclosures, the space-time conditions which regulated their activity while they were free. In other words they would make of their prisons a sort of miniterritory, with as many of the accoutrements as they could manage to duplicate in one form or another. They argue that the animals would then adapt to captivity. But this adaptation leads to the creation of a new kind of animal, one which stands midway between wild animals and domestic animals. Such animals —monkeys, rhinoceroses, and bears, for example—make refuges for themselves, invent pastimes, and even devise practical jokes. For monkeys the favorite game is to hold water in their mouths and then spit it on some unwary spectator. And some lions find it amusing to urinate on visitors who come close enough to their cages to be within range. These "jokes" are, in fact, methods of delineating territory and are designed to dissuade intruders—in this case the intruder being man.

There are some animals incapable of devising pastimes to lighten their captivity. They become torpid and melancholy if they are confined alone, but they seem to enjoy the company of other animals, regardless of the species of animal with which they share their enclosure. R. G. Schillings, the director of a German zoo, put a pair of goats into the enclosure of a rhinoceros suffering from depression. The presence of these animals had its effect, and the rhinoceros quickly regained its zest for life as well as its good humor.

In order to give captive animals something to occupy their time, some zoos provide them with toys. Zoo personnel have learned from experience that much care must be exercised in the choice of such toys. For example, monkeys who had been given sticks to play with soon devised a game of their own: They threw the sticks at spectators. At the St. Louis Zoo, the monkeys have been given electric automobiles with which to amuse themselves, and they have become very adept at handling them, both in forward gear and in reverse. The director of the zoo at Basel faced a special problem when his prize Sumatran rhinoceros, a very rare animal, showed signs of depression and boredom. He had a large rubber ball made, weighing 100 pounds. The animal gave every sign of being delighted with the ball, throwing it against the bars and walls and, despite its 4,000-pound bulk, leaping about with the agility of a mountain goat.

Even human beings can provide needed companionship to wild animals. François Pompon, a famous French sculptor of animals, made daily pilgrimages to the Jardin des Plantes or the Jardin d'Acclimatation in Paris, merely to visit the animals. His presence had a notably soothing effect upon them. It was said that he could speak with the animals, and certainly he had a way with them, for he was amazingly successful in persuading animals to maintain a pose for long periods of time. The animals came to recognize him and acknowledged his presence with roars and other sounds unintelligible to those less gifted than Pompon. Yet the artist never fed the animals. He only spoke to them, in a soft, affectionate voice. When someone asked him how he had been able to win their confidence and affection, Pompon replied: "We have a secret, my animals and I, but I can tell you what it is without betraying them. It is this: They love me and I love them. You have no idea of how much they need to be loved."

Not all captive animals become depressed. Sometimes their frustration manifests itself in the form of aggression, and they become irritable, unpredictable, and unapproachable. Nothing is more dangerous than not being able to predict what a wild animal's reaction is likely to be. The slightest incident, any loud noise, or the presence of an unfamiliar person may trigger a violent reaction even against keepers and guards who have had long contact with the animal. Spectators, too, are not always safe. It may well be more dangerous to come within reach of a caged lion or bear than to meet these animals face to face in their natural habitat.

The proper care of animals, therefore, and particularly of young animals, requires unlimited patience and affection, and the willingness to perform duties which are far from pleasant. Professor Gustave Brandes, former director of the Dresden Zoo, tells in his book, *Buschi,* how he succeeded in rearing a male orangutan which was born aboard a cargo ship in the Red Sea. When the animal was a baby, Brandes fed it the way that a mother orangutan feeds her young. That is, he chewed bananas into a paste and then put his mouth against that of the baby orangutan and slid the paste between its lips. For all this trouble and care, Brandes was eventually rewarded with a perfectly tame male which reached an exceptional size because of the constant medical attention which he had received while in Brandes' care.

In zoos it is necessary to provide at least a minimum of training even for the largest and most dangerous animals. These animals must learn, for instance, to obey certain commands; otherwise the lives of the keepers and guards would be in constant danger. Even this training, however, is no real safeguard against unexpected attack. It sometimes happens that a bear or an orangutan, after years of tolerating the presence of its keeper, will suddenly attack, without reason or visible provocation. The reason for the attack in such cases may well be that the animal had never truly accepted the man, for the emotional relationship between prisoner and guard is as precarious as it is complex. It is a relationship in which man must constantly be the dominant party. He must be the animal's superior in every sense. He must never lose face and he must ever be on the alert.

It is a commonly accepted opinion, with respect to this relationship of mutual sympathy between man and animal, that animals are invariably grateful for food. Here again the common opinion is erroneous. Most animals feel no gratitude when they are fed by visitors. Monkeys, for example, delight in snatching away bananas and peanuts from visitors—stealing them, in other words—and then fleeing instinctively after their larceny. To animals, food is not a gift, but a conquest. Man, therefore, hopes in vain to improve his standing in the eyes of animals by offering them food.

There are some curators of zoos who believe that they have found a method of sparing their charges the physical and psychological effects of inactivity by training them to perform before audiences in an American-style animal show. This method is advantageous for two reasons. First, it allows the animal both to engage in physical activity and to obtain the approval and affection which it requires. Second, it usually means that the animal is freed from its enclosure for a certain period of time and allowed to mingle with other animals. But it also has this disadvantage, that in practice it merely adds one more form of servitude to those already imposed on the animal, one more form of degradation to which the animal is subjected.

Between 1871 and 1900 there was a public infatuation with trained animals. It was the time of the great trainers—Henry Martin, Van Ambourg, Crockett, and the Pezons—whose exploits have been chronicled by Henri Thétard. The most interesting aspect of this infatuation, however, is not the numbers which the animals were taught to perform, but the contact thus established between the trainers and the lions and tigers, which are perhaps the most intelligent of wild animals. The trainers touched these great predators, stroked and caressed them, in the exercise of an art which had flourished two thousand years before and then had been forgotten. But what was the purpose of this renewed contact? What inspired such courage and skill on the part of the trainers? What evoked man's intuitive skill in handling animals? The ambition to make a tiger jump through a hoop, a lion walk a tightrope, an elephant stand on its head. Animal training did not mark a resumption of the natural relationship between man and animal. It established in its place a relationship which teetered on the brink of the absurd. "No animal is ridiculous," Edmond Jaloux said, "except when man obliges it to be ridiculous."

In our own time we have seen another revival of animal training. We have now turned our attention to the marine animals in our aquariums and marinelands. Instead of lions and tigers, we are training dolphins, killer whales, and pilot whales. We are teaching them tricks—antics which involve no risk to the trainers, but a great deal of danger for the animals. The more the trick is contrary to the animal's nature, the more the spectators applaud. In the old days the star of the circus was the lion who walked the tightrope or the bear who rode a bicycle. Today the star is the dolphin who jumps through a flaming hoop—the dolphin, whose skin is too sensitive to endure even the slightest burn.

It goes without saying that such spectacles are wholly alien to the spirit in which a *rapprochement* between man and animal should take place. This spirit requires that man respect that which is exceptional in the animal and that he oppose anything which degrades the animal or reduces it to the level of the absurd.

Yet it must be said that if these spectacles have any merit at all, it is that they serve to establish a certain familiarity—however violated it may be—between man and animal. If one reads the lives of the great animal trainers of the late nineteenth and early twentieth centuries, what impresses one most is not the courage of these men, but their utter confidence in the animals. They confronted animals reputed to be completely intractable. Having discovered that the animals had been mistreated, they calmed them and reassured them. And, having discovered that the animals were afraid and that they needed above all to be loved, they loved them. It was this basic sympathy which enabled the trainers to demonstrate the intelligence of the lion, for example, and to show that the lion's memory and reasoning ability could be used to teach the animal to perform. This sympathy—and two peculiarities of human beings: man's upright stance and his voice. Man, on all fours, and face to face with a wild animal, is in imminent danger of death. But so long as he stands upright and confronts the animal, man has a chance of mastering it. By the same token, the human voice is able to influence animals. Most trainers talk to their animals, usually in a soft voice. They call the animals by name, and speak to them in a certain tone. One famous trainer, Vincent Trubka, was knocked to the ground by one of his tigers and saved himself only by talking to the animal.

The training of animals, like the keeping of animals in captivity, dates to earliest recorded history. Sargon I, King of Assyria (2048–2030 B.C.), kept animals. And Pithana, King of Kussar, in the nineteenth century B.C. established at Nesa a veritable zoo of bears, wild boars, lions, leopards, and deer. There is a curious vestige in our language of this ancient Oriental practice. The word "paradise" derives from the ancient Iranian *paradaiza,* and long before it was used to designate the abode of the blessed, it was the name of the enclosure in which the kings of Persia kept their animals—and where, presumably, those monarchs believed the animals found true happiness. At the time of the Greek historian Xenophon (430–355 B.C.) there were still such paradises in Anatolia.

The mighty pharaohs of Egypt, for their part, assigned to their priests the task of training ferocious wild animals to participate in their preferred pastimes: war and the hunt. The favorite lion of Ramses II was immortalized on one of the pylons of the Temple of Luxor, where we may read its name: Antan Necht.

Many princes in later centuries followed the example set along the banks of the Nile. The kings of France, from Charles V to Louis XIV, prided themselves on their menageries. (Louis XV, when he visited the menagerie established at Versailles by the Sun King, complained that there were too many turkeys.)

The mental torture that we inflict upon animals by holding them in captivity for the delectation of visitors dates from the dawn of human history, and it is far from coming to an end. To the contrary, it is increasing, and collections of animals have become all the vogue. Private zoos and preserves have multiplied alarmingly in the past few years. Animals are imprisoned far from their native habitats and where the conditions which prevail are those neither of the menagerie nor of freedom. In 1970 and 1971, for example, in France alone, more than 200 private zoological parks were opened, most of them wholly commercial in nature.

Generally, these private preserves in France are the property of owners of *chateaux* who establish them as a means of meeting the increased maintenance costs of their estates.* Their purpose, in other words, is to profiteer at the expense of the animals. More often than not the space available to the animals is so limited that these "parks" resemble zoos more than preserves. Such collections of animals, it seems, represent the latest stage in the relationship between man and animal. They offer man, who is at once the victim and the prisoner of his technological civilization, a caricature of the jungle along with every convenience. In fact, they are almost perfectly suited to the tastes of today's city dweller. Without stepping from his automobile, without danger and even without inconvenience, a visitor and his family can drive through these outdoor prisons and gape at the inmates. Without leaving his own country or interrupting his routine, and at a minimum of cost, man now has access to an exotic vision. And he has the comforting certitude that as soon as he has satisfied his mysterious longing for life in the wild, he can drive through the gates and be restored to his own environment. It remains to be seen whether this sort of arrangement will wreak less havoc on the human mind than it does on that of the animals.

The Thoiry preserve in France is the exception rather than the rule, by reason not only of its size but also because of several unusual conditions found there, such as the mixing of several species of antelope within the same enclosure, and the fact that all the tigers are also kept in a single enclosure. The methods employed

*Some of these preserves have led to scandalous situations. On one of them the owner simply abandoned his animals and left them to starve or to die of disease, and the place became a death house. Only thirty of these private parks are approved by the French Association of Zoos and Zoological Gardens.

at Thoiry reveal a subtle understanding of animal life and are based on the hierarchical concept; that is, upon the recognition of the authority of a dominant animal. Such methods, one hopes, bode well for the future, for they may insure the survival of animal life and also a maximum degree of respect for that life. In that respect, Thoiry is a model preserve. Yet even there it is not possible to preserve the wildness of the animals. Six or seven species of antelope, for example—not to mention some Watusi cattle—share the same quarters during the winter, and this necessarily effects a change in the attitudes of the animals.

Another example of remarkable behavior: A herd of gnu imported to Thoiry divided itself into two rival groups, one comprising about twenty individuals and the other, four. In the wild, when a calf is born, the entire herd of gnu forms a circle around the mother until her offspring is born. At Thoiry, when one of the females in the small group went into labor, the other three animals were too few to encircle her. The larger group therefore approached, warily, and formed the circle until the calf was born. Thereupon, the rivalry between the two groups was resumed.

In the United States—and especially in Florida—there are a number of public preserves within which are kept exclusively African fauna: lions, zebras, elephants, giraffes, and other animals, none of which is native to America. The curators of these preserves, however, have gone to great lengths and expense to duplicate the natural habitats of these animals. They allow the animals to roam in comparative freedom over wide areas, and they are at pains, whenever possible, to allow various species to mingle. Their approach seems to be to provide the animals with the best—that is, the most natural—living conditions possible. The ideas being implemented in such preserves are those of the ecologists and of many nature lovers, and it is possible that we are witnessing, in such places, the beginnings of a true revolution in the art of wildlife conservation.

Seven of the seventeen largest zoos in the United States—those which house 2,000 animals or more—have developed and are implementing a program which may be reduced to two principal points:

(a) Reduce the number and variety of animals so as to increase the space devoted to each species and to re-create their natural habitat;

(b) Acquire and breed above all those species which, in nature, are threatened with extinction.

This program constitutes a radical departure in the attitude toward animals on the part of the curators of zoos. There is less and less of the exhibition value of animals, or of the impression that particular animals make on visitors, and more and more concern with allowing animals to live in captivity as they lived in the wild.

Such ideas are not entirely new. In 1940, the Bronx Zoo opened an "African plain" in which, for the first time, predators and their natural prey—in this case, lions and antelope—were allowed to roam together in a single enclosure surrounded by a moat. Later, at the Milwaukee Zoo, families of lions were loosed in the same enclosure as their herbivorous victims, and families of tigers with their natural prey, gazelles. And, in 1972, the innovative Bronx Zoo inaugurated a section called "The World of Birds," in which the climatic and botanical habitat of each species was duplicated.

Perhaps the best example of captivity in a natural habitat is that which obtains at the Arizona-Sonora Museum, near Tucson, which houses some 700 animals—all of them native to the surrounding desert. Since the animals never leave the climate in which they were born, the museum is much less costly to maintain than its equivalents in such cities as New York. The

Arizona-Sonora method is one which deserves to be studied in other parts of the world.

Several American zoological societies are actively encouraging the establishment of similar zoos far from civilization, in the wide open spaces of America, where land can be had cheaply and where, consequently, the animals can be allowed considerable space. These institutions would lie, philosophically, somewhere between the conventional zoo and the wildlife preserve.

The San Diego Zoological Society has already opened one such preserve to the north of the city: the San Pasquale Wild Animal Park, which covers some one thousand acres. So vast a zoo, however, has problems of its own. It is sometimes difficult to find animals which are ill or injured, and it occasionally happens that a month or two passes before the guards realize that young have been born and lie hidden in the bush. But these disadvantages are minor when compared to the great advantages which, under this system, accrue both to the animals, who live in a semicaptivity much less cruel than the cages of zoos, and to the public, whose contact with animals becomes more meaningful.

Speaking generally, the captivity of animals, whether in conventional zoos or spacious preserves, plays a role of undeniable importance in the preservation of species in danger of extinction. One might even build a strong case for the belief that captivity is, after all, better than death. The Przhevalski horse, for instance, which was the favorite game of our prehistoric ancestors, seems to have disappeared from the wilds; or, at least, not a single specimen has been seen for the past ten years. The species, however, is not extinct, because specimens living in captivity at the Prague Zoo reproduce regularly. Another, more striking example is that of a species of stag, known as Father David's stag, which abounded in northeast and central China three thousand years ago. By the middle of the nineteenth century, the only specimens left were those in the Imperial Gardens of Peking.* Today approximately 400 of these Asiatic stags are alive and well on the estate of the Duke of Bedford in England, and reproduce freely. The last specimens in the Peking Zoo died in 1921, but in 1964 the London Zoo presented the People's Republic of China with two pairs of the animals. There are also specimens today at the Los Angeles and San Diego zoos. Paul Geroudet, scientific consultant to the World Wildlife Fund, has observed that the experience with Father David's stag "will lead people to believe that species threatened with extinction can be more surely saved by being bred in captivity than by confining them within preserves or by the adoption of a system of protection. Certainly, breeding in captivity has advantages, and these should not be neglected. Yet, nothing should be preferred to a free animal, living in its natural habitat. We can keep orangutans, tigers, bears, and many other animals in captivity. We can keep them alive, make them reproduce, and establish whole families of captive animals. But they will never be anything more than prisoners. Our efforts at conservation and rehabilitation must be aimed primarily at preserving the wilds. And the future of the wilds will not be found either in a cage or in a zoological garden."

We have already observed that never before has the general public been so aware of the necessity for protecting animals, and never before has everyone been so eager to declare his love for animals. At the same time, as we have said, never has there been so much ignorance and so many misunderstandings with regard to animals. The explanation of this paradox, it seems to me, lies in the uncontrolled development of urban life.

*Father David, a French naturalist, in 1866 succeeded in obtaining two hides, which were studied in Paris by the zoologist H. M. Edwards.

Only dogs and cats, and a few caged birds, can now survive in our cities. Yet, it was not very long ago that things were different. Visitors to New York City in the nineteenth century registered astonishment at the vast numbers of chickens, pigs, and cattle freely roaming the streets of that considerable metropolis. And in my own lifetime I have seen veritable farms, with farm animals, in the Grenelle and Vaugirard sections of Paris.

The consequences of this loss of contact with nature are important both for the present and for the future. This is the age of awareness so far as the environment and animal life are concerned. It is also the age of ignorance and error with respect to nature and animals. It would be foolish to expect that in our ignorance and misunderstanding, we will be able to devise the proper methods to save what is threatened in nature. Young people exhibit great generosity and great ardor when they campaign to save the otters of Alaska and the whales of Baja California, and they must be praised for their efforts. But they must also learn the difference between an animal that is truly free in its natural habitat, one that is enclosed in a preserve, and one that is held prisoner in a cage.

The loss of real contact with animals leads us to fabricate images of animals in our imaginations; and most often these images are not only devoid of all reality but dangerously misleading. Children read stories of talking lions or see jungle stories on television in which these fearsome predators are presented as nothing more than large pussycats. We adults have passed on to them the affliction with which we are all more or less burdened—the neurosis known in America as the Bambi complex.

And yet, though we may have succeeded in changing the animals we hold in captivity, there is no evidence that such change manifests itself in greater tolerance for human beings on their part, or in a desire for peaceful coexistence with the human race. There is nothing in the past of the lion or of the bear to predispose them to endure peaceably the spectacle of humans filing past their cages for hours on end. Captivity has not taught them to spare the human young who come within reach of their paws. A wild animal is a wild animal, and even Walt Disney Productions, Inc., cannot teach a real lion to be forbearing or a real polar bear to be gentle.

It is perfectly understandable that a child might wish to pet a lion, and I expect that it would be useless simply to forbid a child to do so. It must be explained that a great cat is not simply a large version of his pet at home, and that to go near it is extremely dangerous. This will not, as some parents believe, inspire the child with a neurotic fear of animals. It will merely put the child in touch with reality and teach him the respect for the character and power of animals which is, after all, their due.

The petting of animals is itself a delicate art, and it is an art which even expert trainers exercise with great care. Anyone who has had experience with animals is aware that any hesitant, timid movement on the part of a human excites the wariness—that is, the aggressive instinct—of an animal. One well-known animal trainer, Jim Frey, explains how he goes about petting an animal: "You must lay your hand flat on the animal's head, shoulder, or flank. If the gesture is direct and open, the animal will know that the trainer is his friend, that he intends no harm, and also that he feels no apprehension. . . . Every movement that seems hesitant, purposeless, nervous or reticent, defeats the purpose of the caress." Frey, of course, has the advantage of being known to his animals. Even so, he never abandons his caution. "I've got into the habit of using my left hand to pet them," he tells us, "even though I'm not left-handed. It seems to me that, if worse comes to worse, it's better to lose my left hand than my right."

I think that most people when they see a beautiful animal in a zoo feel an impulse to stroke it. It may be that being members of an urban society we have come to regard wild animals merely as a source of distraction and amusement—which shows how deep is the chasm which now separates us from the animals which for thousands of years were an integral part of our environment. Or it may be that, with all our good intentions with respect to animal life, we want to express our sympathy and affection. We believe that animals will always welcome the human touch—whereas the truth is that any movement on the part of a human often strikes fear into the animal. The animal reacts accordingly—and bites. That should not surprise us. Most animals have no reason to believe that the human hand is an instrument of benevolence, and no experience which teaches them the meaning of a caress. I remember once I was swimming in a creek in Guadeloupe, among a large group of sea turtles. I could think of no better way to express my affection and admiration than to try to pat them on their heads. They did not appreciate my sentiments. Their bite is quite painful.

Nonetheless there are some animals which are more tactile than others and which, apparently, enjoy being petted by humans. With such animals, petting is often an important part of the training process. This is the case with killer whales and dolphins, whose extremely delicate skin is quite sensitive to a gentle touch. It is also true of the octopus, whose sense of touch is highly developed. But we must not conclude from this that these animals are sentimentalists, no matter how much they seem to enjoy our caresses. A much surer way to win their affection and their trust is to offer them a fish or a crab.

The whole question of what pleases or displeases an animal is a very mysterious one. After tens of thousands of years of living cheek by jowl with animals, we still have almost everything to learn—in this area, as in others. It is almost as though men and animals lived in two different worlds, without communication, separated by a gulf of ignorance.

True aggression is rare among animals. Usually, animals do not attack unless they have concluded that flight is impossible and that their attempts to frighten off an intruder have failed. Specialists in African fauna tell us that an elephant, when it catches the human scent, does not necessarily react by charging, but by pretending to charge. I have seen the director of a wildlife preserve demonstrate this phenomenon. He walked boldly toward the large female who was the leader of a herd. The animal immediately came thundering toward him at a full trot. In my heart, I knew that my friend had seen his last day. When the charging elephant was 150 feet away, the director turned around and ran as fast as he could toward the trees. That was enough to satisfy the elephant. She stopped, then returned to her charges and herded them away.

It takes a great deal of provocation before a wild animal's desire to flee is overridden by its desire to attack. If we could but persuade ourselves of the truth of that statement, and act accordingly, we would be spared many tragic errors. To avoid such errors, we must acknowledge, first, that the reactions of animals are not the same as the reactions of human beings. And then we must attempt to discover what triggers those reactions.

Probably the deadliest enemy that man faces in the presence of an animal is his own fear. Human fear is the Damocles' sword of animal trainers. Animals sense—that is, smell—human fear. "When a man is afraid," writes Dr. Méry, "his cutaneous PH—that is, the acidity of his skin—is radically affected. If one animal, more nervous than the others, perceives that change, it will attack."

Until very recently our attitude toward animals was characterized by determined anthropomorphism. We insisted on attributing human vices and virtues to animals—as though nature were nothing more than a copy of the fables of La Fontaine and Aesop. According to this simplistic morality, the carnivores—especially lions, tigers, and panthers—were enemies, to be struck down. And, within himself, man still has a strong tendency to cry "Wolf!" at the slightest provocation.

Perhaps the worst manifestation of this spirit is that we bring up our children to believe in the superiority of human beings over animals; and, what is even more ridiculous, in so doing we pride ourselves on being modern and scientific. How much more scientific it would be to inculcate youngsters with respect for animals, and with wonder at their abilities and their capacity for adaptation and survival. But how can we teach our children to feel what we do not experience ourselves?

Love and respect for all life should be the legacy of this generation to future generations. Everyone says so. If we continue to follow current trends, the world of the future—twenty, or fifty years from now—will be well stocked with zoos and preserves. And in those zoos and preserves will be life—animal life, and probably all the animal life that remains. One wonders what emotional value these concentration camps of animals will have for the world of the future. One wonders what our grandchildren will make of these life forms deprived of their legitimate heritage. The most tragic thing, perhaps, will be that our descendants may well be satisfied with animals in cages. They may come to believe that there is no other way. They may even come to believe that there has never been any other way.

"Ecology" and "the environment" are the great questions of our day. We hear them discussed in boardrooms and bars, in classrooms and at cocktail parties. Everybody is concerned with finding solutions and answers. Yet, few people, so far as I can tell, have bothered to articulate the basic question to which all these solutions and answers must conform. It is this: How can we bring our young people to participate in the life of nature—in a world where that life is daily becoming more feeble, in a world where animals are either held in captivity, or are being modified, or are becoming extinct?

Psychologists and educators agree that animal contact is necessary to children, that animals play the role in human childhood that they did in prehistoric times, as intermediaries between man and the world, between man and life itself. But in fifty years, what animals will there be left for the child? There will be dogs, no doubt. Dogs bred to occupy as little room as possible, and to be as docile and inoffensive as possible. Teddy dogs, we might call them.

Docility is not really the most desirable trait in an animal. A child must discover what an animal really is. He knows only that it is not an object, and that it is not an adult human. But, in order for him to situate an animal in its proper place, the child must encounter a certain resistance in the animal. He must come to realize that it is not only a living being, but a living being with a nature of its own. To bring ourselves to admit the independent existence of animals is a stage of human development which is generally ignored today.

Konrad Lorenz has declared, with understandable pride, that none of his children were ever afraid of animals, and that no animals were ever afraid of his children. He also states that something will always be lacking in the life of a human who, as a child, did not live with animals. I am of the same opinion as Dr. Lorenz. But I should explain that the Lorenz children, from their earliest years, lived with six dogs, a cat, a badger, some geese, and a dingo (an Australian wolf). In those circumstances, Lorenz could plausibly state that "contact with animals is the open door to nature." Today, however, that door is not necessarily open to the city child. What usually happens instead is that the child picks up erroneous ideas from the adults around him on the "animal-object." The animal is then momentarily showered with affection—and then abandoned when the family goes away on vacation. Or, if the child is a girl, the pet dog or cat becomes the child's doll, or even her "baby"—those classic buttresses of a mawkish desire to "love" and "be loved."

It has not been said often enough, or openly enough, that in some instances—and such instances will become increasingly frequent—the presence of an animal in the home may be more harmful than otherwise in the emotional development of the child. The problem of the relationship between child and animal is complicated by the fact that almost all children have a predilection for pictures of animals, or for stuffed animals. Many children even like real animals. Many animals, on the other hand, choose children as their masters. They put up good-naturedly with the most atrocious treatment and never waiver in their affection for the miniature tyrants who lord it over them. Everyone knows of dogs or cats which, though short-tempered with adults, will endure the whims of a child with perfect equanimity. Such reactions are, on both sides, of surpassing complexity.

What is known for certain is that children experience a need to touch a ball of fur or of feathers. It may be that animal warmth is a complement to, or a substitute for, maternal warmth. And the consequences of such contact may be either desirable or undesirable. It may result in deep emotional attachment, or in a manifestation of the ego—a tendency to selfish treatment of the animal, or even to sadism.

Sometimes this reaction is encouraged by parents, who believe they are doing the proper thing in obtaining a large number of animals for the child. What usually happens in such cases is that all of the animals are neglected and mistreated, and become unhappy. Occasionally they turn on their young master, unless they are lucky enough to die before reaching that stage. I have encountered many cases of this kind, in which parents mistakenly interpreted their children's fascination with animals as an affectionate response. I have known children who were given, successively, baby chicks, ducks, hamsters, an owl, a monkey, a turtle, fish, and a chameleon. (All in an apartment in Paris.)

An attachment between a child and an animal is desirable only if the child's affection is durable and sincere, and if he is made aware that this relationship implies responsibilities. But, since parents are generally unaware of the existence of such responsibilities, there is little chance that the child will learn of them.

CHAPTER THREE

No Extra Charge for Lions

The protection of an animal or of a plant will be ineffectual so long as we do not also preserve that organism's conditions of life.
—W. KÜHNELT

PRESERVES and national parks have been established in great numbers in the past few years, in Africa, Asia, and America. The purpose of these parks is primarily to attract visitors rather than to protect animals. Consequently, the animals in preserves quickly become very different from what they were in their natural state. Obliged to live in a state of territorial chaos, relieved by man of fear and of the need to feed themselves, they multiply rapidly; and, in so doing, they are made to contribute to the degradation imposed on them by man. Is it really this caricature of an animal—a caricature whose mentality has sometimes been distorted since the time of its birth—that we are fighting to "save?"

We are obliged to conclude, however reluctantly, that wild animals must sooner or later disappear from the face of the earth. They belong to another time and to an earth which no longer exists. We can no longer even hope for the establishment of "integral natural preserves"—a sanctuary where the integrity of both fauna and flora would be respected, where no new or alien species would be introduced, and into which man himself would never set foot. Such a concept, which would serve to prolong, at least at a local level, the vestiges of wild life, is already anachronistic. It has been rendered so by the twin monsters of industrial development and tourism, and the last possible sanctuaries have either been destroyed already or are irreversibly compromised. After all, who is there who would dare fight to defend "nonproductive" land and "useless" animals?

Here and there among the yellow grass, scrawny, white-thorned mimosas push feebly toward the overcast skies. The distant tornado seems to add supplemental freshness to the early morning air of the African plain.

The minibuses have already left the camps and lodges and are raising clouds of ocher dust on the sightseeing paths. The people in the vehicles are determined to take the animals unawares as soon as they awake.

The tiny vehicles race along the paths, each driver trying to outdo the others in speed and daring, trying—with the professional chauffeur's instinctive feel for what would bring a large tip—to get his charges as quickly as possible to where the lions have hunted, to the pool where the hippopotamuses yawn, to the path which the elephants are already following in search of scarce vegetation. For it is the dry season—which is also the season for tourists.

On the modern-day safari, photographs have replaced the head of the water buffalo and the horns of the eland as the trophy of the great white hunter. For the tourist, it is at once a symbol of his talent as a photographer, of his sophisticated familiarity with distant lands, and of his intellectual curiosity with respect to animals. What the photograph does, in effect, is to prolong in time the photographer's confrontation with the lion—a confrontation which in fact lasted but a few seconds.

And so, the minibuses and the jeeps are crowded with

tourists clutching satchels and bags and telephotographic equipment which can either be carried on one shoulder, like a rifle, or mounted on a tripod, like a machine gun. All these tourists are men and women who, not too long before, were sitting in their living rooms, studying brochures lavishly illustrated in color with photographs of lionesses sporting with their cubs, and elephants charging, and hippopotamuses opening their enormous mouths. Their purpose in coming to Africa was to effect a conciliation between their city dwellers' dreams and the reality of the jungle. Woe to the travel agent who, after so many promises, fails to come up with the promised ration of animals on-the-hoof! For not just any animal will do. There is a hierarchy of values, which is generally recognized, according to which lions, elephants, and rhinoceroses are particularly attractive. The hippopotamus has a low rating. And the giraffe is more valuable for its ability to astonish than for the pleasure which its appearance excites.

Inevitably, animals are sighted—the hartebeest (the South African antelope), the gnu, and other modest herbivores. They, however, are not the main attraction. And, as though they themselves sense their relative insignificance, they do not bother any longer even to turn their heads as the gaping tourists speed past in search of the embodiment of jungle royalty, the lion.

The members of the "safari" are not long deprived of this glorious sight. They see a pride of lions lying in a clearing, their eyes half closed, their demeanor one of consummate boredom. The animals do not condescend to glance at the vehicles, for they have seen many such, and they have seen so many humans, that man, and the odor of gasoline, are now part of their universe. Are these the wild animals of the tourist brochures? The ferocious predators of the jungle? The "savage beasts"? No. They are no longer any of these. They are large pussycats. Or rather, they are spectators in a bizarre zoo, a zoo in which the exhibits are driven past the spectators in mobile cages.

It happens occasionally on such expeditions that the lions, weary of being observed, rise slowly, every movement a gesture of contempt, and move away through the underbrush. Not infrequently, a vehicle ignores the rules of the preserve and follows the animal. Then, a lioness picks up her cub in her mouth and goes off to hide it deeper in the brush.

In these preserves, where animals no longer know either hunger or thirst, where trucks bring them cases of food and tanks of water, where the scent of man is no longer a prelude to death, our civilization has created a topsy-turvy world in which everything is askew—and particularly the relationship between animal and man.

This alien universe was invented in the nineteenth century by big-game hunters such as Theodore Roosevelt and Fred Selous. There were historical reasons for its creation. At that time, antelope were being slaughtered en masse in order to provide food for work crews, and the pursuit of ivory was wreaking havoc on the elephant population of Africa. In these circumstances, the preserves were established as a means of preventing the animal population of Africa from being wiped out.

The first animal-protective societies were founded by retired officers in Kenya and the Indies—officers who themselves had been big-game hunters at a time when the game was in no danger of becoming extinct. Gradually, and belatedly, these men became aware that the larger animals were indeed becoming fewer and fewer; and, at that point, they recognized the need to protect them. Joyce Joffe, in his *Conservation,* cites the case of Colonel Richard Meinertzhagen who, when he was in Kenya in 1904, felt that his day was off to a bad start unless he killed three rhinoceroses before breakfast. Thirty years later, Colonel Meinertzhagen had become the most ardent member of the Fauna Preservation Society; and, until his death in 1967, he remained a militant defender of animal life—the same animal life to the disappearance of which he had contributed so greatly in earlier years.

In the twentieth century preserves began to multiply. Their stated purpose was to spare the animals the trauma of captivity in zoos and keep them "at liberty, but under surveillance." The establishment of these preserves took place at a time when big-game hunting had become too expensive, and also when the development of Africa was inexorably reducing the space available to wild animals.

Most of the African nations, when they gained their independence from the colonial powers of Europe, quickly realized that tourism was a major source of revenue, and that animals constituted one of the principal attractions for tourists from Europe and America. Regrettably, the African republics seem less concerned with respecting their local fauna than with preserving the raw materials of the tourist industry. The exhibition of animals in their "natural habitat" is now as much an adjunct of tourism as hotels and nightclubs. It is a spin-off of a leisure-oriented civilization.

In America the development of animal preserves has had a somewhat different history. That development had its start in 1831, when George Catlin proposed the creation of a national park for the purpose of preserving the natural beauty of Yellowstone. Catlin, interestingly enough, was neither a hunter nor a biologist, but a painter of landscapes. He had lived among the Indians, and he had studied their language and their customs. And he had come to love the beauties of nature. His sole purpose was to preserve

Yellowstone so that later generations might enjoy its beauty. It was not until the year of Catlin's death, in 1872, that Yellowstone National Park was established by Congressional Act.

It is of some importance that American parks differed in their origin and spirit from those of Africa—the Kruger preserve, for example, which was conceived essentially as an animal preserve. The American Congress was specifically concerned, not about animals, but about nature, when it set aside the more than two million acres of Yellowstone National Park, with its waterfalls, geysers, and hot springs. And that same spirit prevailed upon the establishment of Yosemite National Park with its glaciers, Mariposa Grove with its sequoias, and other parks. The fact is that at the time these parks were established, the concept of protecting animals—or, indeed, the need for such protection—was unknown. Nonetheless, almost by instinct it seems, hunted animals began to take refuge in the parks. The grizzly bear, for example, is now found nowhere except in North American preserves.

The operation of these preserves differs from that of Europe in that, in the United States, the preserves are largely owned by the people as a whole, rather than by individuals or corporations. They are public parks, sometimes operated by the state governments (the state parks). And, because they are public, there is a certain ambiguity which reigns in them. It is difficult to tell whether the parks are operated for the sake of the animals or for that of the public. In other words, they reflect the same dichotomy as is found in man's own attitude toward animals in the twentieth century.

It sometimes seems that the most important consideration in the operation of the parks is to attract the largest number of visitors possible. And, in their effort to increase the number of yearly visitors, the parks multiply the "attractions." There are circus acts, beauty contests, Indian exhibitions (more or less authentic), souvenir shops, and even street carnivals.

The park authorities have no lack of arguments handy to justify their mode of operation. A great deal of money is needed, they explain, to maintain the park's roads and to pay its personnel and to care for the animals. It appears that it matters little what methods are employed, so long as the park generates sufficient income for proper maintenance. And, they assert, even if people come only to water ski or to see the beauty contests, they always learn something about animals generally and especially about local animals.

Obviously, the merits of such an approach to parks and preserves may be debated heatedly and at length. We may content ourselves by saying that, even if one succeeds in keeping the parks from looking like cities, the simple fact of allowing restaurants and attractions of various kinds demonstrates the existence of a dangerous misconception, and one which necessarily leads to other misconceptions. For by the development of the areas set aside as public parks, the objective of bringing together man and animal is frustrated for both parties. A developed park is, in essence, a forgery. It is a forgery in much the same sense that a painting may be a forgery, or a piece of furniture. A forged work of art is dangerous, not because its monetary value is less, but because it corrupts the taste and the judgment of visitors to a museum; it causes them to admire an object which does not deserve their admiration. The same thing may be said for some of America's parks. They have deformed the attitudes of both the visitors and the animals.

There is no end of stories to illustrate the extent of that information, and many of those stories concern bears. That is to be expected, for bears are remarkably intelligent, cunning animals, as well as dangerous ones. It has not taken the bears long to conclude that the tourists in North America's national parks are an unending source of sweets and food of all kinds. Usually they content themselves with digging in garbage heaps. Occasionally they approach automobiles to beg for food.

A ranger at Yellowstone National Park recently reported that he came upon a man and a woman having lunch in the park. The woman was seated in an automobile, holding a sandwich. The man was outside, trying to persuade a large grizzly to occupy the driver's seat so that he might snap a picture of his wife having lunch with a bear. The bear was reluctant, so the man was pushing and pulling with all his might. Fortunately, the ranger intervened before the ridiculous scene turned into a tragedy.*

At Yosemite Park, the curator decided at one point to do away with garbage dumps and replace them with incinerators. The bears were outraged, and they created such a disturbance every night that the garbage dumps had to be reinstated.

These are charming bear stories, to be sure; and that is precisely one aspect of the problem. Tourists are unwilling to believe that these intelligent, apparently friendly animals are at all dangerous. The rangers work very hard, but in vain, to persuade tourists that giant grizzlies are not really Smokey the Bear. And so every year there are accidents. Most of these occur when visitors, intentionally or not, somehow tease the animals. One tourist amused himself by holding a piece of cake under a large female bear and then proceeding to eat it himself, under her very nose. The bear reacted in the most natural way possible: She ate the man's arm.

This was by no means the first, nor the last, accident

*Visitors, it seems, have corrupted not only the manners of the bears, but their tastes as well. At Yellowstone, bears will no longer accept plain sugar. They insist on sugar candy.

of this kind. Bears which are exposed to human beings often become quite dangerous. They must then be captured and taken to some spot far away from the tourist routes. If they wander back to the areas frequented by visitors, they are usually shot.

It is important to note that these accidents arise from the general but mistaken impression that bears are not dangerous because they seem very tame. But there is a difference between being tame and being trained. Bears are not afraid of men, and they seem to mingle with humans on a basis of familiarity. Yet for all of that they remain unpredictable animals. They have not been trained to respect man and to obey him. They have simply found a trick by which to obtain food from tourists. But the tourists are in serious danger if the bear becomes irritated or is impatient and decides simply to take what it wants. Such behavioral subtleties are difficult to convey to a public which is naturally disposed to indulgence and trust where bears are concerned.

The problem is that parks and preserves have developed haphazardly and in keeping with local conditions and circumstances. There is no unified concept of the role which they should play, and no real effort to educate the public in this respect. This is surprising in view of the fact that the parks in the United States are frequented by Americans in numbers which, at least to Europeans, seem beyond belief. In 1967, for instance, the national and state parks of the United States were visited by 139,676,000 tourists. Yosemite National Park alone, on a single weekend, was flooded by 40,000 visitors—most of whom came in automobiles which blocked the highways for miles around.

We are tempted to say, "Wonderful!" But is it indeed wonderful? What precisely do people get out of such visits? What happens when families decide to "see America first" and spend their vacations touring the great national and state parks of the United States? Here is the answer of Joyce Joffe: "The vast majority of visitors try to take in as many national parks as possible in a single trip, spending only a day in each, viewing the scenery through the windscreen, stopping only to take photographs, and keeping to roads and camping sites. These people never wander into real wilderness. Is this the end product of the great heritage of which Americans are so proud?" What Mr. Joffe is saying, in effect, is that Americans have turned their parks into extensions of their cities and suburbs. They are places in which to drive, to eat, and to sleep. And, of course, to take pictures.

The pity of it all is that contact between men and wild animals could offer twentieth-century man the most marvelous possibility for a return to nature. But it must be a new contact, one in which material circumstances and psychological consequences have all been studied and taken into account. The parks and preserves, in their present form, do not meet these requirements. Wild animals confronted by tens of millions of human beings every year do not stay wild for very long. And here we must be careful not to confuse wildness with ferocity. Ferocity is not characteristic of animals in their natural state. To the contrary, animals become aggressive and ferocious while in captivity. By a wild animal I mean one which is free; one whose territorial requirements and natural defenses are taken into account and respected. An animal which is compelled constantly to endure the human presence and human supervision in its daily activities and wants—such an animal is no longer wild, though it may well be ferocious. It has been modified by man. It has become a caricature of its species. Its natural habitat has been disrupted by the superimposition of a human environment. It cannot be expected that the animal emerges unscathed from constant exposure to human prejudices, misunderstandings, ignorance, and errors, any more than it can be expected that the animal's habitat will remain unpolluted by its mandatory allotment of sandwich wrappers and empty bottles. Man apparently is not content to have spoiled his own environment. He must now go on to spoil that of other species.

These are facts of which the authorities in American parks and preserves are becoming increasingly aware. There are now roads and paths closed to tourists, so that the animals will not be disturbed. In some parks, automobiles are not permitted, and visitors must tour the park in special vehicles. Such measures perhaps represent the first step at least toward a partial solution of the problem. Our errors and misunderstandings are so long-standing, however, and so deeply imbedded in our minds and hearts, that we cannot expect them to be rectified immediately, in one fell swoop. It is useless, in my opinion, to attempt to correct attitudes by making new and stricter rules governing the behavior of visitors to parks. The only effective approach to the problem, it seems to me, is to attempt to educate rather than to punish.

Many parks, for example, now have regulations prohibiting, in the most absolute terms, the feeding of animals by visitors. These rules are universally ignored—not because tourists wish deliberately to harm the animals, but because no one has bothered to explain to them that if the animals become entirely dependent on humans for food during the summer, they may well die during the winter, when there are no humans around to feed them. This is precisely what occurred at one Canadian park in the Rockies. The squirrels became so accustomed to being stuffed with peanuts by summer visitors that they neglected to store up provisions for the winter—and starved to death.*

It may appear in many respects that so far as the immediate future is concerned, the preserve is the ideal solution in that it provides a shelter for animals whose living space is so restricted elsewhere, and also facilitates that emotional *rapprochement* between man and animal which is apparently one of the needs of our time. In practice, however, the attitude toward preserves, both internally and externally, is predicated on a contradiction in terms, or at least upon a serious misunderstanding of what is involved. In Africa, as well as in the public parks and preserves of America, visitors and tourists—the numbers of whom increase greatly every year—are usually left in almost total ignorance of the most elementary facts, not to say of the subtleties, concerning animal life in its natural or wild state. The tourist believes, and is led to believe, that the purchase of a ticket gives him the right to behave in whatever way he wishes *vis-à-vis* the animals who live in the artificial world to which he has purchased admission. In other words, he regards his ticket as a means to satisfy his own particular emotional needs, regardless of the needs and nature of the animals themselves. Even the altruism of our time, apparently, is based on selfishness. Everyone wants to do good—to help the developing nations, to send milk to undernourished children, to protect elephants and baby seals. But what we really want is more to ease our own consciences than to ease the lives of other people and of animals. Along with our milk and machines we ship political doctrines. And along with our preserves, we acquire that ease of conscience which allows us to believe that, having "protected" the animals they are ours to do with as we will.

*Cited by Pierre Civet, "Quatre Parcs dans les Rocheuses," in *La Vie des bêtes*, no. 173.

The fact is, the "paradise" into which the tourist is transported is hardly more than a zoo, and a carnival zoo at that. It is manifestly impossible to give the visitor what he wants, simply because the habitat of the animal, in its natural or wild state, excludes the presence of visitors. To place wild animals on exhibition, whether it be in zoos or parks or preserves, is to do violence to their psychological structure and balance. The animal is the product of its natural environment, and the intrusion of man, the exploitation of animals for the sake of attracting tourists, serves only to destroy that which attracts tourists in the first place.

When we speak of the "freedom" of animals, or of animals being "at liberty," what we mean is precisely that the animals are free not to encounter man; that they are at liberty to flee. Most preserves, and particularly the preserves of West Africa, are concentration camps of animals in which the prisoners are on continuous display for the sake of the tourists. I do not mean to imply that these preserves are surrounded by barbed-wire fences or that the animal is physically unable to flee. I mean that civilization—or, more precisely, commercial enterprise—has surrounded the animals with an enclosure more impenetrable by far than simple barbed wire. The animal, when it leaves the preserve, encounters a solid, encircling structure of heavily trafficked highways, resort hotels, campgrounds, and airports.* When animals attempt to penetrate that barrier, the humans in the area are terrified and react by hunting them down. Over the years, the animals have become perfectly aware of the moral boundaries of their prison.

Another aspect of animal freedom is that which allows the animal to indulge itself in the purely animal

*It was at one time not unusual to find lions hiding out in airplane hangars at the Nairobi preserve.

pleasures of chasing and bringing down its dinner. It is no wonder that the lions we see on preserves convey an impression of unspeakable boredom and indifference. For a hundred lions on the preserve, there are perhaps tens of thousands of its natural prey—twenty thousand zebras and thirty thousand gnu. Yet to all outward appearances everyone gets something from this arrangement. The lions get to eat all they want with a minimum of effort. The zebras and gnu multiply wildly and far beyond the limits established by nature. And the tourists, of course, get to see animals described in the travel literature—though few of them ever suspect to what extent the exhibits are staged solely for their benefit.

It is difficult to explain the shock and disgust that one feels, remembering things as they were twenty-five years ago, when, today, one comes across a herd of waterbuck or eland who do not even bother to look up when a line of minibuses drives past. These animals—once so noble, proud, and sensitive—have now acquired the indifference to humans which we expect only in domestic animals. They have not only become accustomed to the sight of man, but they have also lost all sense of flight-distance—the minimum of space that an animal, in order to preserve its life, must always maintain between man and itself, and the violation of which, in the large predators, results in the animal's decision to attack.

One morning, in the Waza Reserve in the Cameroons, I encountered a female elephant followed by two calves. I came quite near to the elephants, and the mother treated me to an impressive display of warning signals. She waved her ears, stomped her feet, raised her trunk—she did everything but charge. These were, of course, an effort at intimidation. I am certain that the mother elephant, in her natural habitat, would have followed up her signals by an attack. On the preserve, however, the aggressiveness which should be a concomitant of her maternal protectiveness had been severely blunted.

The director of lakes and forests of a certain African republic, after listening patiently to these and other criticisms, answered me by saying, "What does it matter if we are changing the animals, as you say? We've created a paradise on earth for our animals in the preserves!"

Unfortunately, it is not possible for man to create an animal paradise. The whole concept is a contradiction in terms, because it is impossible to reconcile human intervention with the fact that the very foundation of animal life is the freedom of each species of animal to appropriate a space in which there is place for every one of its life functions. In this respect, animals are no different from other living beings. Even the starfish in an aquarium always returns to the particular corner which it has chosen for itself, though it may offer no protective shelter.

No preserve, therefore, however spacious it may be, is "natural." Preserves are creations of man. They are not found in nature. In nature, a free animal always follows the same paths—paths which others of the same species have followed for perhaps millions of years— sleeps in the same place at the same time and during the same season. How often I have happened across a well-beaten path in the jungle and followed it, certain that it must lead to a village, only to discover that it was an animal path, hundreds of years old—one of the paths which is sometimes mentioned to prove the existence of tradition among animals. The paths to water holes, to pastureland, and to the migratory routes are unchanging and unchangeable; just as the territory of each animal is strictly delineated. There is nothing less capricious, nothing less flexible, than the life-style of a wild animal.

Paradoxically, the freedom of an animal consists in its being able, without restraint or compulsion, to live its life along these fixed paths, at those given water holes, on those special savannahs, within that chosen territory. And that is precisely why no artificially created preserve, no matter how benevolent and well intentioned its creators may be, can ever provide a wild animal with the purely natural habitat which it requires if it is to remain a wild animal.

In this area we are obviously dealing with the now famous, and much misunderstood, question of territory.* It is well known that animals are bound to a certain area around which, by means of their scent and their excrement, they have erected an invisible wall. For a long time it was believed that animals fought for possession of the females of the species; now, however, it is known that they fight to defend this territory. The vindication of this natural property-right is essential to the continued existence of an animal, for its territory contains the food which is necessary to the animal and which it refuses to share with other animals. The defense of its territory is the animal's way of preventing overpopulation and of contributing to the maintenance of the delicate biological balance imposed by nature. And this is as true of nightingales as it is of hippopotamuses, gnu, or crows. "Animals and their environment *fit* one another," writes Thure von Uexküll, "as a key fits a lock. The constitution of the animal and its corresponding environment is like that of parts of the same organism: it exists in a reciprocal relationship of functional dependence." To this, Professor Roger Heim adds: "When we speak of animals, the

*There are distinctions to be made between shelter, territory, and domain. An animal's shelter is the den or lair in which the animal takes refuge, either habitually or occasionally, when in danger, either to sleep or to give birth. Territory consists of an area which its occupant defends against intruders of the same species. Domain is the area usually frequented by a single animal or by a group of animals. Several domains may overlap without causing conflict.

very term *habitat* necessarily connotes a sense of security." For it is only within the confines of its territory that an animal experiences a remission of that fear which colors its entire life. It is only in that space that an animal feels protected. Therefore, to the animal, any assault on its territory is an extremely serious matter. (Curiously enough, an animal fighting to defend its territory is almost always victorious.) It is therefore likely that life on a preserve must seem chaotic to an animal, and it must constitute a severe psychological shock. The overpopulation which results from the protection of animals within a preserve is an additional disturbing factor. Moreover, the trauma of nonterritorial existence, or at least of finding substitute territories, within a preserve, is a continuous one. As the preserve is modified, as more roads are cut, as more animals are born, as the numbers of tourists increase, the hapless animal must constantly adapt and readapt its sense of territory to changing circumstances.*

This disorientation manifests itself in bizarre ways. One has had only to see the rhinoceroses of the Amboselli preserve wandering aimlessly in the vicinity of the hotels, begging for carrots and lettuce leaves, to appreciate the breadth of the evolution now taking place among hitherto wild animals. One may well ask whether these animals, as they are subjected to the human presence and simultaneously seek out human beings, are still in their natural habitat or whether they have simply become cogs in the machine of the tourist industry.

Examples of the growing dependency of animals on man—not only for material support, but also for psychological support—can be multiplied indefinitely. In some preserves, old water buffalo which are unable

*Some animals succeed in making at least a partial adjustment. Lions, for instance, have learned to walk behind moving minibuses in order to conceal themselves from the grazing antelope they intend to attack.

any longer to battle against younger rivals and which are chased from the herd, seek out the company of the preserve's rangers for protection. They sometimes even approach tourists, who naturally understand nothing of what is happening and are terrified at the sight of these animals which are reputed to be among the most dangerous in Africa.*

Some of the most peculiar problems of the preserves are those presented by "orphan" animals—that is, young animals of all species found and raised by rangers of the preserve. For some reason, the practice of adopting young animals seems more common in the preserves of East Africa than in West Africa. These animals—often bottle-fed until they are old enough to take solid food—are raised among human beings and live in semifreedom; which is to say that they are allowed to roam, and are put into cages only when they do too much damage or frighten too many visitors. They are in a special category on the preserve—a category which one may either praise or damn according to one's approach.

Since such animals are accustomed from the earliest age to the presence of humans, they are generally harmless, although sometimes their playfulness leads to accidents. Some of the animals, when they are fully grown, are, and should be, turned loose on the preserve. Once there, their reactions differ. Some animals return to the "orphanage" for food and protection. Others become extraordinarily vicious and dangerous and eventually they must be shot. Otherwise they will frighten the tourists.

*Professor H. Hediger, curator of the Basel Zoo and later of the Zurich Zoo, measured the flight-distance of an old male buffalo in Ruanda and found it to be 13 meters (about 46 feet)—an extraordinarily short distance for a wild animal of the species. Hediger found during his stay on the preserve that all the instincts on which wild animals depend to escape danger—flight-distance, speed, aggressivity, tactics of intimidation—had been dulled.

Obviously, the attitudes and comportment of these orphans have been profoundly affected by their constant contact with humans during their infancy and adolescence, and it is these animals—whether we are talking about lions, rhinoceroses, elephants or hippopotamuses—which represent most clearly the new varieties of animals more attached to man than to nature.

Thus, we are witnessing, in our time, a new and strange form of conservation: zoos without cages, populated by nonwild animals. Many naturalists are of the opinion that these animal orphanages contribute even more than preserves to the propagation of misinformation and errors with respect to animals.*

Daphne Sheldrick, wife of the first supervisor of the Tsavo preserve in Kenya, has written an excellent book, *The Orphans of Tsavo,* on the orphans she took into her home at one time or another—elephants, mongooses, civet cats, and rhinoceroses. Her husband, David Sheldrick, was well aware of the danger of "humanizing" young animals deprived of their mothers, and he made every effort to prevent the mental integrity of the animals from being affected adversely. He was determined not only that the animals should be capable of living in the wilds, but also that when the time came they should be able to choose freedom without being endangered by their lack of experience. Therefore no effort was made to keep the animals from returning to the wild if they wished to do so; even if it meant that they would never return to their human "family." When the animals reached maturity, they all opted for the

*Ric Garvey, in *Animal Orphanage,* recounts numerous anecdotes which throw into relief the essential speciousness of the relationship between man and these orphanages, such as the establishment created, for the sake of tourists, in Nairobi National Park. This particular institution was set up by the park's first chief ranger, Steve Ellin; but there are other similar orphanages, at Amboselli Park, Rutshuru, and so forth.

jungle—all except one, a rhinoceros named Rufus, who chose to remain with humans and to continue his diet of hardboiled eggs, curried goose, and chocolate.

It is possible, one supposes, to justify the existence of orphanages and preserves by arguing that they do, after all, allow animals to survive in a technological civilization, even though the animals themselves may be transformed psychologically by the experience. This argument, though often advanced, is not necessarily true. In order to see it in the proper light, it might be useful to examine the case of the hippopotamus.

I happen to be very fond of hippopotamuses as a species, and I have spent many happy hours observing them. At Lake Iro and along the Chari I used to wait for them in the early morning hours, to see them as they returned from their nocturnal excursions to submerge themselves in the water. Their skin is relatively tender and the African sun is capable of burning them badly. Therefore, during the hours at which the sun is most intense, they submerge their massive bodies in rivers and ponds in such a way that only their nostrils, eyes, and their tiny ears can be seen above the surface.

On the whole, the hippopotamus is an inoffensive animal as long as one keeps in mind that it is "wild." The unwary tourist who places himself between a hippo and its pond or river may very well be charged and trampled. In the water, however, I was able to get quite close to these animals without alarming them. Nonetheless it happens that a hippopotamus will attack a canoe or pirogue and snap it in two between its powerful jaws, and sometimes it follows up this performance by attacking the humans who were in the boat. Even so, it is absurd and scandalous to kill a hippopotamus unless its meat is absolutely necessary to feed a village, or unless a particular specimen has proved to be habitually aggressive.

For this reason, in what was at that time the Belgian

Congo, a group of well-meaning naturalists succeeded in having a law enacted which provided absolute protection to the hippopotamuses along the Kasinga Canal (which is about twenty-two miles long and runs between Lake George and Lake Edward). The hippopotamuses then began to multiply at such a rate that the alimentary resources of the area around the canal were insufficient to support them. They spread out for several miles into the surrounding countryside and devoured all the vegetation within reach. Consequently, when the rainy season came, all the topsoil was washed away and the entire area remained barren.

The unlimited multiplication of the hippopotamuses resulted, naturally, in the increase of their excrement in the canal itself, and this in turn resulted in a great increase in plankton and plants in the canal, and therefore in the number of fish all the way to Lake Albert. A cannery was established to take advantage of the superabundance of fish, and everyone congratulated themselves on the success of the hippopotamus-conservation scheme. Then it was noticed that the excrement of the fish was attracting hordes of marabou. These became so numerous that they constituted a veritable plague, stripping all the trees bare and covering the whole region with their droppings.

Finally it was conceded that the whole thing had been a disastrous mistake and it was necessary to adopt the only possible solution: A huge number of hippopotamuses had to be shot to restore the natural zoological balance of the area.*

This was no freak ecological accident. In the Murchison Falls National Park, where elephants were "protected," these great pachyderms increased in numbers until they had eaten all the foliage within reach and the jungle had come to resemble a meadow studded with bare tree trunks. When the elephant

*David Stephen and James Lockie, *L'quilibre dans la nature.*

population exceeded the supply of food, the newborn elephants did not grow properly and many of them died from exposure because there was no more jungle within which to take shelter. Those who survived reached maturity very late. Finally, large numbers of the elephants had to be shot in order to reduce their numbers to a level that could support itself on the food available in the area.

When man does not intervene to resolve the crisis produced by his initial interference, the animals themselves, or nature, must do so. There are some 3,000 hippopotamuses packed into a thirty-mile stretch of the Rutshuru River—approximately one hippopotamus for every fifty-three feet of bank. Their existence is one constant, unrelenting struggle for food, and there are often fights to the death over space. In the Tsavo Preserve, in Kenya, following a dry spell some 20,000 elephants died of hunger and thirst, along with more than 300 rhinoceroses.

The fact is that Africa is no longer large enough, and, especially, no longer "wild" enough to support unlimited numbers of large animals such as elephants, rhinoceroses and hippopotamuses. Formerly these animals roamed over large areas. Today they are concentrated in regions where they are relatively undisturbed and where the land is not yet under cultivation by man. In order to appreciate what this means, one must realize the extent of the devastation that an elephant can wreak in a limited area. It is not only the elephant's appetite which is in question, but also the way in which the animal goes about feeding itself, shaking trees, breaking branches, stripping off the bark, and sometimes uprooting sizable trees. When elephants could move over vast stretches of Africa, it was possible for the vegetation to grow back after the passage of a herd. But now the damage is too great, and too localized, for nature to be able to make adequate repairs. In Uganda's Murchison Park, for instance, there is hardly an acacia tree left that is not broken, dying, or dead. And at Luanga National Park, in Zambia, which covers some 5,000 square miles, and where there are now some 13,000 elephants, one is struck by the fact that the problem to be met is not that of protecting one particular species, but rather of preserving a complex whole which comprises flora, fauna, space, and climate.

Perhaps it would be more accurate simply to say that the giants of Africa are anachronisms in the modern world. Elephants, rhinoceroses, and hippopotamuses roamed the earth in the Pleistocene era, along with the mammoth, the mastodon, and the aurochs. The aurochs disappeared quite suddenly in Europe, and even more so in America, between 11,000 and 8000 B.C.; and it is by no means clear that prehistoric hunters were responsible for that phenomenon. The fact is that the size of these animals, like that of the elephant, rhinoceros, and hippopotamus, was in keeping with the amount of space and the vegetation available. Now, however, the African giants are relics—relics the existence of which we can only hope to prolong more or less indefinitely.

The greatest and most immediate obstacle to their continued existence is not man, but the birthrate of the animals themselves. In some preserves the number of animals has become enormous. In Kruger Park, in the Republic of South Africa, there are approximately 200,000 impalas, 12,000 buffalo, 12,000 zebras, 10,000 gnu, 6,000 elephants, and 6,000 koodoos (a large antelope). On the Serengeti preserve, in Tanzania, there are approximately 500,000 gnu, 500,000 zebras, and 500,000 gazelles.*

*The Serengeti Park is vast—but not vast enough to contain such huge numbers of animals, as evidenced by the fact that many of these animals go beyond the park's boundaries in their seasonal migrations.

In this chapter we have dissertated on the evils of preserves. We have talked about the corruption of wild animals by contact with man. We have cited instances of the disastrous consequences of man's well-meaning but wholly misguided efforts to protect certain species by unnatural means. And we have ended by demonstrating that, far from having learned from our mistakes, we are in the process of duplicating them. What conclusions are we to draw from all this?

I should say to begin with that—anything in the foregoing pages to the contrary notwithstanding—I am not opposed to the concept of preserves *per se*. I am convinced, however, that preserves, at least in their present form, are by no means the panacea that so many people think they are. It seems to me, then, not that the preserves should be abolished, but that remedies must be found for the ills that beset them.

Such remedies exist, and they are within the realm of practicality. In fact, they have been devised by a number of well-informed preserve personnel, and some of them have already been applied.

The first of these remedies is to establish in the heart of each preserve or park a sanctuary which will be closed to visitors—especially to visitors in automobiles. This closed area is intended to be not only a place where the animals may feel secure, but also an area of rest and recuperation for animals which otherwise would be continually on display. Here, of course, there is a space problem. Lions and elephants obviously need an immense amount of room, otherwise they will not be able to be contained within the sanctuary. For that reason it would be best to devote an entire preserve to animals that we are desirous of protecting, and to forbid any visitors in that particular preserve. This is the formula applied in establishing integral natural preserves, where protection is absolute and to which only caretakers and scientific researchers have access.*

The theory of the integral natural preserve is quite simple. The difficulty in implementing that theory arises not from any intrinsic impracticability but rather from the fact that man's devotion to "ecology" and "conservation" has a tendency to vanish, with astonishing rapidity, when the choice boils down to either saving the animals or making a fast dollar. A case in point is the Nimba Mountains preserve. This preserve, in Guinea, was the prototype of the integral natural preserve. Indeed, at one time, it was the only such preserve on the entire continent. It is—or rather, was—situated along the frontier common to Guinea, Ivory Coast, and Liberia, near the village of Nso (whose busy, colorful marketplace testifies both to the prosperity of the region and to the striking beauty of the inhabitants).

The Institut Français d'Afrique Noire (French Institute for Black Africa) constructed a magnificent research center on the preserve, designed and built in conformity with local architecture and of local materials. The center contained both research facilities and accommodations for visiting scientists. I was fortunate enough to spend some time there, and I was delighted to discover that the preserve contained everything needed to make of it an unspoiled slice of Africa truly worthy of being protected. The primeval forest still covered a part of the mountain, and elephants from the north came there during the dry season for refuge. Buffalo grazed on the elevated plains and panthers and chimpanzees abounded in the magnificent forest.

The preserve was of exceptional interest to ethnogra-

*There is a variant of the integral natural preserve, known as a supervised natural preserve, such as that of Kala Maloué in the Cameroons and that of Aouk Akouale in the Central African Republic. The supervision of such preserves is rendered extremely difficult precisely because they are remote, and, as may well be imagined, poaching flourishes.

phers as well as naturalists, for it contained several extremely interesting places of worship. The Nimba Mountains were a center of local religious faith. There was a lake containing sacred fish, and a sacred hill (Bassou) on which lived sacred monkeys to which the local populace brought sacrificial offerings.

Today there is hardly anything left of the preserve. As chance—or mischance—would have it, the Nimba Mountains were composed largely of iron ore remarkable for its purity (68 percent) and the Liberian government, which had not established a preserve on its side of the mountains, called in an international consortium to exploit the wealth represented by that ore.

Scientists, indeed, were given permission to make an inventory of the natural wonders of the region before they were destroyed forever. "Researchers representing the specialties came from all quarters, but the flora and fauna were as abundant, and the mechanized exploitation of the area so rapid, that nature was destroyed before it could be studied in depth."*

The irreversible destruction this wrought inevitably affected the Guinean side of the mountains—so much so that the preserve, which no longer exists in practice, has lost its entire population of buffalo, chimpanzees, and panthers. In 1968 a road was built through the jungle so that prospectors and engineers might study the mountains which lay in the territory of Guinea. It was discovered that these slopes were even richer in ore than those of Liberia. From the moment of that discovery all hope was lost that the preserve might be reestablished. The fauna had already fled. Now the flora would be destroyed. The work of destruction is well under way.

*J. G. Adam, "Etat actual de la végétation des Monte Nimba en Libéria et en Guinée," in *Adansonia,* ser. 2,10 (2), 1970.

Another way of saving certain wild species, and even of making use of them, is to allow them to multiply in preserves until the number of animals begins to exceed that which the preserve can support. The excess animals would then be slaughtered to provide meat for the local population. Obviously, I am referring to a systematic and rigidly controlled slaughter, and not to the sort of hunting which makes no distinction among its victims.

The U.S.S.R. has been using this method for several years with respect to the saiga antelope, which at one time was on the road to extinction. This animal was quite common in Western Europe thousands of years ago, and hunters at the close of the Paleolithic era reproduced its likeness on the walls of the Rouffignac caves. By 1930, however, the saiga had become so rare that the Soviet government afforded it total protection against hunters. Today the number of these antelopes has reached some 2,000,000 specimens. They are permitted to live in the wild state, but every year 500,000 of them are slaughtered for meat.

Similarly, in South Africa herds of eland and springbok (a South African gazelle) exist in semifreedom and furnish an appreciable source of meat.

In such national preserves as Serengeti in Tanzania, where there is sometimes a million head of zebras and antelope, the preserve is so crowded that the vegetation is utilized in its totality. Yet, somehow, there is never any sign of overpopulation in proportion to the food supply and there is no permanent destruction of the flora. When it comes to wild animals, apparently, nature somehow provides—though no one knows quite how this is done. In the same vein, other authorities record that "in the Nairobi preserve, along the waterways, the land is able to feed as many animals as the best pastures in Normandy. And in Rhodesia and South Africa, a hectare of land [2.5 acres] gives a better return in wild animals than in cattle."* Fiasson assures us that this is due essentially to "the remarkable adaptation of a fauna which thrives where domestic animals would die of hunger. Thus, wild animals make better use of the alimentary resources of a given area."†

A third solution to some of the problems presented by preserves may be achieved by transferring animals from one preserve to another in order to maintain a biological equilibrium and to assure that all the animals will have sufficient food and water for their needs. This type of movement was employed in the period 1959–1965, under the project name "Operation Noah," during the construction of the Kariba dam on the Zambezi. The method employed involved putting the animals to sleep and then loading them on flatcars and transporting them to their new homes.

There have been refinements in procedure since Operation Noah, and, though not all of the problems inherent in this method have been solved, there have been instances of animals being saved from extinction by being transported. One such species was the white rhinoceros of the Umfolozy preserve in South Africa, which was transported to Rhodesia where it has now begun to multiply. The major drawback, obviously, is that even if the animals are not traumatized by being moved (which is by no means certain), they undergo the severe shock of what is known as translocation; that is, of being thrust suddenly into a new world to which they must adapt. Still, the animals survive, and survival is preferable to extinction.

All of the solutions given above present certain difficulties and problems, either because the remedies they offer are incomplete, or because they offer a

*Stephen and Lockie, *L'quilibre dans la nature.*
†*Animaux sauvages.*

postponement of the crisis rather than a resolution of it. It seems to me that the only really viable solution may be to accept the fact that there are two variants of the same species of wild animal: the "wild" animal of the tourist industry and the wild animal as it exists in nature. We must admit that these two variants differ widely in mentality and comportment. Then, we must logically conclude that there should be two kinds of preserves: one for the public and the other for the animals.

CHAPTER FOUR

The Hercules Complex

Those things which we regard as our basic attitudes toward the world are often exercises in confidence on the youthfulness of our minds.
—GASTON BACHELARD

OF all man's relationships with animals, the most complex is that which binds him to wild, predatory animals, and especially to lions. The lion has always been an object of human terror and awe; and, historically, the act of killing a lion has conferred a semidivine character on the killer. Today the lion killer, and even the photographer of lions, still enjoy a kind of protohistoric prestige. This, at least, has not changed; for man has always had need of wild animals to fortify his self-esteem.

Until the end of the nineteenth century, fortunately, there were enough lions to go around. But today there are lions only in Africa, and they are not quite as dangerous as they were. They roar a great deal, though, and this apparently is enough to attract large numbers of thrill seekers and great white hunters. In any event lions are disappearing. Mythology, archaeology, and psychoanalysis have done more for big-game hunting than all the travel agencies in the world.

Well and good. But somewhere along the way, our mighty killers of lions forgot something rather important. They did not take into account that the killing of lions would result in the uncontrolled multiplication of herbivores, and that the multiplication of herbivores would contribute to massive deforestation and to a serious ecological imbalance. The middle span of the twentieth century is now reaping the consequences of that lack of foresight. We live in an age when, literally, the deer is more dangerous than the tiger.

I have known many lions in my lifetime, and they were all different from one another. They were individuals, not only in size and coloration, but also in their personalities. I have observed them as fearsome predators, silent and terrible, in search of a victim. And I have seen great-maned beasts as haughty and disdainful as fashionable hairdressers. I have known indifferent lions, timid lions, and curious lions; young lions who were lazy and old lions too feeble to protect themselves from flies or even to forage for food. And I have seen "loner" lions who, for lack of other food, became man-eaters. These encounters took place over a period of twenty-five years, in different areas of Africa; but they all have one thing in common: Not once did I feel endangered by the presence of a lion, and not once did a lion give me reason to be afraid. In other words, I have been extraordinarily lucky.

A quarter of a century ago, lions were still very numerous in Chad and in the north of the Cameroons. They displayed no hostility, only mild curiosity as they watched us go past. I was not surprised at their indifference at that time, and I am even less surprised now, many years later, when my experience with lions is considerably broader. Generations of moviegoers have been persuaded that lions attack humans on sight. The truth is quite the opposite.

Along the Niger River, during the dry season, herds of cattle and buffalo drift around looking for fodder. Most often, the man in charge of a herd is no man at all, but a boy of ten or twelve years. The sole weapon is a stick. Lions also suffer from hunger during the dry season, and they usually follow the herds, waiting, watching for an opportunity to pounce on a weakened cow or buffalo. To protect the herd against the lions, there is only the boy with his stick. The boy knows perfectly well that if a lion attacks his herd, the worst possible thing he could do would be to run. Flight immediately stirs a lion's aggressive instincts. The boy knows that he must stand fast and face the attacker, for he belongs to a pastoral people and he has in his blood both love for his herd and contempt for the lion. And so, when the lion does attack, the boy resists. He throws stones at the animal and, if he can get close enough, he strikes the lion with his stick. The boy's courage, however, is not the most astonishing thing. What is really remarkable is that the boy is almost always victorious over the lion. There seems to be something about a human being, standing erect, shouting, wielding a stick, which overawes even a voracious lion. Unless, of course, the lion is an old one on the verge of starvation or one which has been wounded by a hunter who had not the courage to follow the wounded animal and finish it off. In either case, the lion has lost its fear of man; and, in the latter case, the fear has been replaced by hatred.

Generally speaking, however, a lion does not attack human beings unless it has been wounded, and female lions attack only if they sense danger to their young. Even so, it would be a mistake to underestimate the danger represented by these predators. Their attack is truly terrifying, and the charge may briefly attain a speed of about forty-five miles per hour. Moreover, they are armed with formidable weapons. Their speed, strength, and weight (usually between 600 and 800 pounds), their uncertain and unpredictable temper, make them awesome adversaries. A lion with a bullet in its heart and three or four more in its lungs is quite capable of leaping on a hunter and felling him with one stroke of its great paw. This very thing happened in Gao, a few days before my arrival there. A lion had been riddled with bullets, and the hunters, made careless by confidence in their aim, approached the wounded animal. The lion sprang up, ripped open the leg of one man, and wounded several of the others before it finally succumbed to its wounds. (One of the hunters captured the entire scene on film.) This supreme rage in the face of death, this all-consuming hatred of the hunters who had brought him down, is probably that which is most noble in the lion.

Today, in Africa, lions are found only in the Sudan and the Sahelian regions. In Asia there are no more than 250 specimens, all within the Gir preserve which is located on India's Kathiawar peninsula. At one time, the Asian lion was found in great numbers in Iran, Turkey, Arabia, Afghanistan, and Pakistan. In ancient times there were some even in Palestine, Macedonia, and Greece. Cave paintings and fossils attest to the presence of lions also in the Iberian peninsula.

The North African lion—a truly magnificent, black-maned beast, like the Abyssinian and Kalahari lions—disappeared not more than a hundred years ago. In the middle of the nineteenth century, during the French conquest of Algeria, they were still numerous. Some French officials and settlers then took it upon themselves to free the natives from the threat presented by the lions. One such man, Jules Gérard, known as "the Lion Killer," not only shot a great number of these animals, but left to posterity a book of recollections and recommendations explaining why, in his opinion, lion hunting was a duty which devolved upon man. Gérard nowadays comes across a humbug, but, in his own mind, he thought of himself as a second Hercules. The qualities necessary for a man to hunt lions successfully, he informs us, are: "youth, a strong arm, a solid stance, a keen eye, an iron will, and a love of good."

In the same lofty tone, he draws on his experience to advise those who would follow in his footsteps: "Once the lion has caught sight of you, it will always keep its face toward you. If it happens that your first shot has not brought him down, then the lion will spring upon you and, if he reaches you, knock you to the ground on your back. He will straddle you and hold you to the ground with his claws. But this will not, of itself, kill you. If you have aimed carefully before firing and your bullet has not been deflected by any object, you will come out of it with only a dozen or so strokes of the lion's claws. These will heal, so long as the mouth of the lion has not touched you, and so long as his death agony has lasted only a few seconds. In any case, always keep in mind that you have a knife. If you have not dropped it when the lion knocked you to the ground, use it. Strike swiftly, hard, and aim at the animal's vital spots."

This rather optimistic view of lion hunting will bring a smile to the lips of anyone who has ever indulged in big-game hunting. Even so, I know of at least one case which bears out M. Gérard's conception of lion hunting. In the spring of 1972 I met, at Fort Archambault, a guide named Meunier who had a decided limp. Meunier's story was simple enough. He had taken a hunter to a spot very near a lion, and, instead of signaling the hunter to fire, had said "fire." The lion, of course, heard Meunier's voice, and charged instantly.

Meunier, a conscientious guide, jumped between the lion and the hunter and fired. But it was too late. The lion was upon him, seized his rifle in its jaws, and, with one stroke of its paw, knocked Meunier to the ground. The guide took hold of the lion's head and struggled to hold off the great maw yawning a few inches away. The guide's hipbone had already been pulverized, and he was certain that he was done for. He could hear the hunter's rifle pouring a steady stream of rounds into the lion's body, but without apparent effect. Finally, he felt the lion's neck go limp, and the great body suddenly slumped, crushing Meunier beneath it.

The guide spent several months in the hospital recovering from his wounds. Today he is back in business, guiding hunters in the Chari region and in the Aoûk Valley. His attitude is that hunting can be justified only if the odds are even; that is, if the element of death enters into it on the part of the hunter as well as on that of the hunted. Truth to tell, for the past twenty or thirty years the only one who has been in danger, other than the lion, has been the guide. I know of at least one guide who was killed because his client insisted on filming the lion's charge. The client, presumably, got his film.

The factor cited above may "justify" lion hunting, but it does not explain it. That is, it does not explain what it is precisely that pushes an otherwise normal, sensible man to spend a great deal of money in order to be given the opportunity to kill an animal so noble, so worthy of our respect, and now so rare, as a lion. The answer, as I have implied above, is that for uncounted centuries man has regarded hunting as a noble undertaking. The struggle of man for domination over all the creatures of the earth has traditionally been looked upon as a semidivine undertaking, as the work of gods and demigods. When the earth was overrun by "monsters," this attitude was perhaps understandable. Now, circumstances have changed, but the attitude remains. Indeed, the function of lion killer seems to have become more praiseworthy as the danger involved has decreased. Perhaps the explanation is that the killing of lions now requires a great deal of not courage or strength, but money. And money is the supreme virtue of the twentieth century.

To kill a large animal, therefore, has become a luxury. And, in the hierarchy of contemporary values, luxury and nobility are easily confused. Hunting still has about it an aura of archaic glory. The hunter enjoys a prestige somewhat analogous to that of the knights of old—to the slayers of dragons—and, perhaps more directly, analogous to that of the lion-slayer par excellence, Hercules.

The first of the labors of Hercules was to kill the lion of Nemea. In that protohistorical era, it was a justifiable exploit. Greece and Asia Minor were infested with lions. Now, a hero appears to protect his fellow men from the threat represented by animals—a threat which always has been thinly submerged beneath the surface of human consciousness. The name of this hero, this superman with which every hunter has since identified himself, was Hercules,* who embodied in the highest degree the concept of human victory over the animal kingdom. He also embodied man's millennia-old dream of safety from attack by animals; for Hercules, once he slew the lion, made a tunic of its hide and thereafter was invulnerable.

It has been a long time since there were lions on the shores of the Mediterranean, but the Hercules complex still persists in European civilization and in its daughter-cultures beyond the Atlantic. That having been said, one must confess that it is not always easy, within that context, to analyze the motives which impel a twentieth-century man to embark upon an African safari. There is probably no single motive, but rather a mixture of motives based upon fear, vanity, and egotism, as well as upon respect for and awe of a magnificent and powerful creature. All these motives and partial motives cover, I think, a conviction which has remained with man since his home was a cave; that to kill a courageous and powerful enemy is automatically to acquire the

*The Hercules-figure also exists in other ancient cultures. The Punic equivalent was the god Melkart; and that of the Babylonians was Gilgamesh.

courage and strength of that enemy. And, somewhere among those motives, there lurks another, less honorable: to destroy what is beautiful, which is one of the worst, and yet one of the most frequent, temptations to which human nature is subject.

In the eyes of the general public, the lion is indeed the prototype of the virtues that are traditionally regarded as male and heroic. It is, moreover, the incarnation of proud virility, a splendid creature at the peak of its strength, representing an unlimited potential for violence. Thus, the hunting of the lion becomes, as it were, a settling of accounts, a struggle to the death against a formidable rival. It also represents a deliverance from fear and doubt and humiliation, akin to deliverance from tyrants or brigands.

One can easily see how complex are motives, both conscious and unconscious, which impel a man to undertake the killing of a lion. How naïve it seems, therefore, to speak of the "adventure" or the "fun" of big-game hunting. Even the word "adventure" barely touches on a single aspect of the mass of fears, ambitions, superstitions, and symbols which control the relationship of man with the Lord of the Jungle.

Man's determination to demonstrate his superiority over the lion has now entered a new phase, which manifests itself in the enclosure of lions within preserves. It is entirely possible that the lions themselves would be the last to protest against this arrangement, for they are, by nature, lazy creatures, and life on a preserve encourages indolence and inactivity. It also serves to emasculate the lions, speaking metaphorically, by blunting their aggressive instincts to the point where many lions have formed friendships—rather distant friendships, to be sure—with the rangers on the preserves, and even with the general public. Some of these animals have become quite famous for their "friendliness"; Hildebrand and Hadubrand, for example, and Brunette and Blondie, at the Nairobi preserve.

These lions are no longer the product of their natural environment. They are rather the invention of man; or, more accurately, the product of two of man's inventions—the automobile and the camera. That they have learned to tolerate automobiles and the humans in those automobiles is to say very little. What is more interesting is that they have apparently learned to perform for human spectators. It is impossible for someone who knows lions to look on these animals, with their attitude of utter indifference, their manner of rising and going to nip at a female, their elaborate yawns, their habit of stretching out like enormous pussycats—it is impossible to see all these things without feeling the gnawing suspicion that, somehow, the whole thing is nothing more than affectation and pretense. This, of course, is the rankest anthropomorphism; but we must, after all, make use of human terms to speak of animals. I do not say that lions are affected or pretentious; I say only that, on certain preserves where the struggle for life or for territory no longer plays a major role, they *seem* pretentious and affected. Nor am I the only one to have received that impression. The wife of one of the first administrators of the Serengeti preserve once told me: "Our lions are perfectly capable of doing just about anything that is expected of them—everything, that is, except eating you alive. And I don't doubt that they would do even that if we asked them to."

The notion that lions, out of an eagerness to please, or from some less discoverable motive, could pretend to be what they are not, is not one whit less incredible than a host of other notions that are generally accepted as true. One such notion is reflected in constant references to the "terrible and formidable jaws" of the lion. The fact is that the teeth of the lion are comparatively small—much smaller than those of the leopard and the cheetah, for example. Its real weapon is not its mouth, but its paws, with their long, curved, and retractable claws. In an attack, the lion tries to knock its victim to the ground with a stroke of its paw—as all trainers and guides well know. It does not use its mouth to kill the victim once the latter is on the ground, but rather depends on a blow with its shoulder, and the weight of its body, to do the job. The belief that a lion pursues its prey is also a fable. The lion knows quite well that its ordinary victims—antelope, gnu, and zebras—are all faster than he is (although the female lion is capable of greater speeds than the male).

The idea that we have, perhaps from jungle movies, of lions prowling about ready to attack and devour anything that moves is an old wives' tale. A lion will do battle with another animal, such as a rhinoceros or another lion, only if there is no way in which to avoid such an encounter. In almost every instance the lion prefers simply to walk away rather than to fight. And yet, the lion is undoubtedly courageous; more courageous, for instance, than the tiger. The tiger is more aggressive than the lion because aggression is inspired by fear; and the lion, to all appearances, does not know the meaning of fear. Even in its quest for food the lion is a model of temperance. Like other animals—including such ill-reputed creatures as the shark—it does not hunt continually. When it has found a victim such as a gnu or a zebra, it feeds, then it rests for a day or two before hunting again. And it prefers as its victim a relatively weak animal which it can bring down with a minimum of effort and difficulty.

The above may explain the apparently strange confidence exhibited by herbivorous animals in the presence of lions so long as the lions show themselves openly and make no attempt at concealment. Herbivores seem to sense that the only real enemy is a hidden enemy. If a lion strolls openly onto a plain, in full view, the gnu, zebras, and antelope look up for a moment, then continue grazing. There is a well-understood rubric of the wild which dictates that a victim must be taken by surprise, which, at least for the predator, is more certain and less tiring a method of hunting than pursuing the victim. Thus, when a lion appears in the open near a herd of antelope, the antelope are aware that the lion is not hunting, and that they are safe.

When it comes to hiding, however, lions are quite ingenious. In the Manda preserve, I came across two full-grown lions, each one squeezed behind a tree, like children playing hide-and-seek. They were watching two eland grazing nearby. The eland, needless to say, were completely unaware that they had been selected for the lions' dinner. Our arrival spoiled the game for the lions, and the eland bounded away.

There has been considerable difference of opinion over whether lions hunt during the day or during the night. The truth is quite simple. When lions were hunted over the whole of Africa, they became nocturnal hunters, for much the same reasons that the few remaining wild elephants now wait for dark in order to venture out in search of food: They sensed that it was safer to move about under cover of darkness than during the daylight hours. Now, however, on the preserves, and especially during the past fifteen years, lions have been reassured with respect to the behavior of humans, and they have become what they once were: diurnal hunters. I do not believe that they hunt during the heat of the day. They seem to prefer the early-morning or late-evening hours. The reason may be that there is less chance of the victim being frightened off by tourists.

Lions are not picky eaters. Generally speaking they are satisfied with whatever food they can procure without too much effort. "The Lion may well be the king of beasts," observes T. C. Bridges, "but when he is hungry he will eat wood rats, locusts, and even garbage. The lion who holds the world's record in this respect is the one which ate the flannel vest of a badly washed, sweaty bearer. When a tiger turns into a man-eater, it is usually because it is old, toothless, and mangy. The African lion needs no such excuse."

Lions never attack full-grown elephants or rhinoceroses. They do try, however, to choose victims which will supply the largest amount of meat and, at the same time, offer the least resistance. The compromise thus effected has made it possible to establish, statistically, their preferred victims. At the head of the list comes the gnu, which weighs about 450 pounds; then the hartebeest, at 300 pounds. Zebras, because they are so swift, are only in third place, even though they weigh in at over 500 pounds. Finally, there are the eland, at about 300 pounds.

Not infrequently, lions, rather than take the trouble of hunting for their own dinner, will steal the prey of others, and especially of jackals and hyenas. (The hyenas, however, have their revenge. Sometimes a pack of them will pursue, and eventually bring down, an aged lion.)

There is no tale more widely believed than that which maintains that the lion and lioness are models of devotion so far as their young are concerned. It is easy to see how this belief originated. One has only to see the lion romping with his offspring, allowing his cubs to nip at his tail or climb onto his back, or the lioness licking her offspring with every sign of tender affection. When it comes down to the serious business of eating, however, one gets a somewhat different impression. When a victim is killed (in a well-organized pride, the females take turns hunting) the lion cubs are sent sprawling by a cuff of a paw if they dare approach the meat. The older, stronger lions eat first; and if the cubs still insist on coming too near, they receive another harder cuff which sometimes knocks them a distance of four or five yards. This parental brutality when it comes to feeding, and the fact that the cubs eat only if the adult lions have more than enough to satisfy their own hunger, may well account in large part for the high mortality rate among young lions.

On the other hand it is equally true that female lions, as jealous as they are of food, take great pains to teach their young to hunt for food of their own, by demonstrating how to hide and above all by demonstrating the technique of the kill. For, strange as it seems, cats are not born with a knowledge of how to hunt.* It is an acquired skill. When a ranger in the Amboselli preserve turned loose a female lion he had raised from birth, he found it was necessary to spend several weeks teaching the animal to hunt. Left to itself, the lion had neither the skill, nor apparently the desire, to kill for food.

It is often said that the female lion is the one which shoulders the burden not only of rearing her young but also of teaching them to hunt and in hunting, herself, in order to procure food for the pride.† To a large extent this is quite true. The role of the male lion, however, is of equal importance for the pride. It is their responsibility to defend the space in which the pride lives and which is necessary to its survival. They mark the extent of their pride's domain by urinating along its boundaries. And, if other lions ignore those boundaries and wander into the pride's space, the males defend that space. Their proper role, therefore, is to assure the integrity of the space which is necessary to the pride's

*This fact is still disputed: Examples have been cited of young lions who have hunted without having been taught.

†Lions generally live in groups, or prides, of five or six specimens. Occasionally much larger prides are found. In Kruger Park, for example, there is a pride consisting of some forty lions.

survival. In other words the male lion protects the family group while the female lion provides for it.

This family group often consists of a male in his prime, and of three or four females and their young. The young are conceived when the female ruts, which occurs once a month. She then gives off a characteristic odor and marks her territory with urine mixed with a secretion from the anal glands—a combination which has the effect of making the male extremely amorous.

The male, however, does not always win the prize immediately. The female puts him off with ruses and coquetry, and sometimes with solid cuffs of her paws. Finally, a couple forms, and their union generally is respected by the other members of the pride. The couple then withdraws to a "bridal suite" of their own choosing, where they remain undisturbed for a week, neither hunting nor feeding.

So long as the male is young, strong, and vigorous, he reigns like a monarch over his harem of females. As time goes on, however, he finds his rule challenged by younger and stronger rivals, and gradually the harem disintegrates. Thereafter, the male, once lord of all he surveyed, becomes a loner.

There was a time when the lion preserves of Africa were not characterized by the air of calm, and even apathy, which strikes the visitor today. Kruger National Park, for example, suffered many vicissitudes before its boundaries were finally established and its existence recognized in the first years of the twentieth century—some thirty years after the founding of Yellowstone Park in the United States. Kruger was the first of the African preserves, and its establishment was due in large part to the tenacity of the man who was to become its first superintendent, Lieutenant Colonel J. Stevenson-Hamilton.

Kruger National Park, from its earliest years, was

home to a large number of lions. The superintendent was a man of intelligence and good judgment, and he was careful to keep the lion population at a level that was sufficiently high to insure that the park would not be defoliated by an overabundance of herbivores. In 1936, for example, there were some 600 lions on the preserve—enough to kill approximately 9,000 herbivores per year.

Colonel Stevenson-Hamilton was the first superintendent to realize that visitors to the park were in no danger from the animals so long as people remained in their automobiles.* In the first edition of the guide which he authored, *Kruger National Park,* Stevenson-Hamilton explained: "The lions realize that automobiles are without interest for them so far as food is concerned. Automobiles have no odor which they can perceive, since it is probable that the smell of petrol covers all others. Nonetheless, an automobile is a strange object, and initially it awakens a certain amount of curiosity which quickly dissipates. The lion, when it is neither frightened nor angry, and when it is not in search of food, is an indolent and easygoing animal. It prefers to live quietly without becoming involved in what is going on around it—like other cats, for that matter. For that reason, it looks upon an automobile in much the same light as a house cat regards a mechanical toy."

In the heart of Africa there is a modest village named Fort Archambault. Fort Archambault is the center of wild-game hunting in Black Africa, and it is there that guides come to wait for, or to solicit, their clients. Twenty years ago, in the village's only hotel, the guides used to gather in the evening to exchange stories about these clients. These were not "tall stories," for the men

*At that time lions hunted only at night, for the reasons pointed out earlier. Today, on the preserves, they hunt during the daylight hours. This is another behaviorial modification brought about by the creation of preserves.

gathered around the bar knew one another very well, and observed one another in their work. There was little opportunity for exaggeration. I was there one night, listening to the men talk. In the yard of the hotel, the still-bloody heads of slain antelope were propped up against the walls. Mud-covered jeeps lined the roadside. The guides had cleaned and oiled their rifles, and now settled down for an exchange of information and confidences. A good friend of mine told us the following story:

"One day I received a letter from a man in Bordeaux, asking me to organize a lion hunt for him. To be accurate, I must say that the man who wrote did not seem particularly keen on big-game hunting as such. What he wanted was much more definite and more limited than that. He wanted to kill a lion. I replied by cable, and we arranged to meet on a certain day. I went to the airport, and I was able to spot the man immediately. He was your typical amateur, loaded down with cameras and rifles, wearing a brand new sun helmet and boots polished until they shone.

"He seemed extremely nervous. He told me that he wanted to go out and get his lion immediately, and he was quite angry when I explained that we would have to wait until the next day, and that he should get a good night's sleep beforehand. I had a great deal of trouble in calming him down. I tried to make him talk about other hunts that he had been on. It turned out that the extent of his experience was that he had once, as a boy, killed a rabbit.

"I did everything I could to persuade him to start out with something a little less dangerous than a lion, but he absolutely refused. He was interested only in lions, he told me.

"By then, I was very much intrigued by this man. He had a special reason for wanting to kill a lion. Perhaps even a secret reason. In any case, he seemed completely sure of himself, certain of his aim, and, above all, absolutely determined to kill his lion. There was nothing I could do but agree to take him out. The more I tried to dissuade him, the more nervous and upset he became.

"I examined his rifles. They were magnificent—but absolutely new. They had obviously never been fired, and had been bought for the occasion. My client, I concluded, was rich. Indeed, he was willing to pay anything that I asked if I agreed to be his guide. That, of course, is not necessarily the prime consideration. There are some people who are rich, and crazy or stupid into the bargain.

"The only reason I even considered taking this man out was that my trackers had just reported sighting a small pride of lions at about a morning's march from Fort Archambault. There was a male in the pride, which seemed to be what this man was after. It would not be easy to approach the lions, of course, but, with a good wind and a bit of luck, I would be able to lead my client to a lion that he could have no complaints about.

"The next morning, in the jeep, I made a last attempt to persuade the man at least to try his aim and his rifles on something less dangerous than a lion; on a gnu, perhaps, or a warthog. He refused. In fact, he was quite angry. 'I don't care what you charge me,' he said. 'You can make me pay for a ten-day safari, or a twenty-day safari. Whatever you want. But, for God's sake, let's get on with it!'

"By then, I was as angry as he was. All right, I told myself. Have it your own way.

"We left the jeep and began walking, following our trackers. We walked for about three hours, not even stopping for lunch. We ate our sandwiches on the move.

"The man hardly spoke the whole time. When he took a drink of water, I saw that his hands were trembling. It was not an encouraging sign.

"The approach was perfect. The head tracker took us to the rear of the pride of lions, and slightly to the side. The male was there, stretched out on the ground, yawning and scratching himself. There was a second, older male farther away, ahead of us.

"I led the man to within about ten yards of the animal. I practically had to drag him. He refused to move forward, and with every step he made a strange, groaning sound, pointed his finger at me, and rolled his eyes like a madman. I couldn't understand what he was trying to say.

"Finally, we were in position, crouching behind a thicket. By then, the lion had risen and was sitting upright. His right profile was toward us, and he looked like a statue of gold. I felt as though we were about to commit a murder.

"I showed the lion to my client, and made a sign indicating that he should raise his weapon. Instead, he made a gesture which conveyed unmistakably what he had had in mind: 'No, not me,' the gesture said. 'You. Go ahead. You kill it.'

"I was astonished. The man had come all the way from France. He had paid a large sum of money in order to kill his lion. And now he refused to do so. I had my own weapon ready to use in case he missed, but it was contrary to my principles to fire the first shot.

"It was my turn to try gestures in a last attempt to persuade him to fire. He understood me quite well. His response was to hide his rifle behind his back and shake his head violently.

"The lion was, for the moment, a perfect target. It had not moved an inch. But I knew that the situation would not last. I was ready to get up and drag my client off into the brush and back to Fort Archambault. He must have read my thoughts, because he folded his hands as though praying and whispered desperately, 'Please, you kill it!'

"The lion heard his voice. He rose and looked fixedly in our direction. I could see his body tense. I had just enough time to raise my rifle and fire. The round struck the lion between the eye and the ear, and the splendid animal crashed to the ground.

"The young lions of the pride ran off. The older male remained there, looking at us and roaring. I was determined not to fire again. I began shouting, and he moved off, reluctantly.

"Without looking at the man, I walked forward a few steps and put another round into the lion's head. When I lowered my rifle, the man was standing next to me, clutching his camera. He thrust it at me, then stooped down and raised the lion's head and, with a brusque gesture, ordered me to photograph him in that position.

"I was furious. I handed the camera to my bearer and said, 'Take a picture of *Monsieur.*'

" 'No,' the man cried. 'It will spoil everything. *You* take it!'

"I took the photograph.

"We pitched our tent a hundred yards from that spot. When night fell, and the bearers and trackers were skinning the lion, I opened a bottle of champagne to toast our 'victory.'

"By then, the man had calmed down. His hands no longer trembled. He had a vague smile on his lips. Our camp, surrounded by the sounds of the jungle at night, seemed an oasis of peace and security. It seemed an opportune moment to find out what I wanted to know.

" 'Now,' I said, 'Tell me why.'

"He smiled as though in a dream.

" 'Why, what?'

" 'Why you came so far and spent so much money, and didn't fire a shot.'

" 'For this,' he said, tapping the camera with his index finger. Then, in great excitement, he shouted: 'It's because of my wife! She has a lover! Now I can go back to her and show her the photograph and tell her, "I'm a lion killer! Be careful how you treat me!'"

"He took a plane back to France the next day. I have no way of knowing the end of the story."

If I have gone into some detail concerning my friend's account of his client, it is because the story is indicative of the incredible pride that a man takes in the killing of a lion, of the vanity that the killing feeds, of the self-confidence that it engenders. And, obviously, the more fearsome the animal, the greater the "benefit" a man derives.

Everyone is aware, certainly, of the lengths to which the tensions of modern life, and of marital life, can drive a man. What is interesting, in this context, is that man, to escape from such a situation, still has recourse to prehistoric means. He kills an animal—or, in this case, sacrifices money in order to pretend that he has killed an animal—so as to regain the respect of his wife. This, it seems to me, must be interpreted as proof that deep in modern man there exists a nostalgia for a life of physical danger and of struggle against wild animals. The choice of the lion as a victim is particularly significant and is perfectly situated within an historical perspective. The lion is the exemplar of nobility and courage, the most feared animal and, in the eyes of most hunters, the most dangerous adversary in the jungle. The glory conferred by the killing of a lion has its origin in the dim mists of history, at a time when it was somewhat justified by the disproportion between the power and strength of the lion and the feeble weapons at man's disposal. To attack a lion was an undoubted act of courage; and the courage of the man resulted in the divinization of the lion, as it were, by proxy. Man, to become like a god, must slay a god. It is this ancient concept which inspired my friend's client in his determination to become a killer of lions, or at least to pass himself off as such in the eyes of his philandering wife.

In that particular case the man was at least willing to sacrifice a great deal of money to acquire a smattering of vicarious glory. There are many cases in which people are not willing to do even that. A few years ago, a young Parisian couple devised an ingenious way to make money. They acquired a lion cub and went from restaurant to restaurant offering, for a modest amount, to photograph people holding the cub. Everyone was wild about the idea. The favorite positions were holding the cub against one's chest, or draping it over one's shoulder. It was, one must admit, a tempting opportunity. The cub evoked exotic places, adventure—and, at the same time, offered the pleasure of holding a warm furry animal.

The idea caught on. Apparently there is no end to the number of lion cubs that may be rented or bought in Paris. Both materially and psychologically, the venture, based as it was on the vanity of the public and the prestige of animals, succeeded beyond the entrepreneurs' wildest dreams. The cub, however, was obviously miserable. Dragged from café to café, night after night—probably in a slightly drugged state for greater safety—handed from person to person like a package, it existed in a constant state of fright and insecurity. Finally, the Prefect of Police, in a burst of sound judgment, forbade this kind of photographic minisafari; and that was the end of this twentieth-century manifestation of the Hercules complex.

In 1955 I accompanied a caravan of fifty trucks carrying supplies from Tunis to Sebha, the capital of Fezzan, in the eastern Sahara. The distance to be covered was some 3,500 miles, across an implacable desert, over dunes and rocks, in the full heat of the African sun. Our route lay through the Hammada el

Homra, a region without roads, without water, and without oases. The normal duration of the journey was from ten to twenty days depending upon what occurred en route.

The caravan looked like a circus traveling across the moon's barren surface. There were seventy-five men, thirty-five 10-ton supply trucks, a provisions truck, a radio truck, water trucks, and fuel trucks. The leader of this motley assortment of vehicles and humans was an old Sahara hand universally and affectionately known as Monsieur Gauthier. In his jeep, he went back and forth along the convoy, sinking into the sand, hurtling over rocks. I was his guest—and his passenger.

Gauthier knew, in at least four languages, the vocabulary of invectives and curses in common use in the Sahara in order to make reluctant engines start, to make bogged-down trucks rise miraculously out of the sand, and to whip sleepy drivers into action.

For two days we drove through an absolutely empty desert. On the third day we reached the Hammada. The horizon seemed to stretch into infinity as we drove over a lake, not of water but of minerals, which shimmered in the sunlight like a compound of fused metals.

In the distance we could see a reddish line against the horizon: the first patch of vegetation. We would feast on gazelle steaks that night, we assured ourselves. We were still many days' journey away from Sebha, and everyone dreamed of fresh meat. In this area hunting was a necessity arising from a primitive human urge; the urge of nomads roaming a desolate waste, hungering for their ration of meat and blood.

Here and there we caught sight of "pastures" —patches of yellowish dusty *drinn* punctuating the boundless stretches of sand. The ligneous growth appeared almost lifeless. It had been four years since the last rainfall.

We zigzagged from pasture to pasture, hoping to find gazelles grazing on this miserable grass. But we saw none.

Toward sunset I glimpsed a silhouette in the distance; it seemed to be a small, slender animal of some kind. The jeep headed toward the spot I indicated. The animal began to move away at a trot. It seemed to flutter over the sand. I saw that it was a cheetah, and I immediately regretted having pointed it out to the others, having betrayed it. But it was too late.

"Shoot," Gauthier shouted. "Shoot, for God's sake!"

How could I fire? The cheetah had slowed a bit to turn and look at us. Then it ran again, confident in its ability to outdistance us if need be.

I thought of cheetahs I had seen. The cheetah held captive at Agadès, who had looked at me from within its cage, its dark golden eyes sad and despairing. The cheetah at Lai which loved to romp with our hunting dogs and delighted in jumping on my back.

The animal before us was in the prime of life. Perhaps three years old, large, slender, splendidly muscled. His head was small, round, finely molded, and topped by pointed cat's ears. As he ran, his paws barely touched the sand.

The jeep roared, accelerated. The cheetah turned to look at us once more, as though to say that, after all, the game had gone on long enough. He was running at full speed now, but the distance between him and us was narrowing.

"Fire!" Gauthier shouted again. "Fire, I tell you!"

I fired. My aim was so poor that I have no idea where the round went. I reloaded hurriedly.

"Give me that," Gauthier said, and snatched the rifle from my hands. There was a shot, and I saw the cheetah stumble, then fall.

Until my dying day, I shall never be able to forget the look in its eyes as we approached; a look of inexpressible astonishment, sadness, and incredulity in the face of death. Then the golden eyes closed, and in a moment its magnificent pelt seemed to lose its luster.

I could not eat that night.

There are many people who would argue that there was nothing wrong in what we did; that the cheetah is, after all, a wild animal, ferocious, predatory, dangerous. The same people have no trouble in summoning up indignation over the massacre of the American bison in the nineteenth century, or over the slaughter of elephants in Africa a little later. But these animals, they explain, are herbivores. They do not kill other animals. They are "nice" animals.

It should be said once and for all that predatory animals kill without hate and without malice. I have had for many years a photograph of a panther, taken at the very instant that the animal was about to seize a monkey. The panther's features are totally at peace, its jaws closed. Innocence, and even gentleness, are evident in its eyes as it faces its terrified, cringing, shrieking prey. The panther killed as all predators kill; that is, in order to eat and to survive.

Man, who kills for sport or for pleasure, cannot say as much for himself. Forty or fifty years ago, there were tens of thousands of tigers in the forests of India. Today, there are several hundred remaining. The rest have been sacrificed to sport and pleasure. Those which remain are scattered about here and there. In eastern Pakistan and Nepal, for example, I doubt that there are a hundred surviving specimens. The Bengal tiger, the Java tiger (of which only twelve are alive today), the Sumatran tiger, and the Chinese and Indochinese tigers are all on the endangered species list. It is too late for the Bali tiger, for it is already extinct.

Such is the fate of a predator which has no natural enemies except man. Yet, it is not the tiger hunt which is primarily responsible for the disappearance of the tiger,* but the growth of the human population† and, perhaps more than anything else, the demand for tiger skins from which fur coats are made for ladies whose husbands can afford the exorbitant price. These skins were usually obtained by poisoning the tigers, so as not to harm the pelts. Recently, however, the Indian government has taken steps to halt the export of tiger skins.

It may be argued that the tiger is an animal which is not only dangerous, but also quite useless to man. That is debatable. Man, if he is to maintain his psychological and moral equilibrium, must preserve the fauna which has constituted his environment for so many thousands of years. As it is, we have been only too successful in our determination to expand our living space at the expense of the animal kingdom. On the other hand, the survival of some of the great carnivores indicates that that victory may not be altogether without saving grace. It is only the protection and preservation of all species, however, that can demonstrate ultimately that man is worthy of being master of the planet, for only then will it become evident that man is aware of, and has finally taken into account, the biological equilibrium of his world.

The predators that we have hunted, slaughtered, and poisoned played an essential role in the preservation of that equilibrium. If they had not constantly limited the increase of antelope, deer, and buffalo, these herbivores would have multiplied in catastrophic fashion. And this in fact is precisely what is happening in certain preserves. The herbivores, free from attack by predators, are breeding at an alarming rate, and, in the

*Though this has certainly made a major contribution. When George VI of England visited his Indian Empire, he and his suite killed thirty-nine tigers in eleven days.

†In the past thirty years, the population of India has doubled, to 700 million.

foreseeable future, the flora of these preserves will consist of nothing more than a lawnlike carpet of green. At that point man will either have to allow the animals to starve—or kill them himself. If we may draw a lesson from this, we may say that, without predators, today there would not be a forest or a jungle on the face of the earth.

This is not sheer speculation. In the Galápagos Islands off the western coast of South America, there are no carnivores. When visiting merchantmen turned a few goats loose on the islands, it took only a few years before the vegetation had been so drastically reduced that the famous giant tortoises of the Galápagos became extinct through starvation.

It is almost axiomatic that whenever man has tried to impose strict controls on the number of carnivores, catastrophe has resulted. The classic example, perhaps, took place in the United States, during the administration of that famous big-game hunter, President Theodore Roosevelt. In 1906 Mr. Roosevelt declared the Kaibab plateau, along the northern boundary of the Grand Canyon in Colorado, to be a refuge for a herd of 4,000 deer. His purpose was ostensibly commendable: to protect the deer from their natural enemies—pumas, coyotes, and wolves.

In the years which followed, the second phase of Mr. Roosevelt's plan was implemented, and hunters proceeded to destroy hundreds of pumas and coyotes and to wipe out entirely the local population of wolves. Thereupon the herd of deer began to increase disproportionately and to eat everything within reach. By 1920 there were 100,000 deer. By 1922, 60 percent of the herd had died of starvation, and the entire area had been devastated to an extent that appeared almost irremediable. "If the natural balance between predators and prey had not been modified," one authority concludes, "there would have been no problem, and the result would have been a large population of deer which would have been self-containing."*

Instances of the catastrophic results which occur whenever man tampers with nature's balance could be multiplied indefinitely. The open season on coyotes in California produced a veritable Biblical plague of rats and rabbits. The Macquarie Islands were the scene of a tragicomic series of such events. First, cats were imported to reduce the number of rabbits, but the cats chose to kill birds instead of rabbits. Then dogs were imported to kill the cats; but they ignored the cats and attacked the seals.

Such instances of tampering with nature are hardly new in history. One of the most loudly voiced complaints contained in the records of the States-General, on the eve of the French Revolution, concerned the abuses which resulted from the fact that it was the exclusive privilege of the upper classes and of landowners to hunt. The slaughter of animals, it seems, was somehow regarded as a prerogative of the aristocracy. (Such attitudes are by no means confined to pre-Revolutionary times. Hunting remains one of the more ridiculous pastime amusements of royalty. The former King of Spain, Alphonso XIII, killed 1,200 pheasants during a single outing. And Ibn Saud, King of Saudi Arabia, massacred 100 gazelles in one day.)

Man's passion for hunting has not escaped the attention of psychoanalysis. The use of firearms, we are told, represents a vindication of a man's virility. The rifle is the death-dealing penis. This hypothesis seems confirmed by the fact that, though there remains comparatively little game, there are huge numbers of hunters; and, by all accounts, hunting licenses are issued in increasing numbers each year both in Europe

*Robert Orr, *Mammals of North America.*

and in America. The aristocratic prestige of the hunt has survived, even though its risks have been abolished and even though its victims may be nothing more challenging than a frightened deer, a rabbit, or a pheasant. Even the panoply of *noblesse* has survived in that most elaborate of ceremonies, the fox hunt, which Wilde once described, so aptly, as "the unspeakable in full pursuit of the inedible."

Given the psychological and social significance of the hunt, it should not be surprising that, in the past two thousand years, some one hundred species of mammals have become extinct; or that, nowadays, species are disappearing at the average rate of one per year. Two hundred and seventy-one species are threatened with imminent extinction, of which eighty-eight species are mammals, and another thousand species are listed as endangered. The *Black Book* of the International Union for the Preservation of Nature and Natural Resources contains a list of the species which have become extinct since the beginning of the seventeenth century. Of the 4,226 species of mammals, thirty-six have become extinct since the year 1600; and a hundred and twenty more are endangered. Of the 8,646 species of birds, ninety-four have become extinct during the same period, and an additional 187 species are regarded as endangered.*

It seems that the fauna of the American continent have been the principal victim of the human predilection for hunting. The asphalt pits of the La Brea ranch, near Los Angeles, have been discovered to contain a large number of fossils dating back more than 10,000 years. These fossils provide us with rather precise data. The excavators discovered not only the bones and the stone arrowheads of the first Amerindians, but also the

*We know of many species which became extinct before 1600; but for these we are not certain of their precise coloration or of their anatomical details.

remains of fifty-four species of mammals dating from 8000 to 4500 B.C. Of these fifty-four species, twenty-four are extinct today, notably the saber-toothed tiger, the giant lion, the camel, the imperial mammoth, and the mastodon. All these species were still alive when prehistoric man first set foot on the American continent. In all fairness, however, it should be said that the extinction of a species is not necessarily the result of human intervention. It seems that the life span of a species of mammal, as a species, is about 600,000 years. But it is undeniable that man's interference has often been instrumental in greatly reducing that span.

It is often said that the accelerated pace at which species are becoming extinct is due solely to the use of effective modern weapons. Certainly, the development of new and more efficient ways of killing animals is the principal cause of this phenomenon; but it is not the only cause. We must also take into account a certain psychological element. For thousands of years, magical and religious considerations prevented man from slaughtering animals blindly and without counting the number of them. Nature and nature's balance was protected by a human system of rites, beliefs, and taboos. The gods of the hunt, the animal-gods of man, were the great game wardens of primitive human society. Now, however, in the West, we have repudiated the magico-religious character of the hunt; and, since these controls no longer obtain, the slaughter of animals has increased disastrously.

Before the advent of civilization, and before hunting was reduced to a mere technique, the killing of animals was a religious undertaking. The risks it involved were less from the animal that was hunted than from the supernatural forces put into motion by the animal's death. To eat the meat of an animal was, in effect, to eat a being to which man was related. To be a carnivore was to be a cannibal. The chief problem was not to kill the animal, but to persuade the animal of the legitimacy of its death. Thus, the Eskimo of Alaska asked the whale for its consent before they killed it. The Ainu were required to expiate the death of the bear. Within that framework, the hunt was not a mere duel between a man and an animal. It was an encounter between man, backed by his gods, and the animal, who, man was certain, was equally backed by its own gods. We may call such beliefs superstition, magic, religion—anything that we wish. The fact remains that for thousands of years they protected the animal kingdom by limiting the number of man's victims and by allowing for the replacement of those victims.

It was not really until the modern era that hunting began to be regarded as a sport to be undertaken for its own sake. The consequent secularization of the hunt has had disastrous effects, because we are no longer constrained to limit the number of animals killed or to provide for their replacement (except by game laws, which, as often as not, are observed in the breach). The gods of our ancestors, on the other hand, while they presided at the killing of animals, simultaneously insured their multiplication. Whether they were the gods of the animals or animal-gods, they guaranteed respect for the creatures which they incarnated or by which they were incarnated. Thus, Runda, the god of the Hittites, was the god of the hunt and also the protector of animals; as was Artemis the huntress.

In the same vein, the major rites of the hunt took place neither before nor during the actual hunting, but afterward, when remorse followed the satisfaction of desire. "The hunter," R. Lantier says, "kills only with regret. He looks to justify his act. He must make use of every possible means to placate the spirits which he has offended, by lamentations, by the ritual preservation of certain parts of the body. . . ." But the death of an animal in ancient societies required more than expiation; it also required certain operations aimed at replacing the animal. And man, for thousands of years, lived under these magico-religious obligations which, more than any of our present-day rules and regulations, assured the preservation of species. The Yakoutes had a saying: "The man who kills too many bears will perish at the hands of a bear." And, according to a Samoyed legend, their god grew angry at a hunter who, having already killed a fair share of reindeer, began tracking a white bear.

The notion of expiation is particularly interesting in illustrating this mentality. After the death of an animal, the man who killed it was expected to pay, in one way or another, for the death. "Animalicide," as Lévy-Bruhl called it, was of the same gravity as homicide, and the killer of the animal was required to undergo purification so as to reestablish the order of nature which had been upset by the animal's death. This took the form of paying homage and honor to the victims, which, in turn, was supposed to result in the continuity of the species and in a supply of new victims.

The celebrated scene at Lascaux which depicts man paying with his own life for the death of an animal is perhaps an expiatory offering. It may have been hoped that the representation of that exchange would spare man from having to pay, in fact, for a life with a life, from having to balance the death of an animal with his own death.

Such attitudes are no longer imposed by our religion, customs, or superstitions. We have replaced such things by what we claim is the rule of reason and, sometimes, by "heart." Is it too much to expect that, in our minds and our hearts, we may find the means both to preserve the species and to insure their multiplication?

Someday man will realize that whenever he attempts to control the natural balance of the earth he loses a bit of his environment. And someday he will learn that when a species of animal becomes extinct a piece of our universe has been lost forever. We do not realize these things yet. Or, in any case, we continue to cause the extinction of species. We continue to hunt, to exercise our vanity and to demonstrate our virility in the stupid, cruel, senseless slaughter of our brother-creatures. We continue to pollute our rivers and streams and oceans, we continue to foul our air. And, above all, we continue to multiply relentlessly. Our cities spread; our highways cover the earth. Soon there will be no place for animals in this world.

Some men believe that grass, trees, and forests, the air, the sun, and the seas are the gift of God. That may be. But they are also the result of a very delicate balance of nature; a balance so precarious that the disappearance of a single species may bring down the house of cards on which human survival itself depends.

CHAPTER FIVE

The Secrets of the Cave

Our most profound relationship to art lies at the metaphysical level.
—ANDRÉ MALRAUX

MAN, long before he began to domesticate animals, had come to regard them as somehow annexed to himself. The essential factor in the exercise of this annexation was not the human hand, but rather the human mind. Courage, cunning, tenacity, and ingenuity were of infinitely more value in this undertaking than the fist or the spear. Man, it is true, taught himself the art of hunting; but he also learned the meaning of doubt, anguish, and superstition. The animal, as victim, enmeshed man in the infinite web of the irrational. In that sense, both art and religion are creations of a culture of hunters.

It is obvious from prehistoric paintings and sculptures that man, by the end of the Paleolithic era, had come to regard animals as the symbols and foundations of human beliefs. He attempted, so to speak, to make animals share with him a burden the weight of which he had begun to feel: a burden of anguish concerning the afterlife, a burden of fascination with the sacred. Prehistoric man's images of an apotheosized animal kingdom were enclosed within the walls of caves in order to protect one of the great secrets of man: the fear of death.

Thus, the animal was deified and became something more than an animal. It became a religious object, a symbol, a myth, an image. It has retained something of this character even today, in a world where man himself has lost whatever of the sacred he once had about him.

In France's Perigord region, there is a charming little village named Montignac. Nearby is the Vézère Valley, which is famous for its prehistoric caves.

On September 12, 1940, during World War II, four youngsters—hardly more than children—were walking near the village, on a plateau which rises a few dozen yards above the Vézère River. Two of the four young people—Ravidat and Marsal—were natives of the region. The third, Agnel, was visiting relatives. And the fourth, Coencas, was a refugee.

The boys were accompanied by a dog; a rather dull, ill-humored, and snappish dog which, as it happens, was to become the hero of this story.

The dog ran ahead of the humans, sniffing at the ground, darting this way and that in the underbrush. Suddenly it disappeared from sight. The boys guessed immediately what had happened. Several years before, a storm had uprooted a fir tree, leaving a large, deep hole in the ground. No one from the village had ever bothered to go down into the hole, but in order to keep their animals from falling into it they had covered it with pieces of wood. The dog apparently had either misjudged its step or one of the pieces had given way under its weight.

The boys leaned over the hole and called the dog. They heard a bark, distant and muffled. The animal was alive, they concluded, but unable to climb out. They decided to go down after it. The biggest and strongest of them went first, climbing down the side of the hole until he reached the bottom. The others followed. At the bottom of the hole they saw a dark corridor. There was no way of knowing if it was a bottomless pit or simply an underground cavern. Yet they could still hear the dog barking. There must therefore be at least a ledge. They decided to go on.

The corridor led to a chamber, where they were greeted with manic enthusiasm by the dog. One of the boys lighted a match and looked around. "There's more," he said.

Off the chamber, there was a gallery hidden in darkness. From the echo, they judged it to be quite large. It would have been a marvelous place to explore, but it was getting late and there were no more matches.

"We'll come back," one of them said. "But let's not tell anyone about this. It's our secret."

The boys did return, this time with ropes and a flashlight. In the dim light they saw a fantastic sight: paintings of huge black bulls, heads lowered, paws spread. Images of horses and deer covered the walls and ceilings. Fascinated, gaping in wonder, they stayed as long as they could, going from wall to wall, finding paintings of bison, aurochs, and other animals, all so vivid that the animals seemed to leap from the walls.

The boys were vaguely aware of what the paintings were. Several caves with painted or sculptured walls had already been found in the vicinity. But there had been none like these.

They climbed out of the cave, silent with astonishment. They had already decided to tell only one person what they had found: M. Laval, a teacher in the primary school attended by two of the boys.

M. Laval's first task was to try to calm the boys' excitement. Initially he refused to believe their story. Finally, on September 13, 1940, he allowed himself to be led to the cave.

Immediately, the excited teacher notified a professional society of prehistorians. A week later, the Abbé Breuil, a leading prehistorian, arrived; and he was followed, on September 27 and 28, by other experts. A few days afterward, the cave was declared officially to be a historical monument.*

Carbon-14 analysis has been able to situate the Lascaux paintings in time. They were executed between 7000 B.C. and 15,000 B.C.† It appears that the cave was still in use in the sixth millennium before Christ. But in use by whom, and for what purpose?

The artists who painted the walls of the Lascaux cave lived at the end of the last glacial period, in the prehistoric era known as the Recent Paleolithic. They were hunters—which does not necessarily mean that they were nomads. They were not an agricultural people, nor were they breeders of animals, but they were profoundly aware of animals, as is strikingly clear from their work.

It is generally agreed that the Lascaux cave was never inhabited by man. The myth that man lived in caves in order to protect himself from the cold has led to a distorted view of prehistory. The fact is that caves are quite rare, and that shelters under rocky overhangs, enclosed by branches or by skins, and huts, are much more common.

Lascaux, therefore, in all probability, was a sanctuary; a sanctuary which remained in use for some 8,000 years. Those eight millennia were as important in the formation of modern man as, let us say, Babylonian law or Greek philosophy. In this case, as in the others, we are the heirs and the tributaries of the thoughts and emotions which were given visible form in those caves through the skills of unknown artists.

All that we know about these men is that they fled

*During the German occupation of France, the Lascaux cave, as it was known, served as a weapons and munitions depot for the French resistance in the Dordogne area.

†An earlier estimate, which now appears to be incorrect, placed them some 22,000 years B.C.

underground to hide, in the form of images, what they had been able to gather from the world above, from the animal world. We may call that transcendental operation whatever we wish; the fact remains that, by any name, it solved for man the secret of creation. It marked his acquisition of the ability to separate living beings from chaos by means of a faculty which was proper to man alone: abstraction. It is that faculty which has made it possible for us today to gaze upon the forms, colors, and actions of animals which long ago disappeared from the face of the earth. The prehistoric artist still teaches. He preserved and recorded, and then passed on to us what he knew. We are both his heirs and his pupils. In that sense, Lascaux is more than a sanctuary. It is also a library.

Prehistorians never cease to be astonished that, in a single cave such as that of Lascaux, Paleolithic hunters depicted, side by side, so many widely different species. Indeed, it seems quite within the bounds of possibility that the prehistoric artist was concerned with recording the result of his personal observations. Even today, in Africa, we find gnu, zebras, and ostriches living side by side, to the mutual benefit of all. Ostriches and giraffes are the first to perceive danger and to give the alarm. Gnu and zebras, since they are the first to be attacked by predators, by their presence provide members of other species with the opportunity for escape.

It is not impossible that Late Paleolithic man was aware of the association of animal species, an association of which he himself was a part. And it is possible that he knew the secrets which we have only lately rediscovered: the secret of the link which unites both the animals of one species among themselves and the various species to one another; the secret of the biological equilibrium which results from that link; the secret of the role played by the herd instinct in the animal world; the secret of territory and that of sexual attraction.

The history of the human adventure is of disconcerting brevity. It covers only about 4,000 years. And what are four millennia compared to the vast span of human existence before the beginning of recorded history? We know very little about the thousands upon thousands of centuries which constitute the prehistorical period. We do know, however, that the problem which occupied man during that time, and his chief problem, was that presented by animal life.

Man formed an integral part of his biological milieu by killing in order to eat, by his attempts to mitigate the danger posed by the proximity of animals, and by the struggle to dominate the animals. In any event, during those unnumbered centuries, man and animal lived in a state of constant contact and continuous interaction. Beyond a doubt, it was an overwhelming experience, one which took place during that period in which the human mind was being formed, and which was a decisive factor in its formation.

The needs of men and of animals at that time were identical. They both needed food, a secure lair, and protection from the cold. Hence, there was a permanent conflict over the possession of caves, for a place in the sun, for safety from enemies during both the night and the daylight hours. In this conflict, our ancestors were pitted against adversaries far better armed, physically, than themselves. The only way in which man could prevail was to make use of a weapon of another order: his mind.

Serge Moscovici draws a conclusion which seems of capital importance in this respect. It was not man, he states, who became a hunter; rather, it was by hunting that man became man. That is the context within which the development and perfecting of hunting techniques played such an important role in the human adventure. Contrary to what is commonly believed, the efforts of the first humans were in no way aimed at separating man from the animal world, or at differentiating him from it, or even at emphasizing the differences which did exist. To the mind of primitive man, human beings could increase their power only by integrating themselves more fully into that world, divining its secrets, and establishing themselves in it. "Just as we delve into the mysteries of chemical reactions and nuclear fission, so they worked to understand the secrets of the bison, the horse and the reindeer."†

In his struggle to grasp the secrets of that arcane kingdom of animals, man developed means which were unknown to the animals. He trained his hands, he invented tools and weapons of stone, he devised the trap, he arrived at the first notion of mechanics. Under the impact of pain, fear, cold, and hunger, he learned the necessity of cooperation with others of his kind. A tribal hunt required communication, and so he learned to codify his sounds into that complex of conventional symbols which we call language. This development of man's mind, social instinct, and imagination—this rising above what he had been—had essentially but one cause and one purpose. It occurred as a function of the world of animals of which man was a part. In a very real sense, therefore, animals were the subject of man's first scientific effort.

"The knowledge of reality," says Gaston Bachelard, "is a light which always casts shadows somewhere."* In the cave of Lascaux there is such a shadow. It consists of

†*La societe contre nature.*
**La Formation de l'esprit scientifique.*

a secret place wherein human fear and human inferiority lie hidden; a place known as the hall of felines. In another hand, in Lascaux, at the bottom of a well in the center of the cave, there is a representation remarkable for its dramatic sense. It shows a man lying at the feet of a bison. The bison has been wounded and one can see its entrails partially exposed. The man is dead, and his arrow is still visible in the bison's body. Not far from the well, some broken spears were found.

The painting may be the commemoration of a hunting accident or it may be a symbolic composition the meaning of which eludes us. There is no way of knowing. All that we know for certain is that the drama of the event, and the anguish, are expressed with an intensity that unites the two subjects by an effective bond which can never be sundered. The stiffness of the human form, its fragility, its slightness—we might even say its ugliness—is in striking contrast to the puissant image of the bison with its massive head and the perfect curve of its parts. Two forms of life, or rather two orders of life, are joined together in the mystery of death.

That painting is, in a sense, an accurate summary of man's prehistoric life. It expresses his inferiority vis-à-vis the animals with which he shared the earth. It was a physical inferiority, certainly; and prehistoric man was aware of that. But, to the minds of our ancestors, it may have also been a spiritual inferiority. For most of his history, both recorded and unrecorded, man has believed that animals were the repositories of mysterious powers and of secrets which he himself was denied.

It is not difficult to understand, within that framework, how it is that Lascaux seems to intend to convey the complex of relationships by which animals are united, in contrast to the inferior situation of the human minority. It is a concept which is evoked in many subterranean sanctuaries other than Lascaux. Lascaux also appears to represent an effort on the part of man "to participate in the great animal adventure which was being played out beyond the bounds of the enclaves of humanity. . . . When the image of a woman appears in bas-relief in the caves, it may well be that she is represented not only as the source of life, but also as the link by virtue of which mankind is united to the world of animals and to nature."*

At the time in which the Lascaux paintings were executed, the pressure exerted on man by the animal world had almost completely disappeared. It therefore seems very difficult to explain why these paintings emphasize the domination of animals. Man was already well on his way to a position of undoubted superiority. He had become an expert butcher and tanner, and he had developed highly specialized tools.

The explanation may well be that by the end of the Paleolithic era the art of the hunters had attained its highest point of development. Hunting itself was no longer an all-consuming preoccupation, and it had probably become an object of study and analysis. The paintings were executed at the end of an era, when the old, practical problems of safety and food were no longer so pressing, and when the threat presented by animals was much less than it had been during the preceding millennia. During the Magdalenian age the hunter was master of his destiny to a degree never before attained. From a practical standpoint, no other prehistoric period witnessed such decisive progress. The techniques of hunting had been perfected, and anguish over what the morrow might bring seemed on the point of disappearing. And yet, if one is to judge by the paintings, the animal still lorded it over man. Everywhere in the caves we see the animal triumphant, proud. Images of the aurochs, sometimes five yards

*Laming-Emperaire, *L'Art rupestre.*

long, overwhelm the viewer, as do the innumerable mammoths of Rouffignac, and the bison of Altamira.

It would be a mistake, in my opinion, to believe that the Paleolithic hunter was perpetually occupied in doing battle against nature, the elements, and the animals. Many prehistorians hold that somewhat exaggerated view; but it does not seem probable that primitive man spent as much of his time defending himself against nature and against other species as he did in attacking them. Ethnographers have established that today, for example, tribes which support themselves entirely by hunting spend only between 35 and 40 percent of their available time in pursuit of that occupation. They have more leisure than, say, a factory worker, and much more than a farmer.* What preoccupied man then, as now, was the finding of problems in order to overcome them. This peculiarity contributed to man's formation and, at the same time, characterized him. Once he had overcome the threat posed by the preponderance of animals, he did not settle back to enjoy a comparatively peaceful life. He remained obsessed with animals; and that obsession remains with us today, although we are unaware of it at the conscious level. Why does it remain? The answer lies somewhere deep within man. The confrontation between man and animal was of such inconceivably long duration that the hunter was deeply marked by it, perhaps even traumatized, and, in any event, psychologically formed (or deformed). It is through that psychological wound that man's anguish naturally manifests itself.

The practical knowledge possessed by those who were, of necessity, careful observers of the world around them, is doubly manifested in these images in the caves; and it was complemented by speculation on

*Serge Moscovici, *op. cit.*

the nature of the world and on the apparent absurdity to which it led: the rigidity of corpses, rot, and nothingness.* For thousands of years man was both the giver and the receiver of death. His partner in this grisly exchange was the animal rather than human beings. (Wars would only come later—and they would involve no metaphysical subtleties.) The animal, therefore, is at the origin of the irrational in man, just as the animal is at the origin of all that there is of rational efficiency, constructive abstraction, and practical knowledge.

It is only in the light of man's distant past that we can arrive at an understanding of our otherwise incomprehensible attitude toward animals today; of our innate sense of the religious symbolism of animals, of the paradox of our abusive affection for animals. It is only by referring to the uncounted creatures which existed when man's spiritual, intellectual, and emotional life was in the process of formation, that we can understand the place of animals in our lives today. For the animal has always been, and remains today, the most constant and important auxiliary of the human mind.

Animals, so far as we can tell, have no knowledge of death. For man, however, death is the black form of the future. For millennia upon millennia, man observed death; the death of animals in the hunt, and, less frequently, the death of men in hunting accidents. It was the animal which opened the gates into another world; and the death of men was linked to that of animals. It was engulfed in the same mystery. It was the source of the same anguish. Thus, at the base of what is irrational in man—or rather, of what is beyond reason and experiential logic—we find the animal; the same animal which is at the source of man's ability to reason effectively, to think clearly, and to form conclusions which are an expression of reality.

*The subjects of this art are almost exclusively animals, and especially the larger mammals. Insects and plants appear with extreme rarity.

The painting at the bottom of the pit in the Lascaux cave, depicting the dead or dying man and the wounded bison, seems less concerned with the hunt and with the wounding of the animal than with life. Gazing upon that representation, I sensed that it was an effort to re-create, by means of images, the artist's concept of balance in the world; to draw order from chaos; to give meaning to that commingling of animals and men which, through the intermediary of the painting, emerges from confusion and chance.*

The animal, therefore, is at the source of man's art and religion, as it is at the source of that technological sense which first manifested itself in the techniques of the hunt. The animal was the medium through which man thought of himself and projected himself. It was almost as though man, being afraid to bear alone the weight of his ideas, compelled the free animals of the time to share the burden; just as, later, he would compel domestic animals to bear burdens of another kind.

Between man and animal, contact was established at every level: psychological, emotional, metaphysical. This, I believe, is the explanation for the fact that the Lascaux paintings, depicting an enormous number of animals in apparent confusion, are actually a single vast unit. The artist conceived the world as a totality, and a totality of which man was an integral part and, probably, not the most important part.

At this point we encounter a difficulty. If we admit that the paintings are not a random collection of animal images, but a total representation, we must attempt to discover the meaning of that representation. We are in the position of men who attempt to decipher the meaning of St. Peter's, in Rome, without knowing of the existence of the New Testament or of the Fathers of the

*Mme. Laming-Emperaire arrives at the same conclusion: "It seems to me that, if there were ceremonies performed in association with these extraordinary bas-reliefs, they were perhaps ceremonies celebrating love and life." *L'art rupestre.*

Church. Indeed, we have nothing from the prehistoric period. No inscriptions, no events. Nothing but images; images without captions.

Notwithstanding these obstacles, there has been some ingenious work done in this area. A. Leroi-Gourhan, for example, has devised an interpretation based on the number and placement of the animals depicted, their positioning with respect to one another, their groupings, and also the presence within these groups of certain signs. Although it is very rare that a male or female is distinctly depicted in the Lascaux paintings, it is true that there is a balance between the extreme complexity of the animals and certain signs denoting males and females the key to which has thus far eluded us. Even so, Leroi-Gourhan's work asserts the existence of a trilogy composed of man-horse-spear facing a trilogy composed of woman-bison-wound.

According to this theory, therefore, every animal, regardless of its sex, is marked with a secret male or female sign. The cave, then, would be something like a vast chessboard, in which the value of the individual animals is determined, not by the animal itself, but by its location.

Whatever the truth may be, it can hardly be doubted that man, at the time that these paintings were executed, was already in full possession of his intellectual and emotional faculties.

We tend to think of the Sahara as a lifeless, desolate expanse. And so it is, to our benefit; for there, in that virtually untouched wasteland, the traces of prehistoric man and prehistoric animals have survived intact. No one has come to disturb them.

I once traveled, by truck, to a sector of the Sahara which was reputed to be inaccessible: the valley of Oued Mathendous, which is part of Fezzan, in the eastern Sahara. It is true that the Sahara, in part, is a desert as most people imagine it; that it is a stretch of sand and dunes. But the Sahara also has mountains and rocks; indeed, most of it consists of stone. At Oued Mathendous, it was necessary for us constantly to move large rocks out of the way so that the truck could pass. Our progress was so slow that I spent most of the time walking behind the truck, listening to the radiator boil, and thinking that we would never escape alive from the blazing, incredible sun.

At dusk Oued Mathendous took on the appearance of a black, rectilinear cut, stretching out before us across the rocky ground. The setting sun daubed the rocks with red. There was not a shrub, not even a tuft of grass. And there was silence. It occurred to me that Oued Mathendous was like a scene from the Inferno—a sun-seared hell from which there was no escape. . . .

I was doing a bit of digging near the walls of the cliffs when, to my astonishment, the walls seemed to come to life. Everywhere I saw animals; animals cut into the rock, touched by the sun which was low in the sky, sprang into life as I walked toward them across the bed of a river which had died thousands of years before.

The images of the animals seemed very large, very strong. They had been created with a sure hand steadied by authority. The artists who had been there had no doubt confronted those animals in that very spot. There was an elephant, over six feet high, charging. The trunk was raised, ears flapping. A rhinoceros measured slightly under nine feet in length, and a crocodile was somewhat smaller, being slightly over seven feet from its snout to the tip of its tail. There were ostriches, giraffes—all animals which had inhabited this area when the river still flowed. Today there is no longer any water. The valley is dead; and, of the animals, there remain only vipers and scorpions.

The site of Oued Mathendous is the richest in the world in prehistoric carvings. No prehistorian should dare to speak of our ancestors unless he has experienced, in the night at Mathendous, the stupendous impact of those images. For this sanctuary is unlike that of Lascaux. It is not underground. It is a gallery of masterpieces under the open sky. It is not located in the pleasant, green countryside of Montignac. It remains, like a skeletal vestige, in a forsaken land. There are no paintings here, as at Lascaux and Altamira. Instead, there are deep carvings, cut with tools of rock painstakingly rubbed over the surface of the cliffs, countless thousands of times, until the artist was satisfied with the depth and width of the line. And we do not even know by whom, or when, these incredible images were wrought.

I have been to Mathendous three times. None of those visits lasted more than three days. There was no water. There was indeed a well, but it contained only sand. Yet it had once been possible for man to live here with sufficient leisure for him to create these masterpieces. The work, obviously, occupied a very long period, and the dates and styles of the images are very different from one another. There is, however, one dominant style, and it appears to be the most ancient. It is the only style which represents wild animals in their natural grandeur: elephants, rhinoceroses, hippopotamuses, crocodiles, ostriches, antelope, giraffes.

Nonetheless, we sense here the same obsession with animals as in the caves of southern France. Here, too, we feel that man, in order to free himself from that anguished obsession, from that awe and fear of animals, externalized it and gave it visible, tangible form. You can see the fear. But one can also see the awe and the veneration in those monumental works. The spirit of the carvings at Oued Mathendous is precisely the same as that of the paintings, thousands of kilometers away, at Lascaux.

I do not think that Oued Mathendous was ever a site

of extensive human habitation. There are too few tools to be found there. There are no axes and only a few arrows. It seems more likely that it was a sacred valley, the site of a cult. If so, then here as at Lascaux the cult developed at the end of an age of hunting; at a moment when animals were becoming more scarce and when the climate was deteriorating.*

The carvings at Mathendous express dramatically the artists' perception of the percariousness of life; and they show, too, that man is one not only with the animals, but with the whole of nature: with water, grass, trees.

There are, in the mind of man, truths of all ages and all epochs of history. The most ancient of those truths, however, are the strongest and the most cogent. The emotions of twentieth-century man with respect to his dog or cat or canary, to say nothing of a lion in the jungle, are incomprehensible so long as we believe that those emotions originated in the full light of history or that they are able to be separated from the prehistory of the human mind. The truth is that between the time of the Lascaux paintings and the Mathendous carvings, and the latter part of the twentieth century, man has changed not at all. It is difficult to accept; yet, our minds and our behavior attest to that fact.

When man ceased being primarily a hunter and became a farmer and a breeder of animals, he did not suddenly change his attitude toward animals. By the same token, in the evolutionary instant which has passed between the Paleolithic era and our own time, we have not lost the attitudes and emotions which characterized the hunters, artists, and "believers" of the Sahara and of the Vézère Valley. They are in us, around us. They are the stuff of which our days and

*The Sahara has not been a desert for very long. After a brief episode of aridity, which took place around 7500 B.C., it seems that the climate there was quite benign. Traces of Neolithic settlements have been found in the southern Sahara, and sometimes they are quite large.

nights are made, our dreams and our anguish. Yet our contact with animals has in large part disappeared. And for this reason we feel a void within us, an emptiness which we try to fill by petting dogs and cats, or by photographing lions with telescopic lenses.

We no longer paint pictures of animals on the walls of caves or carve them on cliffs. Instead we print them in newspapers and magazines and reproduce them on television. And we sometimes sketch them hurriedly on public walls and in subway cars.

Man, obviously, still needs the animal if he is to find his proper place in creation. Dogs, horses, and lions are not only status symbols. They are not only beautiful, strong, and noble. They are also a means of assurance. They make us feel that we are one with them, as we have always been. They are, so to speak, guarantors of ourselves, of our identity. If we are so proud of our cats and dogs and lions and tigers today, that pride is based on the fact that, once, we were by no means their masters. Once, it was not certain that man would prevail in the conflict between man and animal. Once, it was not man who was the master.

CHAPTER SIX

From the Minotaur to Mickey Mouse

Among the innumerable works of man, the most important, no doubt, is his own person.
—JOHN STUART MILL

ONE of the oldest traditions of religion is that man is created in the image of God. It is interesting to note that man has spent a good deal of his history in trying to improve on that image and that in his efforts to do so, he has turned, quite naturally, to the animal kingdom for help. He has attempted to imbue himself with the power and virtues of animals by donning their skins, by wearing masks, by installing horns on his head, and by eating the flesh of animals. We do not have to go back to the mythology of antiquity for examples. As late as the nineteenth century, Kabyle* women made a practice of feeding lions' hearts to their children. Their motive was the same as that of certain cannibal tribes which ate the heart and liver of dead relatives or of a particularly valorous enemy. They believed that along with the lion's heart their children would absorb the lion's strength and courage. To turn man into animal, or animal into man, was a symbolic unification of the world. The Sphinx, the Minotaur, and the Centaur all represent

*The Kabyles are a confederation of Berber tribes inhabiting the mountainous coastal region of Algeria.

efforts to create a single divine monster out of two living beings.

This hybridizing process, once attempted in temples and sanctuaries and propagated by mythology and art, today is celebrated in our cinemas. We may smile at the naïveté of our distant ancestors; yet, we ourselves are not really models of reason and rationality. Felix the Cat, Mickey Mouse, Donald Duck, and Bugs Bunny are the direct descendants of the sorcerers of the Trois Frères cave, of the mastiff-headed archer of Oued Djaret, and of the knights of the fifteenth century who prepared for jousting by donning helmets crested with horns.

Nothing in man is ever totally eradicated; and nothing ever disappears totally from the animal deformed by man.

The river is still layered with fog. A long, narrow pirogue moves slowly along the bank. In its stern, a man stands pushing the craft by means of a long pole. Rarely, the silence is broken by the crystal-tinkle of a fish leaping from the water.

The man in the pirogue is strikingly handsome. His tattered shirt and torn shorts are unimportant. They are not part of him. His massive chest, his splendidly muscled arms, his broad, strong face make him instantly recognizable as a memberof the proud Bozo people.

He is on his way to Mopti to sell the catch of fish which now lies, neatly wrapped in leaves, in the bottom of the boat. Mopti has been called the Venice of the Niger because of its canals. Mopti's ancient mosque, built on dry land, its thick, vertical counterforts from which wooden pilings rise, dominate the sleepy city which enjoys a glorious past and once attained fame as a religious center.

The dominant position of the mosque, however, is somewhat misleading. Islam once conquered North

Africa and for many centuries has held it in its grip. Yet, it has never succeeded in dislodging the ancient beliefs of the people. The Bozo tribe has preserved its ritual ceremonies, its sacred dances; and, perhaps even as one of its members laboriously makes his way toward Mopti along the Niger, his compatriots on a secret island of the river are preparing the masks for a celebration of the great myth of the creation and ordering of the world. For the masks of the Bozo are those which have had the longest use in all Africa. Those of the Bambara, although perhaps better known, are but an imitation of these.

It is difficult for the Western mind to comprehend the true significance of those ceremonial masks. We seem to be interested only in the blackened sculpture of wood which is a stylized representation of an animal. We regard the mask as an art object, and thus as the stock-in-trade of merchants and the prize of collectors. Yet, the mask itself has no meaning unless taken in conjunction with its skirt of straw, its cowry, its fabrics. It is effective only when it is animated by the one who wears it; only when, to the pounding of drums and the wails and cries of the people, it participates in the collective life which unites heaven and earth, men and animals, the history of the world and that of the first mythic persons who played a role in the ordering of society. The mask is not something to hang on one's wall, whether it be the wall of a hut along the Niger or that of a Fifth Avenue penthouse. It is a device in movement.

Ogotemmeli, the Sudanese wise man who was the first to reveal to Marcel Griaule the principles of black civilization, explained that "the society of masks is the whole world. When the masks are used in a public place, they dance the progress of the world, the very order of the universe."

A Bozo animal mask is indeed an intricate structure, a

catafalque wrapped in lengths of cloth extending onto the ground. The mask, properly speaking, constitutes the forward section of that structure, and it represents the head of an antelope, for instance, or a ram, or a bovid. It is made in such a way as to be able to be moved from within. The catafalque also bears other masks or silhouettes of animals and men, the movements of which are controlled by the men carrying them. Obviously it is not possible for a mask so ponderous and complicated to dance. Rather, it simply moves forward, surrounded by attendants, to the sound of drums. The animal head and the other sculptured figures move in time to the music. The essential thing is the participation of all the people, the feeling of communion of men with the world of life and with the whole of creation.

The use of such masks is a contemporary manifestation of man's age-old attempt to fuse with the world of animals; the same attempt which we know took place in both the prehistoric and earlier historic periods. It is a living testimony to the human past; and the Africans who use those masks, living as they do in more intimate contact with animals and with nature, have retained both that cosmic sense and that intuitive understanding of a material and animal environment which our technological civilization has caused us to lose.

There is nothing strange or alien in the use of masks. Indeed, such use is in direct line with traditions handed down from the dawn of history in Asia and Greece, as has been demonstrated by Leo Frobenius in his study of the influence of Aegean civilization on the evolution of African thought.*

I have retained a vivid impression of the Dogon country—an impression of a chaos of rocks, giant

*One finds such links with the ancient past everywhere in African culture. Among the Dogons of the Sudan, for example, the symbol of the man-universe is a cross, one extremity of which terminates in a ring—the same symbol in use among the ancient Egyptians for a similar concept: the ankh.

boulders, steep cliffs and overhangs, inaccessible black caves. It was here that in 1931 Griaule, Leiris, and Eric Lutten discovered bone-littered caves, hiding places for masks, and even human skulls—"rather fresh" skulls, Leiris said—which have since shed precious light on the religious life of Africa. "Here," Leiris wrote, "there is nothing but the abyss, the open sky, and the underground," as he described the "formidable religiosity" of the cliffs.*

The most significant ceremony of the Dogons is the Dama, a funeral celebration in honor of several deceased. The ceremony lasts for six days and involves a large number of masks, many of which represent animals—antelope, hartebeests, bovids, hares, baboons, ostriches, storks, crocodiles, and, of course, the lord of the jungle, the lion. To these are added another mask, that of the hunter, who is called "master of the meat," and whose responsibility it is to shed the blood of the sacrificial animals.

The use of the animal mask originated in the dim mists of the past, even before the founding of villages. It pertains to such specialized activities as the hunt, and war;† and it is inseparable from the dance, and from death.** The animal mask, the dance, death. Once more, man relies on the animal so that he may confront the unknown and the unspeakable. The strength of the animal represented in a piece of carved wood allows man to venture onto a level of the supernatural to which he would not dare aspire with his face uncovered.

*Michel Leiris, *L'Afrique fatome.*

†The Dogon people were hunters before they became farmers, and the use of masks developed as a means of protection against the *nyama* of the animals killed by the Dogons. The mask altars hidden in the cliffs are sprinkled with blood every three years to ensure that they will preserve their efficacy. Such sacrifices are practiced even more frequently by the hunters, who kill animals—lions, for example—whose *nyama* is especially to be dreaded.

**"The Dance," asserts Griaule, "is inextricably bound to one of the most important events in man's life since the creation: the apparation of death."

Yet, African art, viewed as a whole, unlike Occidental art does not seem so much an attempt to control human destiny or, through that destiny, to attain divinity, as it does an attempt to express and realize the proximity of man and animal. Masks and statues—whether we are speaking of the Shark-King of Dahomey or the long, annulated horns of a male antelope carved by an anonymous Bambara artist—appear as so many attempts to banish the distinction between man and animal.

We admire, quite rightly, the depictions of animals by the ancient Assyrians, Babylonians, and Cretans. Yet these works do not have the same breadth as is attained in African art. Each of the African peoples appears to have arrived at a distinct interpretation, at a new use for the animal. Sometimes the animal is depicted realistically. Sometimes it is stylized to the point of being barely recognizable. But when it is a question of death, or of fertility, or of divinity, we invariably find the peoples of Africa invoking the animal.

The method of invocation is something more than a mere calling upon the animal. It involves the supernaturalizing of man by making of him, as in the Upper Volta, a man-pig, or a man-monkey, or a man-gazelle. The mask and its accompanying regalia allow a man, in the exaltation of the ritual dance, to attain a sacred frenzy which raises him to a superhuman level. He fuses with the animal character which he impersonates, and thus comes to possess its strength, agility, and guile. But it is not only the masked dancer himself who is transformed. The entire tribe, through the intermediary of the dance, is placed in communication with the unknown forces of the cosmos. The animal is the doorway through which man is raised above himself, to a new level. The animal is the key to the secrets of nature and to the secrets of the gods themselves; for the animal is closer to nature, and even closer to the gods, than man. (The idea that man is lower in the hierarchy of creation than the animal may seem preposterous—until we remember that the concept of man's infinite superiority is an exclusively Occidental notion, and a rather recent one at that.)

In much of Black Africa there exists a complex system of magic by virtue of which man and animal are identified in the persons of certain individuals. These initiates are called sorcerers, or magicians; or, if one prefers, witch doctors. In the depths of the jungle there are secret societies which profess and practice such identification. There are antelope-men, snake-men, chimpanzee-men, and, the most feared of all, leopard-men. Some of these societies are quite large, and their adherents are found from Sierra Leone to the Sudan and the Ivory Coast.

The link which binds the members of such confraternities to their animal is quite real, and the responsibilities of membership are taken very seriously indeed. The initiates, who are carefully chosen and trained by the elders, are regarded both as witch doctors and enemies of witch doctors, as champions of justice and as ritual murderers. They are said to be in communication with the supernatural world through the medium of their brother-leopards. This brotherhood is effected by means of a significant ritual of initiation, when novices are made full members of the community. Those who have already been initiated capture a leopard and make a small cut behind the ear of the animal. They then make a cut on the arm of the man to be initiated. The two wounds are made to touch, so that the blood of the leopard and that of the man will mingle. The leopard is then released and returns to the jungle; but, when its man-brother calls, it will return. The link between the man and the leopard is indissoluble. If one of them dies, the other will die also. In acknowledgment of his leopard nature, the man himself takes on the appearance of a leopard. He wears the skin of the leopard, a leopard mask, and is armed with claws.

"In certain societies of panther-men and crocodile men," Denise Paulme notes,* "each new member is required to offer a human corpse to his peers. The victim must be taken by surprise; and the murderer must rake the victim's flesh with iron claws in imitation of the clawing of a predator. He then removes certain of the victim's organs, and these are eaten in the course of a gathering held at night in the jungle, or else they are used to cast evil spells."†

The physical and biological solidarity expressed by such relationships is animated by the same spirit which, during the whole of man's prehistoric period, was expressed by our ancestors in images as soon as they were capable of such expression in paintings and carvings. Prehistoric man devised composite images in which his own self was shown fused with the body of an animal.

There have been various explanations offered for these composites. Some say that they represent disguises worn by prehistoric hunters; others, that they depict ceremonies in which the sorcerer wore a mask. But it seems to me that such explanations do not take into account the frequency and continuity of these images throughout human history. Against that back-

*Denise Paulme, *Les civilisations africaines.*

†Such secret societies of animal-men have an obvious connection with totemism; and totemism, in fact, plays a particularly important part in the entire northeastern part of Africa, in the Middle Congo, and elsewhere on the continent. Yet, one must use the term with caution, for the concept of totemism, so simple on the surface, covers a number of very complex realities. It happens, for example, that the totemism of certain secret societies, such as that of the leopard-men, is at variance with "the primitive form of the totemism of hunting peoples and is associated with ideas of the re-birth and transformation of the dead into animals." (H. Haumann and D. Westermann.) It may be stated that totemic religion has played a large role in Africa, as it did in Oceania. It has contributed to the conservation of animals, and it has effected a psychological rather than a utilitarian *rapprochement* between men and animals. Yet, one should keep in mind that totemism covers a multitude of disparate beliefs and practices.

ground one is justified in suggesting that they represent the indestructible bond which unites man and animal. A hunter, wearing the skin of a bison, is able to insinuate himself into the midst of a herd. But that same skin, when worn by the sorcerer, both takes on strength and life and communicates strength and life.* The shaman of eastern Siberia, for example, wears a headpiece made of the horns of a reindeer, and this is regarded as the most potent part of his regalia. And the American Indian, as is well known, wore the skins and heads of bison when performing certain of his dances. The examples cited are by no means exceptions. The concept of man-animal composites is found in all Mediterranean, African, and Asiatic cultures. It was a constant theme in the religion of Egypt and in the art of India, and it was as familiar to the peoples of Asia Minor as it was to the inhabitants of Greece and Crete.

The species of animals with which man, through the ages, has identified himself, physically and spiritually, are innumerable. There is one composite, however, which dominates all others, and that is the image of the bull with a human head.

The preoccupation of the peoples of the Mediterranean with the bull was based upon their conception of this animal as representing the fertilizing, fecundating male principle. Thus, the great God of the Hittites, the god of the storm and the sky, was represented as sitting astride a bull.

The cult of the bull attained its zenith and its most dramatic expression in ancient Crete. The bull was already the "father," at once loved and hated; the possessor of a huge penis; the male rival who must be destroyed; the consort of the goddess-mother; a being simultaneously worshipped and resented.

From such an image of the bull, it seems but a short

*R. L. Nougier, *Rouffignac.*

step to the creation of the Minotaur, the fabled monster of Crete, half human and half bull, who required an annual sacrifice of young men and women. The Greeks deformed the meaning of the myth to derive from it a meaning tainted by perversion and violence, a meaning in no way flattering to the Cretans.

According to the Greeks, the Minotaur was the offspring of Pasiphae, Queen of Crete, and a snow-white bull. The bull had been sent to Pasiphaë's husband, King Minos, by the god Poseidon. When Minos refused to sacrifice the splendid beast, Poseidon punished him by making Pasiphaë fall in love with it. The Minotaur was born in Pasiphaë as a result of this passion. Minos then ordered Daedalus, his architect, to construct a labyrinth so complex that escape from it would be impossible. Here, the Minotaur was confined; and, every year, Athens was compelled to send seven maidens and seven young men to be devoured by it.* Finally, the monster was destroyed by the Greek hero, Theseus, with the help of Minos' daughter, Ariadne, and Athens was freed from the payment of this fearful tribute.

There is, as we know, a visceral, prehistoric desire in man to identify himself with the animal which is perceived as an emanation of the supernatural or divine. Man, therefore, as he draws closer to the animal world, rises above himself—or loses himself. The significance of the Minotaur, the fruit of the love of Pasiphaë for a bull, is quite clear in its dramatic splendor. It constitutes an episode in man's resistance to bestiality. In order to free himself from the urge which would identify himself with the animal, man—Theseus, in this instance—must kill the animal, the Minotaur. To destroy the monster is to eradicate the reproach which it

*An intaglio carving has been discovered in the Athenian agora which depicts two chained women in the clutches of the Minotaur.

represents. It is to kill that part of man in which guilt and anguish are rooted. This is a drama which is reenacted in every era of anguish, for the monster is undying, and rises again during every period of collective fear. It is not pure chance, as René Huyghe has noted, that the Minotaur and several other monsters figure so prominently in the work of one of the great artists of the twentieth century, Picasso.

The Greeks, in embroidering an ancient Asiatic and Aegean myth in order to create the Minotaur, chose as their subject an animal which the Cretans venerated and surrounding which they had developed an impressive ritual. It is not impossible that the Minotaur indeed devoured virgins, Athenian or otherwise, at least in the sense that the bull, like many other of man's gods, accepted human sacrifice. It seems likely, however, that it was more avid for animal blood than human blood, and particularly for that of those powerful bulls represented with such extraordinary intensity in Aegean art, in which we see the animals entangled in nets or participating in those ritual games which preceded the sacrifice.

These games, the *taurokathapsia,* were played out in theaters, in the presence of elegant ladies and gentlemen lounging on rising tiers of seats. The sport itself, a form of bullfighting, was no doubt dangerous, but more graceful than it was bloody. Human performers, acrobats of both sexes wearing short tunics and high boots, used the momentum gained from the thrust of an attacking bull's horns to vault or somersault onto the animal's back. Sir Arthur Evans surmises that these games, which were fashionable in Crete from the end of the third millennium or the beginning of the second, were a ceremonial prelude to the sacrifice of the aminal; but that is not known for certain. It is probable that the Cretan bull was about one-third larger than the modern bull; and it is quite possible that some of them were trained to perform their role as a moving trampoline for acrobats.

The Cretan art of bullfighting vanished along with Cretan hegemony in the Aegean. It was unknown in classical Greece. Yet the secrets of the *corrida* did not disappear entirely. In Asia Minor, in Thessaly, and in the West, the *bos primigenius* continued to be deified, challenged, and depicted; and it reappeared, as everyone knows, in the Iberian peninsula. Many specialists believe that the "fighting bull," the *toro de lidia,* is the descendant of the Neolithic aurochs, herds of which roamed once from Western Europe to China. Yet, the Egyptians also bred a special line of bulls for fighting; and it is possible that these animals were introduced into Spain by the Arabs during the Islamic conquest of the Iberian peninsula.*

Claude Popelin theorizes that the art of bullfighting was born of the attraction exercised on man by the courage and strength of the wild bull, which challenged man to defy such a formidable animal. That may be. It may also be that the modern *corrida* represents the reappearance of the spirit which animated the *taurokathapsia* of the Cretans, in the sense that its elements of virility, desire, sexuality, and violence make of it a classical tragedy which results in the death of the bull-father who, nonetheless, always rises again. It is known for certain that the modern bullfight, although its present rules were not fixed until 1770, goes far back into the dim mists of history. Even the solemnity of the *corrida,* with its processions and other rituals, indicates that it is a reenactment, in sacramental form, of the age-old struggle between man and animal. The bullfight that one sees in Madrid or Mexico City today, like that witnessed by the Cretans of Cnossos, is a

*Claude Popelin, *Le taureau et son combat.*

ceremony, with established rubrics, which endlessly asserts man's domination of the animal world and solemnly affirms the existence of the chasm which separates him from that world. It also reinacts the ancient duel between man and animal for space; and the mastery of the sand-covered bullring is a representation of the domain which man and animal were compelled to share, and over which they contended.

I am aware of all the arguments against bullfights. The *corrida* is, in fact, an act of cruelty to an animal already condemned to death. It is also dangerous to the men and horses involved. At Tarragona, I saw a horse, a picador, and a matador, all wounded in the same encounter, lying on the ground in their own blood. Everyone in the arena lost his head; all except one old peon who threw his cape over the bull's head, momentarily blinding the animal and allowing the wounded men to be hastily removed. I have also seen bulls, mortally wounded and roaring in agony, refuse to die; and others which were forced to remain in the arena until they fell exhausted to the ground. I would venture to say that I have witnessed more horror and absurdity in the bullring than any of those who protest the cruelty of bullfighting. Yet, I must confess that all that horror and all that absurdity have not been sufficient to make me lose my admiration for the *corrida.* It is not the grandeur of the spectacle that I admire, or even the grace and skill of the matadors; for these do not seem to me to be sufficient justification for the death of a magnificent animal. I have given a good deal of thought to the reason for my continuing admiration, and I think it is because the *corrida* today is the only occasion on which it is possible to see an animal as it truly is; I mean an animal as it exists in its natural purity, free of contamination by humans. The bull seen in the ring, according to custom, must be an animal absolutely innocent of training or experience. In principle, therefore, the bull confronting man in the ring is a wholly wild animal; and that confrontation is the reconstruction of a primitive situation such as can be duplicated in no other circumstances—not even in the course of a hunt in the "wilds," for hunting has no significance, and it is not a contest but a slaughter.

Bullfighting deserves the name by which it is known in Spain: *arte hondo,* the deep art. It does indeed reach down into the depths where man is secretly linked to the world of animals; a world from which he thinks he has freed himself, but to which he is still bound by mysterious ties. So true is this that it is impossible to understand the rules of bullfighting without taking into account man's past. The Spaniard knows this; and a true son of Iberia is shocked and angered when he hears a tourist confess that he has come to the fiesta in the secret hope of seeing the bull win. This is a hope which the Spaniard finds scandalous, or absurd. The *corrida* is a ceremony in which everything has been planned to bear witness to man's superiority over the animal. Its justification is that it reconstitutes and celebrates an ancient human victory.

We tend to believe that our ancestors have left us a legacy of pure reason, a heritage of rational positions, clear concepts, and justified emotions. We forget that along with such positions, concepts, and emotions, we have also inherited their prejudices and fantasies and nightmares. We have received the principle of Archimedes along with stories of werewolves, the alphabet, and a concept of the archetype of the lion. We should not be surprised if, within ourselves, we discover that animals play a major role in our interior life. Our interior menagerie goes back farther in time than writing; and perhaps farther even than the spoken word. In its various manifestations—zoolatry, totemism, animal symbolism, the belief in monsters half human and half animal—it has had as much effect upon us, or even more, than the philosophy of the Greeks, the legal system of the Romans, the geometry of Euclid, or the humanism of the Christian.

Indeed, Christianity itself was largely responsible for the spread throughout the West of that intimacy with animals which we find expressed so frequently in Asiatic art and Asiatic thought. And the Christian Church drank deeply from the Oriental well of symbols, monsters, and fantastic animals which served for thousands of years to nourish civilizations from the Euphrates to the Nile, from Susa to Babylon and Persepolis. Among the Evangelists, we find Saint John represented by an eagle; Saint Luke, by a bull; Saint Mark, by a lion. And Saint Jerome, while in the desert, had as his companion a lion. There is the fish as the symbol of Christ among the early Christians; the Holy Spirit in the form of a dove; and, of course, the Lamb. What may one conclude, if not that man, whatever his religion, finds it necessary to make use of animals as intermediaries?

Christianity, far from sundering the link which binds man and animal, has strengthened it by the use of images of beasts both real and imaginary. It has joined faith to the animal kingdom by a mysterious but nonetheless efficacious bond. The bestiary of the Church includes not only those animals, such as the dove and the lamb and the fish, which one expects to find in cathedrals, contemporary as well as medieval, but also an astonishing assortment of beings of lesser fame. At Charité-sur-Loire, for example, one of the most magnificent of the Cluny priories, one finds a dromedary and an elephant, carved in the place of honor, next to the Lamb. Even stuffed animals are not alien to the Church. At Saint Bertrand di Comminges, there is a crocodile suspended at the entry to the church; and in the sacristy one is shown a unicorn's horn which is the tooth of a narwhal. In the middle of the famous Sainte Chapelle in Paris, formerly one could see a griffin's paw suspended from the ceiling. . . .

Not all of Christianity's animals were imported from the Orient. Local saints are represented with indigenous fauna, and many of them have their own animals. Saint Sernin is shown with his bull; Saint Martin with his donkey; Saint Roch with his dog; and Saint Anthony in the company of his pig.

The animals of the ecclesiastical bestiary are by no means dumb. Bugs Bunny would have held no surprises for a European peasant of the twelfth century. On the contrary, the peasant would have been surprised if someone had told him that animals were incapable of speech. "The peasant," Emile Mâle assures us, "knew perfectly well that, on Christmas night, at the moment of the Elevation of the Host, the bulls in his stable were able to speak."

The most striking illustration of the triumphal harmony finally established between man and animal, in my opinion, is that found on the tympan of the great portal at Vézélay. The theme is the descent of the Holy Spirit on Pentecost. From the hands of Christ, rays emanate and touch the Apostles. Around the Apostles are gathered baboons, Pygmies, and pagans, carrying axes, leading a sacrificial bull. All these creatures—animals, monsters, men—are facing the figure of Saint John the Baptist, who is carrying the Lamb. This work of art sums up admirably the ultimate message of Christianity, that the whole of creation—animals as well as men, and even mythical animals—are the beneficiaries of the redemption. Every living thing is a creature of God.*

The time would come when Saint Francis of Assisi could speak of animals as his brothers. But that time was

*The interpretation is that of Emile Mâle, in his admirable *Art religieux du XIIe siècle.*

not yet. Beginning in the twelfth century, the religious art of the West would discover other themes with which to decorate the temples of Christianity. Gothic art, renouncing Oriental monsters and scenes from the Apocalypse, turned to the vegetable kingdom, to leaves and branches and boughs. Thereupon, the animals were appropriated by laymen for other purposes. However, they did not lose their mystery or their power to protect against harm. We first find animals of various kinds painted on shields which, beginning in the eleventh century, were no longer round but oblong, being intended to cover the knight from the shoulder to the foot. Bands of iron edged the shield and divided it into quarters; and, in these quarters, animals of various kinds—lions and eagles, for instance, as well as mythological beasts—were depicted in vivid colors. At that time the animals did not yet constitute what later would become known as coats of arms. In the eight centuries which followed, however, the entire bestiary was put to use as signs of courage, as emblems of nobility, or simply as fetishes, by princes and lords, cities, and states. The lion was very popular, of course; but so were the hare and the ermine, the eagle and the swan, the bear and the unicorn. In addition to the emblems which appeared on their shields, knights decorated their helmets with a crest of sorts. This was usually a fan-shaped object which sometimes took on bizarre forms: an animal standing on its hind legs, wings, or an impressive pair of horns. The Count of Boulogne, for example, in order to buttress his claim to being lord of the sea, wore a crest made of the baleen of a whale.

The ties between animal and man, in all the diversity of their conception and expression over the centuries, are so close that they have neer been able to be loosed, even in modern times. La Fontaine and Kipling made their animals speak, as did Lewis Carroll, L. Frank Baum, and hosts of lesser writers, and no one was shocked or even mildly surprised. Our magazines, newspapers, and specialized reviews often contain images which blend animal forms with human faces—a combination which the artists of the Oued Mathendous and the citizens of Cnossos would have found perfectly natural.

Animated cartoons and comic strips, depicting animals gifted with speech and endowed with human passions and emotions, are the end product of a tradition articulated in prehistoric times and transmitted intact through the millennia of recorded history. The willingness of audiences to suspend disbelief would be incomprehensible outside the framework of this experience from the Apocalypse to Saint-Sever. What we tend to think of as a twentieth-century phenomenon is, in fact, an heirloom from our impossibly distant forebears. It is an heirloom, moreover, the progress of which it is possible to trace through the ages, for one finds evidence of it frequently.

At Oued Mathendous, in the Sahara, I saw a carved scene astonishingly evocative of the characters of a modern comic strip.* It depicts a rhinoceros lying on its back, either dead or dying. Three other animals, with pointed rodentlike heads, large ears, and long tails, are dragging the rhinoceros. These animals, however, are walking upright, like men.†

There are analogous images in Egyptian art. Francis Lacassin** mentions two papyruses at the Turin Museum which date from 1500 B.C. and which depict animals in a satiric form.

*A skeptical reader, like the skeptical explorer and observer, might shrug off these engravings as a hoax perpetrated by some talented aficionado of animated cartoons. However, experts have concluded that these carvings were executed some 8,000 years ago.

†The animals are almost impossible to identify—perhaps for no reason other than that they have undergone the physical deformation customary in cartoons and comic strips.

**In *Pour un neuvième art: La Bande dessinée.*

In more recent times, it is necessary only to mention such artists and writers as Grandville, Boilly, and, later, Benjamin Rabier in France, and Lewis Carroll in England, to show that the tradition of animation, in either literary or visual form, is unbroken, and that in modern man there still exists, in the phrase of Leroi-Gourhan, "a membership in the zoological world as well as in the sociological world.*

By 1892 the *San Francisco Examiner* was carrying a cartoon strip called *Little Tigers and Bears* featuring a group of very human bears and tigers. But it was left to the movie industry to first popularize the ambiguous role of animals in modern times. In 1919, Pat Sullivan and Otto Messmer produced *Feline Follies,* starring Felix the Cat.

It was somehow appropriate that the first animal movie star was a cat. The cat is an animal of mystery. We are always ready to believe that it leads a double life, and we are always ready to lend it human motives. The ancient Egyptians regarded the cat as sacred; and as a domestic animal the cat has been both exalted as a divinity and feared and hated as a diabolical creature. Man has always tended to regard it as a spirit in disguise or as a human being imprisoned in the body of an animal; and fairy tales have always so depicted the cat. Puss in Boots placed all the resources of the irrational and the miraculous at the disposal of his master. The characters in Felix the Cat retained all of these poetic and historical characteristics. Felix himself no longer wore the boots of his predecessor, but he was every bit his equal as a magician.

Felix's rival, Mickey Mouse, was not born until 1930, in the animated cartoons of Walt Disney. Mickey was a resolutely American mouse. He had an automobile, a house, and relatives. He reflected and represented the

* *Le Geste et la parole.*

spectators' standard of living and their moral values. Moreover, he was immortal and indestructible. He was, in other words, an ingenious and happy hybrid of Tarzan and Babbitt—but a citified Tarzan and an unstuffy Babbitt. And, for all of that, he remained a harmless, reassuring mouse.

Mickey Mouse, as well as the other stars who soon followed him—Donald Duck, Goofy, etc.—is an extreme instance of anthropomorphism. In Disney's world, the animal is totally humanized, wholly assimilated to our way of life and to our way of thinking. Mickey speaks, acts, and dresses like a man. He has a human personality and human passions, He is, so to speak, a human mouse.

It is important to note that Mickey Mouse and the rest of Walt Disney's characters are represented as living in a dreamworld. They are not bound by the laws either of reason or of nature. Donald Duck, pursued by his enemies to the edge of a cliff, abandons his automobile and plunges over the precipice in order to escape. And he does escape. Donald and his brother characters take it on themselves to accomplish what we ourselves are incapable of doing, but what we would like to do and what we would like to see *them* do. In other words, they open to us the world of the marvelous.

Nonetheless, no matter how avid we may be to escape into that world, we remain human beings endowed with reason; and reason is able to criticize, to distinguish between the real and the unreal. Therefore, to escape that critique, the cartoon characters must remain obvious composites; they must be nothing more than travesties of human beings, like the Minotaur and the Sphinx. They are no longer informed even by the moralizing intentions of La Fontaine or the surrealist poetry of Lewis Carroll. They must be bland, inoffensive, facile; and these qualities are obtained by the deformation and neutering of the animal. So, Donald Duck wears the clothes of a man, but retains the head, feet, and wings of a duck as he is launched upon human adventures. The fantasy life thus depicted, however, is governed by strict rules. All themes, episodes, and even all gags, must be stereotyped. Jerry the mouse must be lively, cute, clever, and invincible; he must always escape the stupid ferocity of Tom the cat. And, of course, lovers, whatever their species, after their adventures must be rejoined so that they may enjoy the inevitable happy ending.

It is incontestable that the use of animals as characters in cartoons and comic strips has contributed greatly to the affection of Americans for certain of the species represented. One of the most durable comic-strip heroines, Little Orphan Annie, once had the misfortune to have her dog, which had been her sole companion for many years, stolen from her. Immediately, millions of readers not only protested the dog's disappearance, but also demanded that it immediately be restored to Annie.

The enormous popularity of such cartoons and comic strips is explained not by their moral pretensions, but rather by the fact that they are the occasion for wish-fulfillment on the part of spectators and readers. The small man or animal is always victorious over the big man or animal. The gentle hero wins out over the brute. The good conquers the bad. The teeth of the predatory animals, such as the wolf, are always enormous; and the innocent victim—in this instance, Porky the Pig—stumbles into danger inadvertently and somehow stumbles right out again. It is not difficult to see, within this context, why it is that visitors to zoos tend to categorize animals as good or bad, or to feel special affection for herbivores and especially for small herbivores. These are the "good" animals, and their prototype is the gentle, helpless Bambi.

The escape from everyday reality provided for the reader and spectator—or rather, the satisfaction which he derives from seeing reality set at naught—is increased by the fact that it takes place through the intermediary of imaginary animals. The use of such animals itself constitutes a denial of the reality of animals as they truly are. Mickey, Donald, and even Orphan Annie's dog, are not confined to cages or even in preserves, and yet they are "good." In fact, all they need to make them human is a hat and a voice. This is domestication, as it were, with a vengeance. It turns animals into humans, and the reform relieves humans of the need to know, understand, and respect animals as animals.

This mythical taming of animals, undertaken on such a grand scale by Mr. Disney and his associates (sometimes with conspicuous lack of poetic feeling), has been widely applauded and has gained enormous popularity. It would not be imprudent to say that thanks to that tremendous propagation of imaginary creatures cast in man's own image, the general public's concept of animals has been modified once more. And now, Donald and Mickey and Bambi and all their friends have been released from the confines of the film can, and they are available for inspection, in three-dimensional reality, in a fabled world known as Disneyland; a child-and-animal universe conceived and created by one of the great creative minds, and one of the great businessmen of the twentieth century.

It is difficult to know to what age groups cartoons and comic strips, and Disneyland, appeal. What is certain is that a child, even before he learns to read, is exposed to that world on the television screen and in comic strips, where good intentions, the self-confidence of Superman, the use of violence in pursuit of success, and a touch of sex, are all intermingled for the delectation of the child and the child-adult.*

*David Riesman, in *The Lonely Crowd,* devoted a chapter to this subject: "Fairy Tales in the Comic Strips."

There are some cartoon characters so different that they deserve special mention. One of these is Snoopy, in *Peanuts.* Snoopy's peculiarity is that he is a dog with a human nature; whereas man's effort, throughout the centuries, has always been aimed, not at projecting his own nature into an animal, but at incarnating the animal in himself. Yet, there is Snoopy. He looks like a dog, but he is a veritable embodiment of all the weaknesses, complexes, neuroses, and social failings of our contemporaries. "Notwithstanding an element of puerility traitorously suggested by the graphics," writes Francis Lacassin, "and the presence of an engaging dog, *Peanuts* is a fiercely de-mythologizing comic strip the spirit of which only sophisticated adults can appreciate."

The second of these characters is not an animal; or not exactly. It is Tarzan of the Apes, the hero of a book by Edgar Rice Burroughs, of innumerable films, and of a popular comic strip which first appeared in 1929. From that day to this, Tarzan has been the archetype of the hero striving for justice. He is the ideal of beauty and purity in a world of wild animals living in an environment selected for its cinematographic rather than its natural qualities; one in which the Metro-Goldwyn-Mayer lion would feel quite at home, and in which the lianas necessary to the angelism of the hero are subtly arranged.

If there is such a thing as science fiction, then I suppose Tarzan of the Apes must be classified as nature fiction. His world represents the only collective view of the fauna, the flora, and the unhampered life of the wilds which can be transmitted today by audiovisual means. It comes to the viewer or to the reader from a vast distance, like the light from a distant star, long dead, reaching the earth after a journey through eons of time.

CHAPTER SEVEN

The Blood of Sacrifice

The past is not dead. It is living matter from which man creates himself and shapes the future.
—René Dubos

The greatest service which animals have ever rendered to mankind has been to die in place of man and in man's name, thereafter to intervene with the gods on behalf of humanity. It was for the sake of such intervention that for many thousands of years the blood of animals flowed upon man's altars—blood which, reflecting the ambiguity of the sacred at all levels, was at once terrifying and comforting to man.

Bloody sacrifice is the most ancient and widespread form of religious expression. In it man shares flesh and blood with his gods. Within that context the death of an animal becomes a significant event. Thus it is that even today the slaughter of an animal somehow takes on, or evokes a vague memory of, a sacrificial act. If twentieth-century man is so ambiguous in his attitude toward animals, it is because man, at the mysterious frontier where metaphysics, fear, and faith are mingled, still experiences a vague feeling of guilt over the death of his sacrificial victims.

We walked for two days without being able to ride our camels. The sand was so soft and fine that it ran in rivulets, like water, and swirled around our knees. The dunes were so steep that the camels would consent to climb them only if we approached those endless golden waves at an oblique angle; and then only over a visible path. Therefore, we spent much of our time on our knees, scooping out the sand so that those determined beasts, driven by their shouting, cursing keepers, could move forward in confidence under the blazing, nightmarish sun.

At the end of the second day, at sunset, we stumbled across a blue pool between two dunes. Three stunted palm trees grew next to the water, and, near the trees, there were several huts of woven palm leaves. All around, as far as one could see, there was nothing but a sea of golden yellow sand. This pitiful oasis was the home of the Daouada, a refuge rendered almost inaccessible by the surrounding dunes.

My first glimpse of the scene conveyed an impression of utter desolation. Here was not the petrification of Egypt, but the terrifying curse of a sandy waste crushed under an implacable sun. Nothing seemed to move. Even the women at the doors of the huts did not look up as we approached. We fell, exhausted, next to the brackish water as soon as we had tethered our animals.

We were not entirely at ease. We had heard that the Daouada were not friendly to strangers who succeeded in breaching their ramparts of sand. And I had been told that in recent years they had become even less hospitable than usual. Yet we were received with some degree of courtesy.

No one knows for certain just who the Daouada are, or where they came from. Their chief told me: "We are the people whom God forgot." They are, along with the Toubous, the best bearers in the whole Sahara. They carry their loads on their backs, holding them in place by means of a strap around their foreheads. No other tribe of the Sahara makes use of this method.

It is not difficult to see how the Daouada arrived at

that conclusion; for, indeed, they seem to have been forgotten by everyone. Their location, and their mistrust of outsiders, have protected them from invasions and from colonization. They live, in effect, as though they had always been alone in the world. It may be that they are the descendants of a prehistoric people who inhabited the Sahara when water was more plentiful in that area. In any event they are the poorest and most miserable of all the desert tribes. They possess only the few scraggly palms around the oasis and the scanty crop of dates which these trees bear. Their only other source of food is a small, reddish animal for which they fish in their pond, and which they call a worm, but which is, in fact, a crustacean found in brackish water: *Artemia salina.* They pound this crustacean into a paste; or else they dry it in the sun. In both cases, it makes an unappetizing dish which gives off a strong odor. Yet, apparently it possesses some nutritive power; for the Daouada seem in good health and they show no signs of malnutrition.

The fact that they depend entirely upon *Artemia salina* for their survival has had a great influence on the customs of these people. Since the crustacean cannot be domesticated, the Daouada, in order to assure its continued abundance and constant reproduction, have had recourse to nonrational means. These means consist chiefly in a system of taboos, and in sacrifice; and they reflect a situation and a logic perhaps as ancient as man himself. Man wishes to protect, maintain, and increase the prey which is necessary to his own survival. Fear and superstition, therefore, compel him to offer a gift, a sacrifice,* to a higher power on which the continued abundance of that prey depends. This is the basis of the sacred order: a contract between man and

*The etymology of the word is significant: *sacrum facere,* meaning to perform a sacred act.

an invisible, hypothetical second party. But the gift or sacrifice itself is not enough. It must be accompanied by self-imposed restrictions or taboos which, as a necessary ritual, are both an expression of respect and a means of conjuring good fortune.

This ritual has taken on a peculiar form among the Daouada. Only the women of the tribe are allowed to fish for the red "worms." If a man joined the women as they dragged their nets in the pool, the worms would no longer reproduce. Once every year a camel must be sacrificed and its blood must be allowed to run into the water of the pond, in order to ensure an abundance of the crustaceans. As it happens, the Daouada are the only Saharan tribe without camels of their own. They must therefore buy one at the nearest oasis, with their meager earnings as messengers and porters. It is, by their standards, an extremely costly and burdensome sacrifice. Yet they are quite certain that if they used one of the animals found in the surrounding desert—a gazelle, or an antelope, or even a sand fox—they would find no more worms in their pond. This is in accordance with the primary law of sacrifice: The sacrifice must be both bloody and costly.

The supernatural element which man has detected in animals, and which he believes resides in their blood, has made privileged victims of animals. Man has attached a supernatural, or at least a magical and occult, role to inanimate and vegetable matter—rocks and trees, for example. It would be strange indeed if he did not hold animal life as particularly rich in supernatural possibilities. The animal, in effect, was believed to be in direct communication with a higher world; and thus, the animal was regarded as the bearer of human aspirations to the forces which inhabited that world. This messenger role, however, was one which the animal could fulfill only when it was released from this world by death. Only then could it transmit to those forces man's desire for success in his undertakings, for escape from misfortune, for atonement for an offense, or for appeasement of the spirits of the dead. Such desires were the occasion, moreover, for a gift to the forces of the supernatural; for a sacrifice. And the sacrifice was essentially a part of creation which was turned over, or consecrated, to the gods. The principle was that it was desirable to sacrifice one or more members of the community of creatures so that the others might be spared.

Contrary to what might be expected, and to what is generally believed, the members first selected very possibly were not human beings, but animals. In fact, it seems probable that the sacrifice of animals preceded human sacrifice. Animals, after all, were regarded as being closer to the supernatural world than man was, and therefore as having greater sacral worth than man. This belief is clearly reflected in the cave paintings of the late Paleolithic era.

It was only gradually that in the darkness of prehistory, man took cognizance of the differences between himself and the animals. And, as that awareness grew, the sacrificial value of the animal diminished, and the death of the animal lost its dramatic power. It was not until man himself took the animal's place on the altar that the event of sacrifice regained its importance.* Even then, once human sacrifice came to be regarded with horror rather than awe, the animal once more became the victim and was sacralized for a second time.

*Human sacrifice was by no means a rare phenomenon in the ancient world. The Phoenicians, as is well known, sacrificed children to the god Baal; and the Hebrews were, over a long period, devoted to the practice of sacrificing human beings. Even more surprising, there is evidence that as late as the fourth century B.C. the Greeks were sacrificing children. Both Polybius and Pausanias refer to these "abominable sacrifices," in the course of which the flesh of an infant was mixed with that of animals and eaten. During the ceremony, one man was supposed to be changed into

The return to animal sacrifice was characterized by a new note: The animal was now recognized as a substitute for man. In the Book of Genesis (Chapter XXII) we read of an event which probably took place about a thousand years before the birth of Christ: the sacrifice of Isaac by his father Abraham. When Abraham, in obedience to God's command, had bound Isaac and was about to plunge the knife into his breast, an angel called Abraham saying, "Do not raise your hand against the boy. Do not harm him, for now I know you fear God." Thereupon, a ram was substituted for Abraham's beloved son.*

The reinstatement of the animal as a sacrificial victim in place of man was a decisive moment in human history and in the relationship between man and animal. Man now chose the animal as his representative in his dealings with the divinity. This selection not only explains the animal's role as a religious intermediary, but also sheds light on the conditions and restrictions which surrounded that choice. For not just any animal was an appropriate victim. Man, in order to ensure the success of this adventure into the supernatural, had to sacrifice that which was most precious to him.

By virtue of this substitution, which was the ingenious invention of the priests and leaders of the people, the place of the animal in human society increased greatly in importance. The animal became, in a sense, the

---

a stag, and another into a wolf, the substitution of animal for man being a method of atonement for the "abominable sacrifice." On the island of Rhodes, men were sacrificed to the god Kronos; and on Leucadia, the human sacrificial victim was thrown from a cliff into the sea. Perhaps the best-known instance of human sacrifice among the Greeks, however, occurred shortly before the battle of Salamis (480 B.C.), when, at the urging of the soothsayer Euphratides, three Persian captives were immolated. The New World was as bloodthirsty as the Old in this respect. All the pre-Columbian civilizations practiced human sacrifice. In Yucatan, at Chichen Itza, the tourist is shown the pits into which virgins, covered with flowers and jewels, and rendered almost unconscious by drugs and incense, let themselves fall.

*There are instances of such conscious substitution. In the heart of the Peruvian Andes, on the banks of Lake Titicaca, the natives sacrifice a llama, in place of a man, to the Sun God.

savior of man. As man's replacement, chosen to stand in his place before the throne of the god, the animal became both an offering and a sign of liberation; a substitute and a victim. And, inevitably, it became the symbol of the god to which it was dedicated.

The death of the animal was now no longer the result of the hunt or of a conflict between man and animal. It was a solemn, ritual immolation, undertaken as a means of influencing human events. Within that framework the death of the animal took on an importance among humans which necessarily was reflected in the status of the animal itself. The creature dispatched into the realm of the supernatural, so as to plead man's cause, rendered an invaluable service. It went where man himself was not able to go; and it went there in man's name, so as to articulate a request, to appease hostile forces, or to solicit the favor of the divinity. The animal was, in a sense, man's advocate in the abode of the gods. It was a role at once religious and funereal, which was to characterize the animal, more or less secretly, from that day to this.

In order for the sacrificial animal properly to discharge its function of intermediary and intercessor, however, it was necessary that it be endowed with a certain supernatural character, and this was accomplished by means of rites and ceremonies. This character is one which the animal has borne for many thousands of years. It marks the mystical Lamb of Christianity as clearly as it did Abraham's sacrificial ram. And it is one from which the animal may never be totally freed. In any event, the animal is still, in our eyes, a creature which has access to areas of mystery denied to man. This is evident in our religious beliefs, of course.* And it is also evident, at a much more mundane level, in the attitudes of animal lovers toward

*Examples might be multiplied indefinitely. I will cite only one. In the celebrated tenth-century *Sacramentarium* of Drogon, who was Bishop of Metz and brother to

their pets. I know a man—to cite an extreme example—who is convinced that when his dog sighs it is because the animal has seen a wandering soul passing by.

The role of the sacrificial animal in protecting mankind from danger is clearly set out in some detail in the *Iliad*, when we read that Agamemnon has refused to return Briseis to her father, who is a priest of Apollo. Apollo has therefore punished Agamemnon by sending a plague to decimate his army. Ulysses, in order to placate the god, and in the name of all the Greeks, offers a sacrifice of one hundred oxen, in the first hecatomb.* The officiant at the sacrifice is not the priest, but Ulysses himself, acting on behalf of all men. The function of the priest is merely to ascertain that the rubrics are observed. Even though he kills the victim, separates the entrails, and carves the animal's flesh, his intervention is not essential. In fact, he may be replaced by the *Mageiroi*, who are the butchers and cooks of the sanctuary. The chief personage at the ceremony, the man who assigns the mission to the victim and confers on it the necessary sacred character, is the suppliant himself.

Sacrifices of animals and sometimes even of humans in the Homeric era were not always intended to propitiate the gods or to obtain their intervention for the benefit of the suppliant. Homer tells us that the lovely Polyxena was sacrificed on Achilles' tomb so that she might accompany her lover into the underworld. It

---

King Louis the Debonnaire, we find an illuminated letter in the canon of the Mass. The letter is a capital *T*, and the illumination shows Abel presenting a sacrificial lamb, Abraham carrying the ram which has taken Isaac's place; and, between them, is the priest Melchisedek placing bread and wine on the altar. This is the manner in which a perfectly orthodox illustrator—probably a monk—chose to illustrate the passage in the Mass which reads: "Look favorably upon this offering, O Lord, as it pleased you to accept the offering of the just man, Abel, your servant, the sacrifice of Abraham, your patriarch, and the spotless host of your high priest, Melchisedek." (*Cf.*, Emile Mâle, *L'Art religieux du XIIe siècle en France.*

*The word "hecatomb," which has come to mean merely "a great sacrifice," means literally "100 oxen." It is a composite of the Greek *hekaton* (100) and *bous* (ox).

was not uncommon, throughout the ancient world, to sacrifice both animals and humans so that a deceased person of importance might, in the beyond, be surrounded by the creatures he loved. The practice was in use in China, Egypt, and Asia Minor, as well as elsewhere. It has been a boon to archaeologists that, when they open a tomb, they often find not only the deceased himself, but also his wives, friends, and animals as well as his weapons and much of his wealth—all intended to facilitate the new life which he would live after death.

In Greece, however, it happened eventually that animals took the place of humans in this sharing of the death of a personage of distinction. Their sacrifice at the funeral ceremonies of the deceased then took on a larger significance. They were supposed not only to accompany the dead man into the other world, but also, by their death, and through the shedding of their blood, to confer supernatural strength upon him. Here, as elsewhere, the shedding of the animal's blood was essential. The Greeks even had a term for it: *aimakouria.*

One finds approximately the same successive stages of religious evolution among the ancient Etruscans who, like the Greeks, began with human rather than animal sacrifices. The Etruscans, however, when they sacrificed—whether their victims were animal or human—did so less as an offering to a divinity, or in homage, or in order to commemorate a mythological event, than to discover the will of their god and to foresee the future. For this purpose, the Etruscan *haruspex,* or soothsayer, made use of the sacrificial animal's liver, for the liver was regarded as the seat of life. By a careful examination of that organ, the *haruspex* was able to formulate an oracular pronouncement.*

*A bronze sculpture of the liver, unearthed at Piacenza, testifies to the supernatural importance of the organ among the ancients. The Etruscans, however, were not unique in their beliefs. "For the Babylonians," P. Cles-Reden explains, "the

The nature of the animal-as-victim is apparent from its use not only as a gift to the gods, or as a means of foretelling the future, or as a means of providing comfort and protection in the great beyond, but also from other sacramental uses common in the ancient world, and still known in the twentieth century. In ancient Greece, for example, when two men wished to bind themselves by a very grave contractual oath, they would cut an animal—usually a kid—into two parts, and each man would place his foot on one half of the animal and speak his oath. Then the whole of the animal was burned. The significance of the ceremony was to proclaim: "I am ready to undergo the same treatment as this animal if I perjure myself." Here again there is a substitution, in which the kid takes the place of the man; and the ceremony prefigures a conditional human sacrifice.

The practice of a sacramental substitution has not vanished. In 1972 I was in the North Cameroons, among the Kirdi, an admirable people who have somehow managed to preserve intact their ancient beliefs and traditions. There, there exists a rite of alliance based upon an oath which, if broken, consigns the guilty party to the mercy of outraged supernatural powers. In very important cases an animal is sacrificed-—sometimes a he-goat, the fat of which is then eaten by the two parties to the oath. Sometimes a dog is used, and is cut into two parts, with each party retaining one part as a symbol of the alliance. Bertrand Lembezat notes that: "The oath taken in this manner has an absolute value, and is such that it binds anyone who takes it, even a European. There is a story to the effect that Captain von Raben, who was charged with the defense of the Cameroons against Franco-British

---

liver was the seat of the soul; and for the Tyrrhenians, it was the symbol of the Cosmos itself. The visible divisions of the liver found at Piacenza correspond to the divisions of the universe among the various divinities." (*Les Etrusques.*)

attacks during the First World War, made use of an oath of this kind to form an alliance with the tribesmen of Mount Mora who, in any event, remained faithful to him until the end."*

Animals also have a function in a sacrificial ceremony which one might call a communion banquet. According to some historians of religion, the communion banquet is the only ceremony which truly merits the title of sacrifice. The role of the sacrificial animal in the instances cited above was that of an offering which was consumed by fire after having been killed. Yet it sometimes happened that the assistants at the ceremony, after having witnessed the sacrifice, ate of the animal's flesh. The purpose of this communion was ritualistic: to unite those who offered the sacrifice both among themselves and to the divinity.

There are many instances of such ceremonies. The Hebrews sanctioned the Treaty of Galaad, which determined the boundary between Aram and Israel, by a sacred feast in which the delegates of both peoples participated. When there were public sacrifices every good Greek citizen was expected to take part in the banquet; and noncompliance in this respect was regarded as a grave civic lapse. "The sacred banquet," Marie Delcourt explains,† "was the moment in public life when the members of the group felt closest to one another, and closest to their god. The poorer citizens, for whom these 'splendid hecatombs' represented the only opportunity to eat meat, flocked to them in great numbers. We may get some idea of the quantity of the sacrificial victims when we recall that the altar of Hieron II, which was built at Syracuse in the third century before Christ, was 200 meters long and 20 meters wide."

* *Les Population païennes du Nord Cameroun.*

† *Sanctuaires de la Grèce.*

Indeed, flesh and blood are one of the great themes of man's imagination and of his religions. It seems that for thousands of years man could think of no better way to assuage his anguish than by spilling blood and carving flesh—whether it was his own flesh and blood or that of animals. God became man, and was crucified in the bloody sacrifice of the cross. But Christ, the God-Man, broke with Jewish tradition. He did not forbid his followers to drink the blood of this sacrifice. Instead, he commanded: "Take and drink for this is my blood." In that simple phrase, there must have been a potential of mystery and of horror which escapes us today.

It is no exaggeration to say that the altars of the ancient world literally flowed with the blood of sacrifices, and animals of all kinds were called upon to contribute to this river of blood: bulls, swine, goats, sheep, kids—the only requirement being that they be healthy, handsome specimens of their kind.

In some sanctuaries, such as that of Epidaurus on Greece's southern coast, animals were sacrificed for almost a thousand years, from the fifth century before Christ to the end of the Roman era. At the end of the fourth century, Saint Jerome fulminated against "those who go to the Temple of Asclepius to sleep on the stretched-out skins of the victims." Epidaurus was a center of healing much frequented by the people; and Saint Jerome's reference is to the practice—obviously, among the rather wealthy clients of the sanctuary—of sacrificing a sheep and then spending the night wrapped in its bloody hide. The mysterious air of the sanctuary was intensified by the presence of large yellow snakes—quite harmless—which glided around the recumbent forms of the faithful.

Eventually such sacrifices lost both their religious character and their civic importance. During the

Roman era they became nothing more than a means of providing free food for the poor, who were delighted with the opportunity of obtaining meat without charge. "Educated people," Marie Delcourt says, "were astonished that their ancestors could have been so naïve as to imagine that the gods would feast in their company. They would have been even more astonished had they known that, before trying to eat with the gods, their ancestors had tried to eat the gods themselves."*

Yet even in the midst of Roman skepticism, everything that was part of the sacrificed animal—the entrails, skin, paws, etc.—was regarded as being taboo since they belonged to the divinity to whom the sacrifice had been offered. Even the ashes which remained on the altars were regarded as worthy of respect. "The altar of Zeus, at Olympus, was twenty-two feet in height, and it was approached by means of steps trimmed with ashes which the priests cemented every year with water from Alpheius."† The awe in which the victim was held and the reverence shown even to its remains contributed greatly to the sacred character of the victim, which was regarded as a reflection of the god to whom the sacrifice was offered.

The role of animals in the ancient religions is so varied, complex, and inspired by different motivations, that it is almost impossible to make a simple statement regarding their place in those religions. There must be a distinction, for example, between those animals which were merely sacrificial victims and those which were regarded as symbols of, and were associated with, the gods themselves. Sometimes the same animal fulfilled both functions; sometimes not. Thus, sheep, lambs, swine, and cattle were sacrificed to the gods in general; but innumerable animals were associated with particu-

* *Ibid.*
† *Ibid.*

lar deities: the eagle and Zeus; the owl and Athena; the dove and Aphrodite; the lizard and Apollo; the fish and Artemis; the dog and Hecata; the cock and Esculapus; the peacock and Juno. There were also animals who were the chariot animals of the gods, such as Cybele's lions and the horses of Poseidon and Hades. Not all of these animals, obviously, were worshiped for themselves; it was the god or goddess who was worshiped through the animal with which the divinity was associated. The animal, in other words, was a symbol of the sacred.

During the time of Roman hegemony the cultural center of gravity of the Mediterranean basin shifted from the East to the West. Nonetheless, the attitudes of the East toward animals are readily evident not only in the religious, intellectual, and artistic life of the Romans, but also in their emotional attitudes. Hellenized Romans took into account the flights of birds and the appetite of their sacred chickens before arriving at political or military decisions. What is less widely known is that the whole history of Rome is colored by the influence of animals. The city itself was founded by a she-wolf on a spot indicated by a white sow and her litter of thirty offspring. Its boundaries were laid out by a bull and a heifer, and the city was saved from destruction by a flock of geese. Many Romans regarded these stories as nothing more than fables; yet, the fact remained that every year the first item in the Roman budget was for the maintenance of the sacred geese of the Capitol. And, naturally, there were sacrifices for all occasions and for all the gods. It was one of the more complex responsibilities of the priests to unravel the laws decreeing which animal was to be sacrificed to what god. Vulcan received fishes; Juno, goats. Mars, that warlike god, preferred horses. And mighty Jupiter was offered a young white bull.

The animals used by the Romans in their formal sacrifices were domestic animals. So far as wild animals were concerned, the Romans set out on a campaign of extinction which almost destroyed the large-animal populations of Asia and Africa. It was, in effect, the greatest massacre of animals in history; and the opening of the famous Colosseum in Rome marked the apex of that slaughter: In a single day 5,000 animals were killed. This, too, however, was a sacrifice of sorts; a sacrifice to a new god: the people of Rome.

The Romans went to the ends of the earth in search of new victims for that sacrifice, and no expense was spared. No animal was so exotic or so dangerous that it was not a fit victim for the altar of the arena. The great Indian rhinoceros, for example, was made to do battle with other animals or with men, under the Roman sun.* There are some historians who regard the massacre of animals under the Romans as beneficial. "Thanks to that slaughter," writes Jérome Carcopino, "the Caesars purged their states of the terror of monsters, and by the fourth century the hippopotamus was confined to Nubia, the lion to Mesopotamia, the tiger to the Hyrcanians, and the elephant had disappeared from North Africa. By means of the *venationes* [simulated big-game hunts] staged in the amphi-theaters, the Roman Empire extended the benefits of Hercules' labors to the whole of civilization."

The fact remains that at the time of the Empire wild animals no longer represented a great threat to man, and it seems hardly likely that the massacres in the amphitheaters were inspired by a desire to rid the Empire of predatory beasts. Nonetheless, the senti-

*For over a thousand years after Rome's fall, no rhinoceros was seen in Europe. It was not until 1513 that one was sent to Portugal, as a gift for the king of that country. The king subsequently dispatched the animal to Rome, as a gift to the Pope. The ship carrying the rhinoceros never reached Italy, for the animal attacked the hull of the craft with such furious vigor that the ship sank.

ments of the people with respect to wild animals were ambiguous and even contradictory. The Romans were no longer subject to the terror inspired by the sight of Hannibal's elephants. Indeed, Caesar's litter was surrounded by the great pachyderms; and it was not unusual for important personages, accompanied by actresses and courtesans, to appear in public in chariots to which tigers, lions, panthers, or cheetahs (which were great favorites) had been harnessed. Such animals were a common sight in the city, and they were not very difficult to come by, for in the imperial preserves, to the south of Rome, as many as 11,000 wild animals were held captive at one time.

The history of Rome with respect to animals is not one of unremitting cruelty and slaughter. The Romans, to their credit, had a great affection for domestic animals; so much so that it was celebrated by Virgil in the *Georgics* and the *Bucolics,* as it had been among the Greeks by Homer, Hesiod, and Anacreon. On this foundation the new religion of the Christians built a new affection for the creatures who share the earth with man. The Gospels are full of references to animals—to birds, to fishes, to the dog licking Lazarus' sores, to the Holy Spirit in the form of a dove—all of which forged new bonds between man and animal. Among the Christians there was no more bloody sacrifice,* no more need for animals to die as man's representatives and messengers. Death now came between man and animals symbolically, like a shadow. The animal, in Christian belief, was a symbol of rebirth and of eternal life. The cock represented Christ among the early Christians because it crowed and was reborn at each new dawn. The lamb was (as it had been among the Hebrews) the

*The Essenes, a religious sect the adherents of which lived along the Dead Sea, and the doctrine of which, in many respects, prefigured that of the Christians, had already repudiated the practice of sacrificing animals.

symbol of the Messiah.* It was no longer necessary to sacrifice the lamb in order to obtain a supernatural effect. Now, one had only to call on it, to name it, or to reproduce its image.

Far from doing away with the religious significance of the animal kingdom, the new religion took it over and transformed it by a new gentleness. Animals now were no longer victims. They became figures in religious images, legends, and fables.

Long before the birth of Saint Francis of Assisi, Christians had learned to live in peace and understanding with the animal world. This reconciliation was religious in nature. Perhaps it may be attributed, at least in part, to the monks who spread throughout Europe—which was, of course, still heavily forested—and lived in close communion with nature. They therefore incorporated deer, wolves, boars, and other animals into the lives of those admirable men, the saints, and thus annexed them to the folklore of the Christian nations of Europe.

The elimination of the bloody sacrifice of animals by the Christian Church hardly marked the end of all such slaughter, even at the purely religious level, throughout the world. Even today, the practice is still pursued in Haiti, among the adherents of the various voodoo cults; and in India it is not infrequent. Indeed, it is not unfair to say that man, for most of his recorded history, has characterized his relationships with the gods and with animals by the spilling of blood. However, there is little reason for us to be shocked or surprised by that fact or to regard this phenomenon as the manifestation of a "primitive" mentality. One must recall that, in the

*The rite of the Pascal lamb dates from the time when Israel was still a nomadic nation. The full moon of the Nizan marked the beginning of the year and the migration of the herds toward their summer pastures. It was then that the shepherd sacrificed a lamb.

sacrificial death of animals, in the shedding of their blood, our ancestors were seeking to discover the secrets of life and death; and, through them, they attained at least to a familiarity with death which we ourselves do not possess. Today animals are still slaughtered, but their deaths are perpetrated less nobly and more secretly, within the walls of our slaughterhouses. The doors of our giant refrigerators conceal the carefully carved sections of beef and pork which have been sacrificed to nothing more glorious than the ideals of a consumer society.

CHAPTER EIGHT

The Synthetic Animal

It is not always certain that man, when he creates gods, creates them in his own image.
—PAUL RADIN, *La Religion primitive*

LONG before the animal was useful, it was sacred. Domestication, in fact, first took place in the temples. It was a long-drawn-out, hazardous undertaking, characterized by many errors and failures. For domestication does not consist simply in capturing a wild animal and turning it into a docile, obedient prisoner. To domesticate an animal means to create a new being, to modify its body and its behavior in ways that are unknown in nature. In this sense a domestic animal is a synthetic animal; and, because it is synthetic, it must be fed, protected, and cared for like a child. Not even its love life is its own.

Human pressure, in religious forms, worked upon bulls in Mesopotamia, upon cows in Egypt, upon horses in Mongolia, upon the llama in the Andes, upon the elephant in India. The domesticators—priests—worked to eliminate everything in these animals which might prevent them from becoming contented servants. They banished fear, aggressivity, and the instinct of flight. They had no way of knowing that the synthetic animals thus produced would one day become victims to the afflictions of civilization—to obesity, diabetes, cardiovascular ailments, and psychological disturbances. Controlled biology claims to improve living beings. We should keep in mind that it also degrades them.

On an isolated rock which rises from a dead waterway* of the Sahara, there is a carving of three oxen. The carvings are life-size and the horns are long and slender. The three animals are depicted frontally, facing the observer, and their heads are carved deep into the rock. Their eyes are round holes. The somber, exact lines of the carvings are astonishing. The artist, by giving a peculiar inclination to each head, and by arranging the figures in perspective, has communicated an extraordinary sense of reality to his work. The technique employed is quite refined—one might almost say modernistic. Its daring, and the undiluted purity of its lines, make of this carving one of the masterpieces of the prehistoric period. There is also a secret emotion discernible in the work; or rather, the reflection of such an emotion in the life which the artist worked to communicate to the oxen in conferring individuality, and an air of sweet gravity, upon them.

These figures are there, in the burning Sahara, for a reason. The oxen are in a drinking position. Quite clearly, one can see three lines marking three levels of the water which once flowed here. At each of these levels an ox is graven, with its nostrils precisely at the level of the vanished water. The oxen may well have been drawings for religious practices, to reverse the deterioration of their environment. No doubt they sent up prayers to unknown gods, imploring their help against the aridity which threatened. In any event we know for certain that man witnessed this drama; that after having attained a high level of pastoral civilization,

*The proper term here is *oued*, an Arabic word used to designate a temporary course of water in desert areas. These streams are usually dry; but they sometimes carry a torrent of water and mud after a heavy rainfall.

he saw all of his work, and all of his happiness, destroyed by the climate. The figures of the oxen, therefore, are certainly the measure of the water's disappearance; but they are also perhaps instruments in man's attempts to forestall that disappearance by the celebration of some mysterious cult.

By a curious paradox, it is in the Sahara, the most unrelieved stretch of desert in the world, that one finds today the most convincing evidence of the early domestication of ruminating bovids. I do not believe that such domestication originated in the Sahara; but it surely marked an important stage in that undertaking, as attested by various paintings and carvings such as those described above.

We do not know anything about the religious beliefs of the first Saharan herdsmen; but, if it is true, as some believe, that the descendants of their livestock are now found farther to the south of Africa, then it is also true that that livestock is still characterized by a certain religious importance. Among the nomadic Kanembou tribes, as well as among other tribes of herdsmen in the south Sahara, the ox is not regarded as a source of meat. Instead it is one of the foundations of society and a buttress of the supernatural order. It is a true heir of the animal's prehistoric and essential role in the religious life of man. With respect to the Nuer tribe, to the west of the Kanembou, E. E. Evans Pritchard notes: "It is through his livestock that man establishes contact with his ancestors and with spirits. . . . By rubbing ashes on the back of a cow, one enters into communication with the spirit or ancestor associated with the animal and may then ask for help."

Within this context one may sense the reasons for a religious attitude—still prevalent today in parts of Africa and in India—which forbids the killing of animals. That attitude derives from the very purpose of domestication, which is not to have a steady supply of meat constantly available, but rather to have at hand a means of communication with the other world. Herds were not formed to be slaughtered. Rather, they were formed so that the animals might be cared for and their lives prolonged. One might make use of their milk, or, in the case of sheep and llamas in South America, of their wool. But the herds were not used as a source of meat.

In Africa, among the Watutsi, I had the opportunity to observe a survival of that attitude toward flocks and herds of animals. The Watutsi are an imposing people. The men are usually over six feet in height, and they are famous as gifted dancers (a talent which touristic entrepreneurs have not been slow to exploit). Their homeland is one of the loveliest regions of the continent, and on their lands they maintain a herd of sacred oxen. These Ruanda oxen, celebrated for the size of their lyre-shaped horns, are regarded as the property of the king; and they are known to the Watutsi as *Inyambo.* The role of the herd is exclusively religious. Even their urine may be used only for ritual ablutions (although their droppings are gathered as fuel for fires). Each animal of the herd has a human servant, and no animal is ever slaughtered—an observance which, given the political and economic difficulties endemic in Ruanda, is hardly "practical."

The Watutsi are not alone in Africa in their respect for their herds. In Central Africa, the Maures, the Tuareg,* and the Peul tribes, although they stop short of the extremes adopted by the Watutsi, also have bovids which they never slaughter. They make use of these animals only for milk; and, occasionally, they use them as mounts. Even these, however, are only

*The Tuareg, contrary to what is commonly believed, are not found only in the Sahara. Only ten or twelve thousand of them live in the desert, while about 400,000 live along the Niger.

incidental uses, for they allow their animals to grow old, and their herds contain infirm and very aged specimens which serve neither purpose. When these tribes need meat, rather than touch their own herds they organize a hunt.

Among the Nandi, one must fast after drinking milk, since it would be harmful—not to the man who drank the milk, but to the herd and to their pastureland—if other food were mixed with the milk of the herd. Among the Longarim of the Sudan, there is a high degree of identification between man and his animals—so much so that when a young male reaches puberty, he is expected to choose a young male specimen from the herd which he thereafter regards as his "son," and for which he cares. When the man dies, the ox is slaughtered on the tomb of its "father." No man is allowed to have more than one such "son"; and he is given the name of that offspring. This identification is carried to such extremes that when the son-animals of two of the tribesmen engage in battle, the "fathers" must do the same.

To an African, therefore, it is no simple thing to own a herd of domestic animals. There are the techniques of husbandry to be mastered, of course; but these are the least of it, for they concern only the animals and man. There is something else, and something infinitely more complex; for, in Africa, as everywhere else in man's history, man and animal are not alone. Between them stand the gods. There are traditions, obligations, and taboos, and the whole of them is so complex that one cannot hope to understand them, let alone observe them, without an initiation.

This initiation is particularly complicated and detailed among the Peul tribe. "This initiation," says a Peul text, "begins when a youth enters the corral, and ends when he enters the tomb." The life of an initiate, in fact, is divided into three periods of twenty-one years each.

There are twenty-one years of apprenticeship, twenty-one years of practice, and twenty-one years of teaching. There is probably no profession in the Western world which requires stricter training or more complete devotion than that of the Peul herdsman. It is an educational prowess which aims at the religious, moral, and social formation of the youth, as well as at his technical training. It tests the aspirant at every turn, measuring and developing his willpower, his courage, his tact, and his self-mastery. The use of herbs and vegetables is as important in this training as the veterinary arts, and the adolescent is instructed not only in the secrets of husbandry, but also in those of the structure of the universe. When the student has acquired a mastery of all these things, he is allowed to care for the herd. Then, when he is old, he is made responsible for the training of his successors. And these are the people whom the white man, when he invaded Africa in the nineteenth century, regarded as primitive savages without culture, technical ability, or moral sense.

One of the most remarkable peoples of Africa are the Masai. Or, at least they were still remarkable when I had the opportunity first to know them. They were a proud, nomadic people who insisted on remaining on the fringes of white civilization. Unfortunately, their homeland is in Kenya and in Tanzania, near the most popular of the African preserves such as Serengeti. Tourism, therefore, has had its effect upon them. Nowadays they demand money from any tourist who attempts to photograph them.

The Masai came from the northeast—perhaps even from Asia Minor by way of Egypt and Ethiopia. They have never constituted a nation in the common sense of that term, but have remained simply a human community. Their chief personage is the *moran*, who is a young warrior trained not only in all the secrets of animal husbandry, but also in those of stealing cattle from other tribes. All other forms of activity are forbidden him. The impression thus conveyed that the Masai are a warlike people is the correct one; or, at least it used to be correct. The principal event in the life of the Masai male was single combat with a lion; and, if he survived this encounter, he was raised to the rank of warrior. Today, however, this is an exploit which it is difficult to accomplish, for there are no longer a great many lions outside the preserves.

The Masai have a special reverence for their herds of oxen. They live on their milk (which they drink either fresh or sour), and they bleed their animals with a special arrow and drink the blood from the jugular vein.*

Today, the Masai number no more than 150,000, and they are greatly weakened by venereal disease. They live in wretched conditions with their skeletal herds, yet they have retained their contempt for the civilization of the whites—except when they can obtain the white man's money without working for it. And that contempt is not far removed from outright hostility. They are convinced of their superiority, both human and spiritual, over the white man, and they are simultaneously much attached to their pastoral way of life and defiant and wary of any other way of life.

In the Masai view, man and animal had a common origin, and the Masai language uses the same noun to designate both man and animal. The great religious significance which they attach to their oxen, however, is not peculiar to the Masai. It is common to all the eastern Hamite peoples from Lake Rudolf to the southern part of Tanzania in its various manifestations: the ritual

*The carvings of oxen at the Tararat *oued,* described earlier in this chapter, show specimens of oxen with one of the horns curved downward toward the ground. Interestingly, the Masai train one of the horns of their favorite oxen to curve in the same way.

purity of their livestock, the taboo against mixing water and milk, the use of urine in ritual cleansing, and the taboo against women caring for the livestock.

In the light of such observances it is clear that husbandry is not merely an economic undertaking, but a magico-religious enterprise. It is almost as clear that, in the West, in our attempts to put husbandry on a purely economic level, we have lost touch with the historic realities of that art. It is extremely probable, for example, that man, when he first began to breed and raise animals, did so for religious reasons. The life of the domestic animal was not only respected, but was often also sacred. The first animals that man tamed and kept for himself were perhaps intended as sacrificial offering to the gods.

The domestication of animals was of great importance among the Egyptians as well as among other peoples—so much so that it has been impossible to decide, despite certain similarities, whether the Egyptians were innovators or whether they drew the rudiments of the practices and beliefs from a common Oriental source.*

It appears that very early in time the bull was particularly associated with the worship of the moon—perhaps because the line of its horns is evocative of the lunar crescent. "Wild oxen would thus have been fenced in so that they might be sacrificed to the goddess worshiped by the tillers of the soil. . . ."† Certainly, among the sacred animals of Egypt there is little evidence of utilitarianism in the qualities required. The bull of Ptah, which was raised in the temple of the god,

*René Huyghe, in his extraordinary book *L'Art et l'homme,* has reproduced ceramics which show a striking and mysterious similarity between antelopes on a vase from 3000 B.C. and on contemporaneous pre-Pharaonic ceramics from the Negada period.

†Lucien Febvre, *La Terre et l'evolution humaine.*

was required to have a lustrous black hide, a white triangle on its forehead, and, on its back, a white marking resembling either an eagle with its wings outstretched or a crescent. It therefore seems obvious that long before the oxen became the companion of the farmer in his field, it was an inhabitant of the temples of the gods.

It seems that beginning with the Neolithic period the first Egyptians had several kinds of domestic animals, especially oxen, sheep, and goats. Some of the tombs of these animals date from the Protodynastic era, and this indicates that the Egyptians, whom Herodotus called "the most religious of men," were already making use of animals in their worship. Several Badarian sites of the fourth millennium before Christ exhibit tombs in which men and bulls were buried together. And the man who united Egypt, Menes, the founder of the First Dynasty, chose the bull as his emblem—the worship of which, in the form of the god Apis, spread throughout Egypt. Even before this, however, the country had a totemic religion, and each nome, or administrative division, had its animal protector.

It is easy to lose one's bearings in the complexities of Egyptian beliefs concerning animals and their relationships to the gods which they symbolized. There has never been a pantheon, even in India, which has been so confusing. Even when animals became fewer and fewer along the Nile, they remained omnipresent in the religious beliefs of the Egyptians and were immortalized in carved stone. Throughout the Old Empire, the practice continued of taming and domesticating animals within a religious framework, and was extended to a large number of animals: gazelles, antelope, hyenas, etc. Needless to say, it was a process which entailed many false starts and led to many dead ends. On the other hand, it served as an incubator for new ideas—it played a role in religious ritual and became the basis for a spirituality which developed and spread rapidly. The wild bull, for example, was taken as representing chaos, subsisting on the fringes of the organized world, and it was the ritual duty of the sovereign to lasso this bull. An Egyptian bas-relief depicts Abidos Sethos I fulfilling this obligation with the help of his son, the future Ramses II.

Despite such superficial indications, the zoolatry of the Egyptians must not be taken literally. From it developed a monotheistic religion which included the concept of eternal life and offered man the hope of salvation. For practical purposes, educated Egyptians were no more concerned about the Hapis bull or the ram of Khnoum than modern Catholics are about the Lamb or the Dove.

The pastoral civilization of the Aryans, like that of the Egyptians, gave a place of importance to animals. Traces of that tradition are obvious in present-day India, where even in the midst of large cities it is not uncommon to find a cow lodged on the lower floor of a house. The cow in such cases cannot be said to be absolutely useless, since it does give a bit of milk—but in such small quantities that it is impossible to believe it is kept primarily as a source of food. On the other hand, the cow does represent a decided religious advantage in that it marks its owner as a man of proper religious sentiments. Moreover, it is regarded as a satisfaction and a comfort to have a cow in one's home. The owner of such an animal feels that his worth has been increased by the fact that he has linked his fate to that of the cow.

The love of cows has had serious political consequences in India, in that it was the provocation for the rift between the Muslims and the Hindus of that country. And the demographic problems of India have been aggravated by the multiplication of bovids which have no economic or financial value. There are today some 240 million such animals. In such conditions, it is to be expected that the strain of bovid livestock has been seriously weakened; and, in fact, most of these animals are stunted. Some of them are no larger than goats. Since young bulls are castrated at the age of two, coupling takes place only with very young males, and the calves born of such couplings grow progressively weaker with each generation. Today the government is making efforts to improve the strain, but the people still continue to increase the number of animals in conditions at variance with the most elementary economic laws, but in accordance with the doctrine of nonviolence and of respect for the cow-mother.

One should not conclude from the above that Indians are uniformly kind to animals. The cow of India is not slaughtered, it is true, but it is often treated with cruelty. If it is sick, it is not cared for. And if it bears a calf, it is almost certain to die of starvation. Both male and female buffalo, which are used as draft animals, are frequently beaten severely. And cats, dogs, and goats almost always flee at the approach of a human being, since they have learned that they may expect to be stoned or beaten. (Cats and dogs are regarded as impure creatures, and it is better to chase them away with stones and sticks than to be contaminated by them. This reasoning, however, is not applied in the case of cows.)

The respect of animals, commonly attributed to Indians, is, in fact, an Occidental misinterpretation. The doctrine of nonviolence (*Ahimsa*) forbids only the taking of life. It does not imply any particular tolerance of, or affection for, animals. The consequences of this distinction are sometimes surprising. We see adherents of the Jainist sect, founded in the seventh century B.C., brushing the ground before they walk on it in order to avoid stepping on an insect, and wearing surgical masks so as not to swallow a fly when they speak. Yet one sees troops of homeless dogs, thin as skeletons, roaming the towns and cities in desperate search of food. And in the railway station at Benares, I have seen cows eating cardboard and old newspapers for want of other food.

Despite such inconsistencies it should be clear that in India, as elsewhere, the value of the animal is derived less from the utilitarian advantages which it presents than from the personal emotions which it elicits in man.

If this is so in the case of Indian cows, it is doubly so in the case of the famous Indian monkeys. There are more than 150 million of these animals, living on the fringes of the cities. Since they are regarded as sacred and have nothing to fear from man, they have become a veritable plague. In Delhi they enter houses and offices at will, and they have even ventured into the Ministry of National Defense, where they destroyed an abundance of official documents. A few brave human beings attempted to frighten them off with air rifles, but the monkeys soon became accustomed to these weapons and ignored them. In any case, the rifles soon had to be abandoned because the Hindus protested against the use of these barbaric means. Now, when Indian bureaucrats wish to rid themselves of these marauding descendants of Hanuman, the winged monkey of the god Rama, they must lay their plans in secret and carry them out even more secretly.

Among the ancients, it was left not to the Indians, but to the Greeks to modify the essential relationship between animals and religion, as it was to modify so many other relationships. The presence, at the very origins of Greek religion, of the worship of trees and animals is beyond dispute. Yet it was not a totemistic religion such as existed in other civilizations. There is no evidence that there existed a link between a clan, or a human group, and the animal or vegetable object of veneration. There is no comparison possible with the situation in Egypt at the time of the nomes.

Gustave Glotz has explained very clearly the new

relationships established by the Greeks with their sacred animals, by drawing on the example of the dove. "Beginning in the Neolithic age," he writes, "terracotta doves were fashioned in Crete. Before becoming symbolic ex-votos, these figurines were true idols to which were offered, as expiatory victims, martins, as the enemies of other birds. In those days, the dove was regarded as being sufficiently efficacious to serve as a talisman to the dead; and soon it sanctified the columns and the chapel of the Great Goddess by lighting on them. . . . Then, united to the goddess, it was perceived as an emanation of the goddess; the goddess-dove became, in the goddess, the dove."*

This new concept resulted in the creation not of sacred animals, but of consecrated animals. Henceforth whole herds belonged to the gods. At Apollonia, Helios was the proprietor of a flock of sheep; and at Samos, Hera had peacocks. Aphrodite, naturally, sheltered a world of doves in her temples. Here again, when dealing with the origins of animals we encounter a wall of mystery. All that we can say for certain is that the domestic pig is of many kinds and is found in every part of the world. Man has traveled in company with his animals more than we think.†

There is at least one animal, however, whose domestication is fully documented, and that is the rabbit.** The domestication of the rabbit occurred during the period of recorded history, in the Roman era. The animal probably came originally from islands in the Mediterranean. During Caesar's time hares were captured and held captive in enclosures so that they might reproduce. These rabbit farms remained virtual-

**La Civilisation égeénne.*

†The reasons and the consequences of domestication are intimately connected, and it is interesting to note that of all the domestic animals the pig stands out as extremely "polymorphic and changeable . . . and its domesticability may perhaps be due to its polymorphic nature." (René Thévenin, *Origine des animaux domestiques.*

**The process has been studied in depth by Hans Nachtsheim.

ly unchanged through the Middle Ages. A manuscript from the late fourteenth century informs us that noble ladies were in the habit of hunting rabbits, with bow and arrow, within the confines of such enclosures. It was not until the fifteenth century, however, that the first variations in color began to appear, and it was not until the seventeenth that the silver rabbit first was bred.

Today rabbits are generally divided into two groups, according to whether they are bred for meat or for their fur. René Thévenin lists the kinds of fur, analogous to those of other animals, which rabbits are specially bred to produce: genet, civet, ermine, polecat, marten, sable, mink, otter, skunk, fox, leopard, lynx, seal, otter, nutria, chinchilla, miniver, and many others.

The interest of the rabbit within the context of what has gone before is that it serves to illustrate to what extent a domestic animal may be molded to serve man's needs, real or imagined. It is an artificial creation; and, as such, its genetic balance is always precarious.

The changes brought about in a wild animal through domestication are numerous and profound. First, and quite naturally, there is a weakening of the senses of hearing, smell, and sight. Once the animal is domesticated, it is protected and fed by man; therefore it no longer has to be on its guard against the dangers of its natural environment. It is noteworthy that the brain of the modern domestic animal weighs about 20 percent less than that of its relatives still living in the wild state. Another consequence of domestication is that two very important natural instincts are blunted: the instinct to flee and the instinct to attack when another creature comes within a certain distance of the animal. I say that domestication blunts those instincts, but it does not destroy them entirely. As everyone knows, no matter how long an animal or a breed of animals may have been domesticated, that animal sometimes manifests undesirable reactions. Cows flee, dogs bite, bulls attack men because they sense in them a social (and sometimes a sexual) rival. Domestic animals remain living beings, and, fortunately, they still exhibit the reactions of living beings.

Theoretically the results of selective breeding should render domestic animals incapable of survival in what was originally their natural environment. That, in practice, is not so. When domestic animals are returned to the wild, they regain all those qualities which it is the purpose of domestication to atrophy totally. Thus, the horses abandoned by the Spanish conquistadors in South America have become the justly famous and indomitable mustangs. In this respect there is an interesting phenomenon to be noted. Wild animals which live on remote islands—in the Galápagos, for instance—and which have never had any reason to fear man, are not at all timid in the presence of humans. In the Galápagos, one can approach sea lions, iguanas, penguins, and mockingbirds without eliciting any flight or aggressive reactions. On the other hand, domesticated animals which have reverted to their natural state are incredibly wary of man. There are horses, dogs, and goats in the Galápagos, all of which were abandoned there by visiting ships at some time in the past. All of them—especially the goats—are constantly on the alert for the sight of man, and they flee with amazing speed at the slightest provocation.

It has been said that animals with well-developed social instincts are better subjects for domestication than other animals. It seems to me however that it is wrong to regard such an instinct as a necessary condition for domestication. Group life does not, of itself, make it any easier to domesticate an animal, even though a man succeeds in taking the place of the dominant animal of the group. Bison live in herds, yet no one has ever domesticated a bison. And one of the most thoroughly domesticated of animals is the cat, which is by nature a solitary animal.

Yet, one aspect of the social instinct of domesticated animals manifests itself in one of the most striking and mysterious results of domestication; and that is the affection which such animals show toward man. Many domestic animals demonstrate in very positive terms their desire to be in the company of man, and they will go to great lengths to find their master if they are separated from him. This attachment is formed very quickly, and once it exists, the animal wishes to live on intimate terms with the man. On that basis, it seems certain that contact animals—that is, those which like to rub against others and to be petted—are very susceptible to domestication.*

For thousands of years man has worked at domesticating animals, yet the number of domestic species is tiny when compared to the species of wild animals—hardly more than a thousand to one. If we count only the vertebrate animals, the proportion is a bit higher. Among those, more herbivorous species than carnivorus species have been domesticated. It is not that man has not tried to extend his mastery. Almost all the major species have been experimented with, and many had to be abandoned. Paradoxically, we now have fewer domestic animals than did the ancient Egyptians—though the quality and effectiveness of those we have are doubtless superior.

Historically, the importance of ten thousand years of domestication is that it resulted in a civilization in which the amount of human effort required was reduced by animal collaboration. This result, B. Klatt affirms, is

*Animals show affection not only toward man, but toward other animals as well. Many horses have dogs as their friends. And, in the Tsavo preserve in Kenya, a friend of mine made the mistake of slapping an ostrich on its thigh. He was immediately charged by a young elephant which, as everyone else knew, was the ostrich's personal friend.

"the most magnificent example of experimental biology."

It is difficult for us today to appreciate the importance of that accomplishment. We have rationalized our relationship with animals and we have thus deprived animals of the religious significance which they enjoyed among our ancestors. We have, so to speak, dehumanized our animals, in the sense that we have stripped them of the human characteristics attributed to them by earlier civilizations. In our emotional relationships with animals, we now confine ourselves almost exclusively to cats and dogs. Other animals we regard as no more than economic factors or as means of production.

Nonetheless, we have not yet succeeded in ridding ourselves altogether of our old friends. We may be able to do without wool, leather, and animal fat, but we still have need of meat and milk. Domestication, it now appears, was merely a stage. The following stage is that of the present: the industrialization of the animal and its production in series. Formerly, a cow was given a name at birth. It was called Bossie, perhaps; or, if she was famous, Elsie. Now, she receives a number, and she has become another victim of the agricultural revolution. I have been a first-hand witness to this process of deindividualization of domestic animals, which has resulted in a fantastic increase in production. A cow, left to herself, will bear one calf a year and will produce 45 gallons of milk to feed that calf. Today, cows produce 676 gallons of milk—double the amount they produced in 1910. Some champions give as much as 4,712 gallons. Across the road from my modest country house in Normandy, there is a farm. I have seen the farmer gradually adopt modern methods. His calves, the product of artificial insemination, are imprisoned in cases in which they have no room either to turn or to lie down. Every day at a certain time they are fed automatically, and once a week they receive their vitamin injections. They are the end result of mass production, ready to become products in three months—the perfect synthetic animal. The veal produced by this herd is beautifully white. It is also perfectly bland—which is a pity, since it was supposed to provide a substitute for chickens, which are altogether tasteless.

This new evolutionary stage which we have imposed on our animals, and especially on calves, chickens, and hogs, is not without problems. Our domestic animals have become specialized workers, like men; and, like men, they have become susceptible to the diseases of human civilization. Among hogs, for instance, there have been cases of muscular degeneracy and sudden death, without apparent reason. The pork, in such cases, is inedible. This malady has received the name of Ludvigsen's disease.

Such results are to be expected. Animals created by selective breeding are sometimes monsters, in that they are unnatural. And, because they are unnatural, they are not always viable. In the case of the hog, an attempt was made to obtain the largest possible amount of meat in the shortest possible time. Such hogs are truly manufactured animals. Their bodies are elongated; the hams, overly developed; the thorax, small. Our hogs are no longer allowed to touch the ground or to graze. They are enclosed in boxes, subjected to artificial foods, deliberately rendered obese—and thus made prey to such civilized diseases as diabetes and cardiovascular ailments. However, the daily weight gain among such animals is 50 per cent more than it was among hogs at the beginning of this century. This is not a victory in which we should take pride. Indeed, it is not one in which we may even take pleasure, for biological tampering produces meat which is not necessarily of the best quality. Often, to put it bluntly, we do not even know what we are eating.

So far as the animal itself is concerned, its psychological fragility is almost equal to that of modern man. Hogs, calves, and chickens bred in series have become so emotionally unstable that they can no longer bear to be in the company of their own kind, or to hear their cries—especially the cries coming from the slaughterhouse. And there is a form of transportation sickness among hogs which is sometimes fatal. Is this perhaps a warning? Human beings, when jammed into subways and trains, now experience only vague unease; but perhaps some day we will become as vulnerable as our hogs.

There are many such warnings to be gleaned from these animals which, like ourselves, are the victims of contemporary life. The hog, for instance, has become particularly sensitive to noise: to the noise of other hogs and to the sounds they make while eating. When some hogs are fed after the others, they eat; but they do not gain weight.

In the case of animals as in the case of man, virtually no muscular effort is required to survive. Yet, there is an increased expenditure of nervous energy among both men and animals which induces intense fatigue. Also, overeating, which selective breeding induces in calves, hogs, and chickens, produces a state of fatigue and apathy in those animals, and they become increasingly vulnerable to physiochemical, microbic, sensory, and emotional disturbances.

It is possible that such things prefigure the human condition of the future. How ironic it would be if this were the end to which man had labored for a hundred centuries at the domestication of animals.

CHAPTER NINE

The Horse with Five Lives

The horse has probably changed more in the past 200 years than in the preceding 200,000 years.
—ETIENNE SAUREL

THE role of the horse in the human adventure has varied greatly. It was first hunted for its meat and massacred by the herd. It was a victim, and no more noble or respectable than any other of man's victims. In that respect man did not differentiate between the horse, the stag, or the mammoth. What we call the Age of Reindeer might just as accurately be called the Age of the Horse, for it was the horse which was man's favorite prey.* Then, somewhere in Asia, the priests of an unknown religion made of the horse both a sacred animal and a beast of burden.

It was in the latter role, harnessed to a chariot, that the horse accompanied the Kings of Sumer into the great beyond. A companion in death, a guide of souls, it was also the warlike animal on which, for 3,000 years, victory on the battlefield depended. This product of Asia, perfected by the Mongols, the Chinese, and the

*The ancestor of the horse lived at the beginning of the Tertiary era, some 50 million years ago. It was a mammal about the size of a dog. The horse as we know it seems to have originated neither in Asia nor in Europe, but in North America, from which it crossed the Bering Strait into Siberia. It is believed that there were at least four such migrations into Asia during the prehistoric period; but the reasons for them are not clear. R. M. Denhardt (*The Horse of the Americas*) suggests that the rising buffalo population of North America displaced the horses.

Mediterranean races, eventually found its way into the tombs of Celtic warriors.

The Middle Ages in Europe turned it also into a work animal, thanks to the invention of the horse collar. It was perhaps a less noble occupation, but one which nonetheless had its rewards, for the horse labored so effectively that it contributed to delivering the world from slavery.

Today cavalry regiments ride in tanks, and horse-drawn carriages are but a memory. By all logic, the horse, since it is unemployed, should have been forgotten. Instead it has found a new use. Horseback riding as a sport has become very popular, and horse racing, always popular, has restored to the horse some of the esoteric and superstitious significance which it enjoyed for thousands of years in the past.

Today, it is left to little girls and gentlemen riders to reap, for a few dollars per hour, such benefits as may be derived from 2,000 years of chivalry and 6,000 years of domestication.

In France, near the tiny village of Solutre, there is a great rock which rises from thirty to forty meters above the valley, forming a steep cliff which can be reached only from the other side of the rock. At the end of the Palaeolithic era, the humans living in the Saône valley developed a special technique for the slaughter of horses. When a herd in seasonal migration approached the area they would stampede the horses over the cliff. Today, at the foot of that cliff, over a considerable area and to a depth of six feet, one finds great masses of broken bones. This is the largest graveyard of horses in the world. Archaeologists estimate that between 30,000 and 40,000 animals met their deaths at that spot.

The Solutré horse is quite a bit smaller than the modern horse. It was hunted relentlessly in Europe; so much so that it may well have migrated to Asia to escape the prehistoric hunters of Europe. What saved it from extinction, however, was not migration, but domestication. Toward the sixth or fifth millennium, Mongolian tribesmen from the Altai or the Gobi found that the horse had important uses other than as a prey; and this was undoubtedly one of the most important discoveries of the prehistoric period. The Mediterranean peoples of the Neolithic period had already domesticated the dog, the goat, the ox, and the sheep, but apparently they had been able to do nothing with the horse. It was left to the Asiatics to succeed in this undertaking.

Their domestication of the horse was to have an impact of considerably more importance than that of other animals. The domestication of the hog, the sheep, and the goat did nothing more than provide an easily available supply of food; but that of the horse served to increase man's physical capabilities. It raised him to a new level, both literally and figuratively. It enabled him to move from one place to another at much greater speeds than before. And it increased his self-confidence by allowing him to exercise undisputed authority over a living creature. In other words the domestication of the horse led not only to a physical improvement of the human condition, but to its enoblement. This is the prehistoric source of the prestige which has attached to the horseman throughout human history.

The date at which the particular abilities of the horse were first put to use by man is not altogether certain. It may be much farther in the past than we think; and the process of domestication, at least in its primitive stages, may have begun in Europe, in Neolithic times. In the south of Spain, at Sierra Morena, Henri Breuil discovered a document of great importance in this respect: a painting of a man and a woman each leading perhaps debatable whether or not this document can be taken as proof that domestication was an accomplished a horse by reins. The horses, whose tails seem to be trimmed, appear quite calm, if not domesticated. It is fact in the Neolithic era. It may well be that the horse was being bred by humans, but that it was not yet domesticated; and the man and the woman may have been leading the horses to pasture. In fact, there is no prehistoric document which shows man riding a horse, and none which shows a horse drawing any kind of vehicle. The only certain conclusion that may be drawn from the Sierra Morena painting is that the process of domestication stretched out over thousands of years, and that the prehistoric Occident perhaps played a role in that process before the Orient did.

The domestication of the horse, whenever and wherever it was initiated and perfected, is one of the surprises of the human adventure. Horses, in their natural state, live in herds; and the impression they convey is one of stubborn individuality and dangerous unpredictability. The primitive horse, no doubt, appeared to offer little possibility of conversion into a docile servant of man, and it must have required great daring and ingenuity on the part of prehistoric man not only to achieve the domestication of the horse, but even to conceive and undertake it.

It was in Asia, on the endless spaces of the steppes, that the horse was bred; that man learned to hunt and to make war in the company of horses, and that he perfected the equestrian art. From these activities an aristocracy was born and a religion thrived. The Scythians assimilated the horse to the sun, and sacrificed one of the animals every year in honor of the latter: "After a year of running at large, the animal chosen was captured and then smothered under covers or else strangled with a cord. The queen then lay under the covers next to the dead horse and, by virtue of this mystic union with the animal, partook of the divinity of the throne."*

The Chinese, meanwhile, made a giant step forward in the breeding of horses. In order to defend themselves against the invading Hiong Nou cavalry on their Przjevalsky horses, they mounted a military expedition into neighboring Fergana and Sogdiana and captured some 3,000 specimens of a large warhorse known as the Transoxian horse. These gave the Chinese cavalry a decided advantage over their enemies and enabled them to resist the invasions of the nomadic Huns.

The Chinese, like the Mediterranean peoples, had discovered the primitive war chariot, and we have a model of the vehicle in use in the ninth century B.C. It was drawn by four horses—short, compact, muscular animals, obviously well fed and spirited. The Chinese war chariot, like that of the Hittites, carried four men. The use of organized cavalry, however, did not become current until the fourth century B.C.

The Chinese, by virtue of their talents as breeders of horses, were able to develop the remarkable animals which were later to become one of their chief articles of export. Throughout antiquity, both the Occident and the Orient were in desperate need of horses. The famous route of silk could more accurately have been called the route of horses, so heavy was the traffic in these animals in the direction of Iran.

Apparently there were no mounted warriors at the famous siege of Troy in the tenth century B.C.; and the *Iliad* mentions only chariots. Nonetheless Homer

*Maurice Percheron, *Genghis Khan*. In India, the sacrifice of a horse was considered necessary to the consecration of a king. In such cases, as among the Scythians, the queen was required to lie down near the sacrificed horse.

describes the Greeks as "trainers of horses" and he speaks of Ulysses and Diomedes riding the horses which they stole from the camp of King Rhesus. We may therefore conclude that the Greeks at the time of Homer, although they had no cavalry, knew how to ride.

The only famous horse at the siege of Troy, of course, was the Trojan Horse. The role of that monstrous representation in the Homeric saga attests to the sacred character of the horse at that time, and it also marks an era, a revolution in the life of the peoples of the Mediterranean. The Greeks, in fact, believed that the horse was of divine origin, and they had it sacralized almost as soon as it appeared. It was no longer an animal to be slaughtered for food, but a treasure which conferred victory on the man who was able to train it and speak to it. Success in this training seemed to have something magical about it, to be based on the possession of a great secret. And the ultimate realization of that secret, the embodiment of it, was personified in the man-horse: the mythological Centaur, with the body of a horse, and the trunk, arms, and head of a man.

Yet, it is quite possible that the horse, as honored a place as it occupied in ancient Greece (Alexander, it is said, named a city after his mount, Bucephalus), was relatively rare in that country. We find it depicted in paintings and sculptures of the period, and it figures in ceramics and even on the frieze of the Parthenon. Yet there is no mention of it at Marathon, or at the Battle of Platea. As late as the seventh century B.C. the Athenian army organized by Solon had only a hundred horses. The use of cavalry was a specialized art which the Athenians only learned later from the Persians. By 431 B.C. they had learned the lesson so well that Athens had 1,000 horsemen at its service, and 200 mounted archers. But even then they had neither saddle nor stirrups, and the use of horseshoes was unknown. Man, in fact, was very long in creating the accoutrements which eventually made it possible for him to take full advantage of the possibilities offered by the domestication of the horse. And in that sense it is correct to say that at the time of Alexander and his cherished Bucephalus, man had not yet fully mastered the horse. He still rode bareback—expertly, perhaps, by virtue of the physical conformity of the horse to the human shape, but nonetheless precariously. It was no doubt for this reason that ancient man chose to fight his wars from horse-drawn chariots rather than from the backs of the horses themselves. Within this context, therefore, it is evident that the invention of the stirrup was of major importance. Yet the appearance of this essential appurtenance came comparatively late. There is a Greco-Scythian vase, found at Tchertoulik, which seems to show stirrups of a sort, formed by a buckled strap. There is no evidence of them in Chinese ceramics of the Han Dynasty; but they have been found on Oizotin (Altar) saddles of the first century B.C. Also, the saddles found in Sarmatian tombs of the Hellenistic period had stirrups. Yet, it was not until the fourth century A.D. that the stirrup was introduced into the Orient by the Avars; and not until the ninth century that it was imported into Europe from Byzantium.

It was not only in horseback riding that inventions were late in coming, but in the use of horses for traction as well. Although the chariots of the ancients were comparatively light, four horses were usually required to pull them. The reason was that the harnesses in common use—whether they were Chaldean, Egyptian, Greek, or Roman—circled the necks of the horses without resting on any part of their skeletons, with the result that when the animals pulled, the tracheal artery was squeezed and the horse's breath was cut off. Therefore, the horses were unable to utilize their strength to the maximum, and the traction obtained was minimal. It was necessary to use two or even four horses to do the work of one. It has been estimated that the maximum load of a chariot, to which two horses were hitched, was no more than 1,000 pounds. This situation had far-reaching consequences. Because horses were unable to do a sufficient amount of heavy work, man had to be used; and antiquity could find no way to compel men to do such work except within the framework of that socioeconomic institution known as slavery.

The traction potential of the horse increased enormously when the shoulder harness-collar took the place of the neck-collar, in that the former rested on the horse's frame and allowed the animal to breathe freely. At the same time, two other discoveries had significant effects on the use of the horse: the disposition of a number of horses in single file, so that they might all pull without hindering one another; and the invention of the iron shoe, which protected the hooves of horses and oxen. (The hooves of the latter are even more delicate than those of horses.)

Commandant Lefebvre des Noëttes, the author of the definitive work in this field*, dates modern harnessing methods from the beginning of the tenth century A.D. He bases his study on the discovery of a Latin manuscript of the tenth century which describes that method. The same method also figures in manuscripts of the eleventh century; but it was not until the twelfth century that the modern harness came into general usage, and that the shoulder collar made it possible henceforth for a single horse to be used for work in the fields. By the fourteenth century, the old-fashioned throat collars have practically disappeared from the manuscripts. The horses depicted in these documents now strain forward in the traces, obviously without fear of strangulation. The horse, so to speak, was now pulling its weight in human civilization.

***L'Attelage, le cheval de selle à travers les ages.*

It is fair to state that for two thousand years the West enjoyed a civilization based on the horse. In a more specific sense, we may say that human activity between the tenth and the nineteenth century depended on the horse. In the institution of chivalry—from the French word for horse, *cheval*—the horse gave its name to a supranational way of life and a standard of human and moral comportment which was founded on the fact that it was not only a costly animal, but one which required both skill and special care on the part of its owner.

The medieval code of behavior has as its theme and its origin the use of the horse, and the nobility and military efficiency which that use conferred. Without the horse, none of the factors which we think of as characterizing the Middle Ages—feudalism, the Crusades, courtly love, knighthood—would be intelligible. The horse, therefore, was the rock on which society was built in the High Middle Ages; and that society, and the civilization which it entailed, were dependent on two solemn ceremonies: the dubbing of knights, and homage

The dubbing of knights was not merely the ceremony during which a knight handed a young man the sword, spurs, and gauntlets which were the sign of his rank. It also involved a test of the candidate's equestrian skill, a test for which the young man had prepared from childhood. The knight-to-be was expected to demonstrate his ability in handling a horse by a series of classic maneuvers; then, still on horseback, to demolish with his lance a mannequin of steel made from helmets or shields. This was the essential test of the knight, at least in theory: his ability as a horseman.*

*Different kinds of horses had different uses. Knights, for example, would use only stallions—preferably from Spain, Gascony, Hungary, or Syria. The warhorse, which was used only in combat, was the charger. The palfrey was a ceremonial mount; and, on marches, the knight was mounted on a pacer. The knight's page rode a cob (a thickset horse) and archers rode crop-eared mounts. Women rode hacks. And the packhorse, of course, was used only for baggage.

The ceremony of homage was a logical extension of the conferring of kinghthood, and it consisted essentially in the acknowledgment of the bond which existed between the knight and his peers. It was, in other words, a contract which guaranteed that a man and his horse would not be isolated, and that they would form part of a recognized military unit or caste.

The use of the spur was reserved for the knight, and it was the first piece of equipment that he received when he was dubbed. If later he incurred disgrace, he was degraded by having the stem of his spurs sawed off.

When the knights of the West embarked on the Crusades, they took their horses with them. But neither the knights nor their horses were prepared for the climate of Asia Minor, and many of the animals died or were abandoned. "One saw," recorded Guillaume de Tyr, "many noble knights forced to ride oxen in place of warhorses."

Despite such hardships, the Crusades exercised much influence on the equestrian art as it had been practiced in the West, where force and the use of brutal constraints were the customary means of dealing with horses. The Crusaders were exposed to, and learned, the ways of the Muslims, from whom they learned to handle their horses no less cruelly than before, but more dexterously. It was not until the fourteenth and fifteenth centuries that equitation became a relatively gentle art. In the following century, armor fell into disuse, and both horse and rider gained in mobility and flexibility. Riding schools sprang up in Italy, and it was in that country that Pluvinel, groom to King Louis XIII and founder of the "French school" of riding, was trained. The characteristic of Pluvinel's system, Commandant Rousselet tells us, is that "it teaches the horse to love to obey."

The end of the Middle Ages saw not only the beginning of a new age of horsemanship, but also the spread of horses into the New World. A handful of Spaniards on horseback were able to conquer vast empires in the Americas. It is said that the Indians, having never before seen horses, believed that man and mount were but a single monstrous creature. In any event we know that Cortes, when he landed in Mexico in 1519, had only seventeen horses. From these, and from horses imported by other expeditions, sprang the bloodlines which soon populated the continents of the New World. Many of the Spaniards' horses were stolen by Indians, and the Indians themselves became expert riders. And later, it seems, abandoned or escaped horses became the ancestors of the wild herds which multiplied with extreme rapidity in the New World. For example, in 1535, five mares and seven stallions were released in the Pampas by Pedro Mendoza. Within a short time, wild horses had become so abundant in that region that at Montevideo it was said even beggars rode on horseback.

Of all man's domestic animals, the horse has been the most carefully trained, studied, and modified through breeding. Yet, it has remained the most unpredictable and mysterious of the animals which man has pressed into his service. "Thousands of years of obedience," writes Dr. F. Méry, "have not been sufficient to reassure the horse." And, in fact, there seems always to be a thin layer of panic just beneath the surface of the horse; a nervousness always on the verge of being translated into a kick or a bolt. It may be that the history of the horse has made it unstable. It did, after all, once live free, in herds; and for thousands of years it was man's prey rather than his friend. Perhaps the horses' rebelliousness, and above all its fear of man, is rooted in that dim past. Certainly, no amount of breeding and crossbreeding and training has been able to eradicate those ancient experiences.

Most of our modern thoroughbred bloodlines originated with the famous Arabian horses. According to some authorities, the horses of ancient Egypt and Babylonia were the forerunners of these Arab breeds of Asia Minor and the Middle East, which were smaller and swifter than the European horse. These may have been introduced into the Iberian peninsula during and after the Islamic conquest of Spain in the eighth century. Certainly, it was not until the twelfth century that such horses were imported into the rest of Europe. They were not known across the Pyrenees, in fact, until the time of the Crusades, when the knights of the West were first exposed to their dazzling performances of speed and endurance in the battle for the Holy Land.

Not only the Crusades, but also the Hundred Years' War, and other wars generally, contributed to the mixing of bloodlines. The most remarkable product of such crossbreeding is the thoroughbred from which the modern racehorse is descended. To find the thoroughbred's ancestors, one must go back to the Roman horses which landed with Caesar's armies in ancient Britain. The mounts of later Germanic invaders and those of William the Conqueror's Norman horses, improved the breed. Between the twelfth and the eighteenth centuries, bloodlines were imported from abroad in the form of Arabian, Barb, and Turkish horses. Meanwhile, at the beginning of the eighteenth century, on the basis of exceptional performance, the thoroughbred was developed from the offspring of three foundation sires: the Byerly Turk, the Darley Arabian, and the Godolphin Barb. The racehorse therefore is a rare, delicate mechanism perfected by man; and its financial value is measured accordingly. So far as its biological value is concerned, it may be stated that it represents the ultimate in domesticated animals. That is, it is the most perfect animal created by man.

The passing of the centuries has only increased the reputation and glory of the horse. From the time of the Egyptian pharaohs, immured in their tombs in the company of their horses, until that of Napoleon's cavalry, the horse has been the kingpin of history. During the three millennia between those two points in time, man has worked assiduously at modifying and perfecting the horse to meet his own requirements. At the same time, the horse has changed man at least as much as man has changed the horse. It has dictated human life-styles, social structures, and even human costumes. From the High Middle Ages until the end of the *ancien régime,* it served to determine one's caste and to mark one's social rank. As late as the nineteenth century and even during the First World War, horsemanship was a sign, if not of nobility, then at least of aristocratic worth.

Since that time the horse has not only declined as a symbol of prestige, but also diminished in numbers. In the United States in 1918, there were some 21 million horses. By 1925 there were only 18 million. And by 1939 there were no more than 100 million in the world.

The horse, nonetheless, is far from disappearing. Everywhere in the West—and certainly in France and the United States—men, women, and children are rediscovering the joys of riding. Dude ranches are thriving—even though in many cases the customers are satisfied to look like cowboys rather than to live like cowboys. There is still a certain, and growing, prestige attached to the horse. We have never quite lost the conviction that the horse is a noble animal. And we have retained or revived some of the customs associated with that sense of nobility: the riding habit, for example, which, mysteriously, one sees on the subways as well as on the bridle trails of Central Park.

None of the attitudes and rituals surrounding the use

we make of horses (or of any other animal, for that matter) are without some reason and foundation in history. The twentieth-century horseman, like his earlier counterpart, still hopes, at least subconsciously, to benefit from the aristocratic past, and from the athletic and sexual qualities which are reputed to be associated with horsemanship. The amateur cowboy, like the authentic cowboy of the Old West, is driven by a need for space, for a free and unhampered life. In all cases the horseman finds in his domination of the animal a satisfaction that is perhaps denied him in his everyday life.

Still, one should not complain or throw stones. It is true that the horse has been transformed into a luxury; but at least that transformation has saved it from total unemployment and, to some extent, bodes well for the future of the species. It has been a long road from the heights of the cliff at Solutré to Ascot and the Derby. The way has led from the tombs of the Egyptian pharaohs to the war chariots of the Greeks; from the fields of feudal Europe to the conquest of the Aztecs and the Incas, from the Napoleonic campaigns to riding academies for socially mobile young ladies. Who can tell how many lives are yet in store for the noble horse?

CHAPTER TEN

To Each His Own (Animal)

In discovering a species, we find new relatives for ourselves.
—Pierre Gascar

In every age and in all climates there has been no man, no matter how otherwise deprived, who has not had an animal which was a comfort in his misery and a companion in his loneliness. Civilizations have been born from this fundamental sympathy: the yak civilization of the Himalayas, the camel civilization of the Sahara, the llama civilization of the Andes, the boar civilization of New Guinea. There was even a bee civilization among the Indians of Paraguay.

There seems to be a correlation between the effort which one must expend in order to survive and the degree of man's attachment to a particular species of animal suited to his needs. The harder man must struggle, the more he tends to make privileged associates of animals. In that respect nothing has changed. Urban man in the twentieth century, alienated as he is from his fellow humans and even from himself, finds the affection he requires in the company of his dog or cat.

The strength of this mysterious, age-old bond between man and animal manifests itself in various ways, but especially in man's reluctance to cause the death of the animal which helps him to bear his own life: Tibetans drink the blood of the yak, but exercise the greatest care to ensure that the animal does not die from the bleeding.

Early contact between man and animals of various kinds was facilitated, during the Quaternary era, by the numerous climatic changes occurring in glacial and interglacial periods. In this respect, it is necessary to recall that during the latter periods Western Europe was quite different from what it is now. Its flora and fauna were then not dissimilar to those of present-day tropical Africa with its elephants, rhinoceroses, and hippopotamuses. Then, the coming of glaciers and the lower temperatures which that coming entailed, favored the spread of forests and prairies where deer and bison lived. Many centuries later, East Europe was covered by steppes and deserts inhabited by wild asses, goats, and antelope. Alongside the glacial regions were tundras—the home of the reindeer, the muskox, the woolly rhinoceros, and the mammoth. At the same time, wild sheep, ibex, and marmots deserted the cold mountains for the comparative comfort of the valleys.

Thus, climatic change brought about a change in the living habits of animals and at the same time enabled man to familiarize himself with animals to which he had not been exposed earlier. And with each succeeding climatic change, he was obliged either to follow his accustomed game when the latter migrated to warmer climates or to invent new hunting techniques so as to be able to bring down animals which were new to him. The lot of the prehistoric hunter was therefore not an easy one. We can gain some insight into just how difficult it was by reading accounts of polar expeditions during the nineteenth and early twentieth centuries, from which it is clear that man, in a hostile environment, depends for his survival on a chance encounter with a large animal—a bear, a caribou, or a seal. Certainly, there were times in the prehistoric period when man's continued existence upon the face of the earth was contingent on such encounters.

Man, in order to survive, probably often had to follow the animals in their migrations. Such moves did not necessarily mean better living conditions. It was very likely necessary for our remote ancestors to choose between an abundance of game, or adequate shelter, or a sufficient supply of fresh water. Certainly, his choice was more often than not dictated by chance, by fear of the unknown, or merely by the exigencies of the moment. From these circumstances it appears that man did not always choose to settle in areas propitious to human survival; in areas where game abounded or where the climate was most comfortable. Today the whole earth is known. We know where food can grow, where animals can survive, and where the weather is always pleasant. Yet there are millions of human beings who still choose to live on poor land; in primitive and uncomfortable conditions: the people of Siberia, for example, and the Pygmies of the African jungle. These humans remain where they are, perhaps less out of attachment to their land than out of fear of what lies beyond that land. It seems no less likely that prehistoric man, to whom everything beyond a tiny radius was entirely alien, experienced that fear to a much higher degree. He therefore remained attached to his geological, botanical, and zoological environment; to the same environment which had dictated not only the kind of weapons he developed, but also the customs and rites he evolved.

One may conclude that throughout history, in every part of the world, no matter how hostile the environment and inhospitable the climate, man has encountered an animal capable of enabling him to survive and of bearing with him the brunt of nature's hostility. This holds true both in the sands of the desert and in the frozen polar wastes. Man and animal are bound together by a tacit contract which provides for mutual help and which modifies both parties to the contract.

An illustrative case is that of the reindeer and the inhabitants of Lapland. The reindeer civilization, like that of the horse, began by a misunderstanding. Reindeer, before man learned to domesticate them, were game for hunters. Even under those conditions the animal seemed a heaven-sent creature. It furnished not only meat, but also skins for clothing and tents, oil for lamps, and bones from which to make weapons and tools. It is no wonder that it was the favorite victim of Magdalenian and Mousterian hunters.

How the transition was accomplished from game to domestic animal remains a mystery. We do not know where or when domestication was realized.* It is known that the reindeer was first utilized most successfully in Lapland and in northern Siberia. The Samoyeds of Siberia are undoubtedly the oldest known breeders of the animal, and they used it as a mount, as a draft animal, and as a pack animal. Even today the reindeer is exported from Lapland to Alaska, northern Canada and Iceland, where it is regarded as a domestic animal.†

The reindeer, for all its value, is not the only animal that has come to man's aid in the struggle for survival in the frozen North. In a land nine-tenths of which is covered by ice, the Eskimo have taken two animals as their very own: the dog and the seal.

It would be possible to draw an interesting parallel between the sled dogs of the North and the camels of the desert. In both cases, animals and men had to

*The reindeer was among the general symbols of the moon among all peoples to which the animal was known, and it was man's companion in the afterlife. In the Altai tombs, which date from the fifth century B.C., horses with the heads of reindeer were found.

†There are traces of strontium 90 and cesium 137 in the lichen of the Arctic and in the animals which feed on that lichen. Reindeer, particularly, contain a high level of active strontium and contaminate both the animals and the people who eat their meat. The Lapps, for example, are afflicted with a very high degree of radioactivity.

combine forces to assure the survival of both. Together they lived or died. They traveled together, made camp together, and together formed an island of life, a tight social entity, in the midst of a great wasteland. Sled dogs are very seldom used in the Arctic nowadays and they have become part of the folklore reserved for tourists. Among the natives, the dog has been replaced by the snowmobile and by snow scooters. Most of the dogs are left to wander on the fringes of Eskimo villages, with no one to care for them. Apparently, the masters whom they once served so well have retained no affection for them. In the desert, however, there is no animal comparable to that boon of the North, the seal, which is the Eskimo's major source of food during the winter. The killing of such an animal, which requires hours of patient watching, is a solemn occasion in which both hunters and dogs participate. One explorer who assisted at such a ceremony describes it as follows: "A murmur goes up when Tutaunuak, with his snow knife, cuts into the animal's side and draws out the red, steaming liver. The five other hunters surround the animal and are on their knees in the snow. Before each one of them, the man places a piece of the liver, and then a piece of fat. The hunters remain on their knees, immobile, contemplating these tidbits, which they regard as the most desirable portions of the seal. The pieces of liver and fat remain on the ice as the men offer thanks to Nugliayuk [the god of the Eskimo] for the gift of the seal. As the men pray, the dogs lie behind them, motionless. Before me, I see six men and their dogs worshipping the sea from which they draw their sustenance, just as worshippers of the sun pray to that source of light and of life. The frozen immensity and the vast silence which surrounds them lends an air of astonishing grandeur to the scene."*

*Gontran de Poncins, *Kablouna*.

The three animals which have truly been gifts from heaven to climatically disadvantaged peoples are the llama, the yak, and the camel. All three have in common that they are capable of furnishing meat, wool, and milk; and all three have long been associated with man and have become part of a certain way of life.

The llama is a relative of the camel, and it has the noble but clumsy appearance of the latter; its bony head and long neck. It also has a slightly comical air of dignity about it, and a discernible attitude of contempt for humans—which it frequently expresses by spitting. Its long eyelashes, seductive eyes, and handsome coat give it an ethereal, pre-Columbian beauty entirely in keeping with its history, for the llama was the irreplaceable servant and helpmate of the Incas as well as of several earlier races.

The llama had been domesticated long before the Spanish conquistadors set foot within the empire of the Incas. Indeed, the llama and the alpaca were regarded as sacred animals, and all herds were the exclusive property of the Inca sovereign. For uncounted centuries before the time of Pizarro, the llama had been used as a beast of burden—as it still is in the Andes. It was the animal used by the Spaniards to carry their Incan plunder across the Andes for shipment to Europe; and a steady stream of these stately animals moved from the rich silver mines of Potosi, bearing the precious metal destined for the coffers of the Catholic Majesties of Spain.

The llama is not particular as to its master. It will work for prince or peasant, for the conqueror as readily as for the conquered. Yet, as docile as it is, it manages to assert its independence. For example, it will not carry a burden which is beyond its strength.* If it senses that its load is too heavy, the llama lies on the ground, and

*A normal load is between sixty-five and one hundred pounds.

there is no power in heaven or on earth that can make it rise to its feet. If one tries to do so, then as often as not one receives a glob of odoriferous green saliva in response.

The llama also had an important religious function among the pre-Columbian inhabitants of the Andes, among whom human sacrifice (so common elsewhere in the New World and especially in Mexico) was wholly unknown in some areas and rare elsewhere. The llama and the alpaca, rather than man, were the proper victims for sacrifice to the gods. A white llama was offered to the sun, a brown llama to Viracocha, and a bicolored animal to the thunder god. When the suppliant was not wealthy enough to provide a llama for the sacrifice, he substituted a guinea pig—a domestic animal very common in Peru, even today, where in poor areas it is often found living in the same houses with humans.

Among certain African tribes it is not allowed to kill the animals of one's herd for meat. The same taboo prevails among the Andean peoples, who would never consider slaughtering one of their llamas for food. When they need meat they kill a guinea pig.

There is less romance associated with the yak, which is an animal as useful as the llama, but not quite so charming. The yak is found exclusively on the plateaus of Tibet and on the southern slopes of the Himalayas, from Cashmere, through Nepal and Sikkim to Bhutan. It seems incapable of acclimating itself to lower altitudes. The yak is valued not only as a beast of burden, but also as a source of milk—and of blood. It is bled once a year and its blood is dried and powdered. The powder is dissolved in water and then mixed with barley flour to form a dish known to the Tibetans as *tsampa.* It is not a particularly appetizing preparation, but it has extraordinary nutritive value. The yak, moreover, has an unusual incidental use: Its excrement is used as fuel, since wood is rare in the regions where this animal is found.

Of all the providential animals with which man has associated himself, the camel is perhaps the most curious. Unfortunately we know no more about its origins than we do about those of the horse and the ox.

The first record we have of the camel's presence in Africa dated from 46 B.C., at the Battle of Thapsus. This does not necessarily mean that the animal was in common use at that time. It is possible that the specimen in question was a novelty and that Thapsus represented the debut of the species on the African continent. Centuries later, however, the camel was common among the Arabs, who regarded it as a noble animal. It, along with the horse, was in large measure responsible for the strength of arms demonstrated by the Sons of the Prophet as they spread the Muslim faith throughout North Africa and Asia Minor. Also, like the horse, the camel would probably have become extinct if it had not been for man's intervention. The Arabs realized early along that camels, if left to their own devices, copulate only with difficulty. The sexual organ of the male is quite small and the shape of the female's body is such that penetration is improbable. The Arabs, therefore, not only bred the camel into a sturdy, swift mount, but also developed methods for easing the lot of amorous camels.

The presence of the camel in Europe is a matter of record in the first centuries of the Christian era. It was a participant in the spectacles presented in Gallo-Roman amphitheaters; and its remains have been found in the arenas of Lutetia. It is likely that the animal was introduced into Western Europe by Goths emigrating from Bactria. Certainly, there were camels in the armies of Clotaire II, King of the Franks (584–629). And the Spaniards, a thousand years later, who had become familiar with camels through their contacts with Islam, tried vainly to use dromedaries in Peru at the end of the sixteenth century and especially during the eighteenth century.

Napoleon had better luck with the camel during his Egyptian campaign in 1798. He created a Regiment of Dromedaries which included, besides the camels themselves, four companies each of one hundred men, all under the command of a colonel of cavalry. A half century later, Napoleon III tried to introduce the camel into the southwest of France, unsuccessfully.

There are no wild camels on earth today. Apparently, only the domesticated animals are able to survive. In the eighteenth century, domesticated camels were imported into the deserts of Arizona and New Mexico, and they saw service in the Union armies during the Civil War. Shortly afterward, however, this experiment in acclimation was abandoned and the camels were turned loose to survive as best they could. For a number of years they wandered in the American desert and engaged in periodic migrations. These, so far as is known, were the last wild camels. Today they have disappeared completely.*

One must have ridden a camel in order to appreciate the endurance, courage, and patience of this extraordinarily versatile animal. I have ridden camels across rocks and along the edge of sheer cliffs, as well as across the sands of the Sahara—in temperatures which would have killed a horse but which my camel seemed hardly to notice. I have seen camels walk for 300 miles, on a ten-day journey, without a drop of water and with nothing more than a few dried blades of grass as food. Almost unconscious, and half-dead from thirst, I have walked behind a camel with one end of a rope attached

*More successful attempts at the transplantation of camels have been undertaken, and some of the animals have been able to survive in Zanzibar, in the Canary Islands, and in Australia.

to myself and the other end to the camel's bridle, knowing that though my human companions, in their own delirium, might allow me to remain where I fell, my camel would never desert me. On the basis of such experiences, I have a great affection for the camel. Nature has not given it physical beauty, but it has gifted it with a disposition which, contrary to popular belief, is neither unintelligent nor malicious. Indeed, the camel becomes quickly attached to humans if it is well treated, and I know of few animals as sensitive to the human voice or as gifted with a good memory.

The most impressive and in some respects the most intriguing of man's providential animals is the elephant. Like the reindeer, the yak, the llama, and the camel, the elephant in India has enjoyed a long career as both a utilitarian animal and as a religious symbol. Today, however, that career has come to an end. The elephant has become what in America is known as a shill. It serves principally to separate tourists from their money. The Asian elephant is smaller than the species native to Africa, and therefore less imposing. Moreover, it is afflicted with markings—a mauve discoloration of the upper trunk and forehead—which closely resemble the effects of a serious skin disease, but which are nothing more than the effects of constant crossbreeding with albino elephants in order to obtain the white elephant which was regarded as the most sacred of animals.* No one, not even the sovereign, was allowed to ride the white elephant; and from the time that it was born the animal was fed human milk.

"India," Sylvain Lévi wrote, "is a land in which man is too small for Nature." This is quite accurate, at least figuratively. If man was able to survive in the Indian

*The elaborate headdresses, paintings, and decorations which one sometimes sees on Indian elephants are usually a heritage from the country's past. The native princes used such means to hide the unsightly markings on the elephants' foreheads.

peninsula, it was with the aid of the elephant. We do not know at what point the elephant was domesticated in India. We do not even know if the Aryans, when they spread throughout southern India between 1500 and 800 B.C., knew how to make use of the elephant in their confrontations with the buffalo and lions of that region. We do know, however, that a sacred character was attributed to the elephant at a very early date, as is attested by its existence in the Hindu god, Ganesh. Ganesh is depicted as having the body of an obese human and the head of an elephant; and he is the son of the gods Parvati and Shiva.

Charlemagne, urged on by a desire to imitate the princes of antiquity, asked Haroun al Raschid, Caliph of Baghdad, to send him some exotic animals. The shipment arrived at Pisa in 797, and among other rare animals there was an elephant named Aboul Abbas. It lived for thirteen years at Charlemagne's court, and when it died, one of its tusks was made into a hunting horn which is still preserved in the treasury of Aix la Chapelle.

King Louis IX—Saint Louis—also had an elephant, which he bought in Egypt, and which he eventually presented to his brother-in-law, Henry III of England. Louis' elephant was the first pachyderm to set foot on English soil.

It is important to note that the elephant, despite the centuries during which it has been used as an engine of war and of work, and also as a status symbol for ambitious princes, has never been truly a domesticated animal, since it does not reproduce in captivity. It has always been necessary to capture a wild adult elephant and then to tame it. This, then, is not domestication, but training.*

*There have been two or three recorded births at the Gangala Na Bodio station in the former Belgian Congo. The parent elephants, however, were living only in semicaptivity and the females not infrequently escaped into the jungle and returned later.

The elephant, whatever its value may have been, today is nothing more than a historical curiosity. It is an unemployed animal and has been replaced by the tractor, which is faster and less expensive. One does not have to train a tractor, and gasoline is much cheaper than the 500 to 1,000 pounds of foliage that an elephant requires every day.

The elephant's unpredictable reactions make of it a dangerous helper as well as an expensive one. It is subject to sudden seizures of fear and rage. Even when the elephant was taken into battle, certain safeguards were necessary to ensure the safety of one's soldiers. The keepers of Hannibal's elephants, for example, rode on the necks of their charges holding a dagger in their hands, ready to plunge it into the animal's skull at the first sign of panic. And now that the elephant is a star of circuses, surrounded by noise and lights and crowds, there are frequent instances of attacks by elephants which were always regarded as docile and harmless. Recently, in Paris, an elephant trampled first its keeper and then the director of the Rancy Circus, even though it had shown every sign of being fond of the latter. The newspapers concluded that the elephant had suddenly become insane, since in its years with the circus it had never shown the slightest sign of violence. The wife of the owner of the circus, however, shed considerable light on the case when she explained that the elephant had never accepted its keeper. When it finally turned on the man and trampled him, the director had rushed to aid his employee and had been trampled accidentally.* The elephant apparently had been suddenly overcome with a blind rage built up through years of psychological pressure resulting from captivity. In other words, it was mentally ill. The problem is that the mental illnesses of animals are difficult to diagnose. There is so little that we know about the reactions of animals that most often we cannot distinguish between a healthy response and an unhealthy one. Once more, we run up against that psychological barrier which makes it so difficult to establish communication between man and animal; and when the animal involved is one of the size, strength, and sensitivity of the elephant, that difficulty can be fatal.

*It is generally accepted that every elephant have its own trainer. The same trainer must always remain with the elephant. The essential rule in the relationship between keeper and elephant is that the man must always speak softly, and must even give orders in a low voice without shouting. Above all he must never be rough with the elephant or show anger. The elephant, for all its bulk, is a timid animal. It is, literally, afraid of a mouse.

CHAPTER ELEVEN

Return to Asia

This fervor of humanity, extended as it is to animals, remains the honor of Buddhism.
—RENÉ GROUSSET

AT the beginning of 1973 I returned to the Far East after an absence of five years. I was astonished to find that the tourist industry was booming. Jets loaded with camera-bearing Europeans, Americans, and Japanese, streaked over Ceylon, India, and Bali. Even the Dayaks of Borneo, former headhunters, have become a tourist attraction.

I visited Indonesia, India, Malaysia, Borneo, and Ceylon, and especially those cities which are the crossroads of the Orient: Singapore, Djakarta, Colombo, and Hong Kong. Everywhere I was struck not only by the abundance of foreign visitors, by the growth of the urban population, and by the major technical and industrial changes which had taken place since my last visit, but especially by the incredibly rapid deterioration of the flora and fauna of those places.

Most of the peoples of the Far East are aware of the importance of animals to their lives, but that awareness is not enough at this point. There is much time that must be made up for. During the whole of the nineteenth century, the colonial areas of Asia constituted one vast hunting terrain for big game. Moreover, the population growth of the twentieth century has transformed much of what was jungle and brush into cultivated, inhabited land.

Asia, therefore, has lost a large number of her wild animals. At the same time she has preserved her respect for animal life. Asian culture and Asian religion, whether Hindu or Buddhist, for centuries have regarded the sacred, the human, and the animal as one world. The attitudes which have been formed are too strong to be broken easily. There still does not exist in Asia that chasm of incomprehension which in Europe and America separates man from nature. Life there, in all its forms, is still regarded as sacred; and while "progress" has come to Asia, it has not yet succeeded in persuading the people of Asia to give up the domestic animals which surround them. These animals, no matter how troublesome they may be, and how nonproductive, are still held in honor.

Asia, then, is the last area on the globe where man is still in immediate contact with nature. Whether it will remain so is another matter.

I was at Taman Negara, in the heart of the Malaysian jungle. Before me there was a clearing of tall grass; beyond, a dark wall of trees. It was dusk, the time at which the gaur, the wild buffalo of Southeast Asia, having spent the day in the protective shade of the jungle, leaves his shelter to graze.

I saw the first one, so huge as to be almost unbelievable. I had not heard a sound. Not a leaf crackling, not a branch breaking. It stood there, immobile, standing six feet at the shoulder, a mass of potential violence more fearsome than any African buffalo that I have ever seen. Its massive head and huge shoulders bore witness to a power that nothing could withstand. Yet its horns seemed rather small and somehow insignificant in the frontal view of the animal. The impression of immense strength and power came from the head and shoulders. Looking at the animal, I thought: It is like a great rock.

The bony crest on the gaur's spine formed a hump on its back. The animal's ears were two yellow spots on its dark, almost black hide. Despite the tall grass, I could distinguish a white marking above each hoof—the "stockings," as they are called.

This specimen, the first to venture into the open, was no doubt the old female which was the leader of the herd. She was larger and more formidable than any bull. I watched her, head high, sniffing the clearing. Although the eyesight of the gaur is poor, its smell and hearing are keen. I had already picked the tree that would be my refuge if she decided to charge, but she did not seem to have picked up my scent.

There was a series of strangely gentle sounds, and other gaur ambled into the clearing: females, followed by their calves. Then came the young members of the herd, and finally a large bull. That evening there were eleven animals. The next evening there were seventeen; and the third, twenty. By all accounts I had been extraordinarily lucky.

I say lucky because it is not often nowadays that one has the opportunity to view such a herd. The gaur, one of Asia's most spectacular animals, is threatened with extinction in the more or less proximate future. One must actually see the gaur to appreciate its size and beauty. Some specimens stand seven and one-half feet at the shoulder and weigh over a ton. In Malaysia, the gaur, or Indian urus, is known as the *seladang*, and the Malaysians hold the animal in great fear. However, no one was able to cite an instance in which a *seladang* had killed a human being. I gather that the animal's fearsome appearance is largely responsible for its reputation.

The Taman Negara preserve, where I saw the herd of twenty animals, was established for the protection of the gaur and of other species of rare animals. The Malaysian government, with extraordinary foresight, has transformed its jungle areas, which lie in the heart of the peninsula, into a vast national park. There are no roads, no paths. It is a dense equatorial forest, the only means of access to which is the Tembeling River and its tributaries. The jungle, therefore, has remained a jungle, with all that this implies not only in natural beauty, but also in natural danger and discomfort for humans. There are swarms of mosquitoes and an abundance of snakes—and of leeches. The least dangerous, but the most revolting of these are the leeches, which are so bloodthirsty that they climb into one's boots and shoes and attach themselves to the legs without being felt. Nature has equipped these creatures with an anticoagulant which makes their bloodsucking much easier than it would otherwise be.

There have been efforts made to attract tourists to the jungle, but these efforts have not yet been carried to the point of destroying the leeches. That is something to be thankful for; not only because leeches play a part in the ecological equilibrium of the area, but also because these troublesome parasites discourage the kind of tourists who are concerned more with their comforts and conveniences than with nature.

The twentieth century has invented a new kind of tourism, which one might call zoological tourism. The urge to "see the animals" has made tourism a major industry in Africa, and anyone with a little money to spend can treat himself to the spectacle of sleepy lions, tame rhinoceroses, and overweight zebras. But such attractions are becoming rather commonplace. The animals of Asia have the advantage of being more of a novelty. Moreover, a voyage to the Far East is no longer the expensive undertaking that it once was. It may safely be predicted that the animal preserves of Asia will soon form part of the zoological-tour circuit.

These Oriental preserves are of comparatively recent origin. Some of them—the Teman Negara park, for example, which is blessed with a superintendent as courageous as he is competent—manages both to retain the tranquility necessary to the animals and to satisfy the curiosity of visitors. Many preserves, however, have not yet adopted sufficiently stringent means of maintaining their isolation and of safeguarding the animals. And these are the things which are essential if the preserves are to become havens for species in danger of extinction.

The preserves of the Far East nonetheless enjoy certain advantages. Most of them have preserved intact their natural character, and the density of animal population has been maintained at a reasonable level. In this respect they are far more successful than their counterparts in Africa. The ecological equilibrium has not been upset, and both flora and fauna may still be observed in their wild state. This, perhaps, is what Asia has to offer that is truly distinctive so far as tourists are concerned. On the other hand, tourists who are accustomed to the numerous, half-tame, apathetic animals on display on guided tours through the African preserves, will probably complain that the animals of Asia are too few and "too wild"—by which they mean that the animals have preserved their natural reactions to man's presence, and especially their flight-instinct.

The fact is that it is not easy to embark on an Asiatic safari. There are no minicars in which to ride in comfort through the wilds in search of animals. The Malaysian jungle is not the savannas of Kenya or Tanzania. The animals come and go without being seen by man. In the dense jungle growth, when an animal is encountered, it is by chance or because it has somehow been lured into the open. One must move noiselessly, climbing jungle-covered mountains, pulling oneself along from root to root; then, suddenly, one may hear a grunt nearby. A wild pig, only a few yards away, crashes its way through the undergrowth.

I spent a night on a platform in a tree, in the heart of the jungle. It is an experience which everyone should enjoy at least once in his lifetime; indeed, it is the only way to appreciate the sounds of the jungle, since it is impossible to convey these with mere words. Nightfall is followed by an hour of sudden silence. Then the sounds begin—the frogs, especially, are deafening. Their calls stop suddenly, then begin again with renewed volume. Animal sounds are heard over the unrelenting hum of the insects. Then, the rain on the trees, drumming on the leaves, drowns out the sounds of the jungle. It is a rain which one hears, but never feels. The leaves overhead are like a vast umbrella, and the life-giving water reaches the ground only by streaming down the trunks of the trees.

At dawn I saw a hornbill take flight at tree level, with a great flapping. I was fascinated at the sudden appearance of what is surely one of the strangest birds in existence. It has an enormous curved yellow beak topped by a growth of red flesh. Zoologists can offer no certain explanation for this mass of flesh. There may be some connection with the fact that during the mating season male hornbills fight by smashing into one another, in flight, headfirst. But no one knows whether this crest of flesh is a consequence of this practice or at its origin.

The habits of the hornbill are as peculiar as its appearance. The male seems to have only limited confidence in the loyalty of the female. He cements her into a hole in a tree trunk, leaving only a small hole through which he brings her fruits and berries. In her hideaway, the female loses all her feathers and remains in the tree trunk until her eggs hatch eighty-seven days later. However, she is able if she wishes to demolish her cement wall with her beak—which she does if the male, for some reason or other, stops bringing her food.

There are numerous gibbons in the Malaysian jungle. They are seen rarely, but they are clearly audible in their treetop havens as they play, fight, and shriek. The animals have as much trouble seeing through the trees and undergrowth as humans do, and their cries and calls serve to establish their location and notify other animals of their presence. This is true not only for the primates, but also for such animals as grasshoppers and frogs.

To civilized man the sounds of the jungle are the most significant object of the senses. To primitive man, however, the smells of the jungle were equally important. His senses were not atrophied as ours are, and odors constituted a rich and varied language which he understood: the smell of decomposed vegetation, the acid emanations of ants, the bitter odor of the elephant, the excrement of the wild pig—all these things were, to our ancestors, an integral part of the language of the jungle, as was the smell of camphor given off by a particular tree, or of honey or beeswax.

The Malaysian jungle exists virtually as it was in the time of those remote ancestors of ours. How long it will survive is a matter for speculation. Already the fringes of the jungle are being eaten away in the wake of man's determination to exploit the precious hardwood (Dipterocarpaceae) found in abundance there. The single tourtuous access road is constantly filled with trailer trucks, each loaded with three gigantic logs. And there are always automobiles, trucks, and wagons speeding along in both directions in total disregard for life and limb. The road is literally a highway of death; yet it has made the fortune of Kuala Lumpur, the very modern capital city of Malaysia.

Occasionally one sees a great column of smoke climb

to the sky, spreading over the jungle, black, swirling like a tornado. Then one knows that yet another part of the jungle is being destroyed, by fire this time, to make room for the planting of oil palms and pararubber plants.

At this stage it is not so much a question of whether the jungle will survive, but of who will finally conquer it, the tourists or the industrialists. The Malaysian government understandably is eager to exploit both; but it has already begun to realize that development is a two-edged sword. The existence of Malaysia's tigers and elephants, both of which are the country's stellar tourist attractions, has already been seriously compromised by the infringement of man onto their domain. The tigers roam the fringes of villages at night rather than remaining on their preserves, and this habit results in their death by poisoning. The elephants are somewhat more direct. They lay waste to the plantations which have infringed their domains, and one must have seen a banana plantation after a visit by an elephant in order to appreciate the damage that even a single animal, let alone a herd of them, can do. The problem of the elephants is the same in Asia as in Africa. They require a vast stretch of land in order to find the 500 to 1,000 pounds of foliage that each of them requires every day; and, on all sides, the area available to them is constantly being reduced by human infringement.

The Malaysian government hopes to solve the elephant problem by importing specialists from Ceylon. These experts expect to capture the most troublesome wild elephants and transport them to the Taman Negara preserve. It seems to me that this plan presents almost insuperable difficulties at the practical level. An animal can be immobilized by injecting it (by means of a rifle) with an anesthetic such as M-99; but once it is immobilized there is no way to transport an elephant weighing six or eight thousand pounds across miles and miles of jungle in a country where roads are nonexistent. It is hardly likely that the government will embark on a road-building program merely for the sake of the elephants. Therefore one should prepare oneself for the worst. We may expect to see the elephants of Malaysia disappear from the face of the earth.

Malaysia is not alone in facing this dilemma. All the countries of the Far East have the same apparently insoluble problem. They must choose either to adapt to modern technological and industrial civilization or to preserve their forests, their animals, their traditions, and their human equilibrium. They cannot do both.

This dilemma is epitomized on the island of Borneo, among the Dayak, a former headhunting people.* The Dayak are very poor people. Their only "industry" consists in the capture of orangutans for zoos and laboratories. This is a vocation which the Dayak have pursued with great eagerness and skill, with the result that there are no more than 2,700 orangutans today on Borneo.†

The orangutan is the only large ape found outside of Africa, and nowadays they are found only on Borneo and Sumatra. (Formerly, they were not uncommon in India, China, and Indonesia, where their fossils have been found.) The male of the species reaches a height of about five feet and a weight of over 200 pounds. Its arms are disproportionately long, and when an orangutan is standing erect its hands reach to its knees. These

*They no longer hunt heads, but they have kept those obtained by their forebears, and they display these trophies with great glee for the edification of tourists.

†Seven hundred of these are in the Baka National Preserve, and 2,000 at Sabah, in North Borneo. (These are the official figures and therefore somewhat optimistic. According to nonofficial sources, there are not more than between 2,500 and 3,000 orangutans in the whole of Asia, besides the 300 specimens living in captivity.) Even on these preserves, the animals are not left in peace, for the government has granted timber rights to companies in those areas.

animals are neither so powerful nor so large as the African gorilla, which may stand over six feet tall and weigh over 600 pounds. Moreover, gorillas move about on the ground, while orangutans spend most of their time in the trees.

The orangutan has been described as the most human of the apes, in looks, in the richness of expression of its gestures, and in the intelligence of its behavior. In fact, the accomplishments of the orangutan are remarkable. It was the inventor of the umbrella—for it uses large tropical leaves, which it holds over its head, to protect itself from the rain.

The orangutan, once seen, is never forgotten. Its long hair is flame-colored—almost red; and its face is black, with sunken eyes. It has no nose and its swollen jaw dominates its visage. And (another human characteristic) it has a potbelly.

Its habitat is the primary forest, and it prefers wooded areas at an altitude of 2,000 to 2,500 feet, although it sometimes climbs as high as 4,000 feet. With the destruction of its natural habitat, however, the orangutan has taken refuge in areas where it does not find the plants which are its nourishment, such as the fruit of the durio tree. Indeed, the species numbers so few members today that it is rare that one finds them in their natural habitat. (The difficulty of observing them is aggravated by the fact that the orangutan, unlike the gorilla, is a solitary animal.) Only a few thousand years ago they were found everywhere from China to Java.

The further reduction of the orangutan population is inevitable because of the ease with which they are captured. The Dayak cut down all the vegetation around an orangutan's tree, and when the hungry animal climbs down to the ground they throw a net over it. The orangutan does not fear man and does not attempt even to flee. Moreover, the orangutan multiplies at a very slow rate. A female bears a single baby once every four years, and 40 percent of the young do not survive infancy. Most females do not bear more than three or four viable offspring in their lifetimes. The Dayak will often kill a mother in order to capture her offspring—and then only one out of every six captured orangutans reaches its destination alive. The one surviving animal usually will live only for three or four years in captivity (they are extremely vulnerable to human pulmonary diseases), while in the jungle its natural span is thirty or forty years.

At the present rate, naturalists expect that the orangutan will be extinct by the end of the twentieth century. In an effort to forestall this eventuality, the Association of American Zoos has persuaded its members not to purchase orangutans unless the supplier has obtained an export permit from the country of origin. At the same time, attempts have been made to abolish the animal depots at Hong Kong, Bangkok, and Singapore which serve as clearinghouses for animals to be shipped to Europe and America. Yet, not all zoos and laboratories are willing to accept the ruling of the association, and so the capture of orangutans continues.

The animal most associated with India, and at the same time that which is most imminently threatened with extinction, is the tiger. There are not more than 5,000 of those splendid animals at liberty today in the whole world. In India, according to the official figures, there are 1,827 specimens. In 1930, there were 40,000; and, in 1920, there were 100,000. No animal in Asia except for the lion has been hunted so relentlessly. During a single tiger hunt in India, George V of England slaughtered thirty animals in eleven days. The tiger hunt (it was conducted from the back of an elephant, without the slightest risk to the hunter) was reputed to be the most aristocratic of sports.

Today, experts estimate that the Asian tiger (there are no tigers elsewhere) will disappear within the next decade, for it is doubtful that the efforts undertaken to preserve the species have been successful. Of the seven known subspecies, only one—the Bengal tiger—is not endangered. All other species are listed among those on the way toward extinction. (Here, the Chinese are at least partly to blame. The bones of tigers, ground into powder, are thought by the Chinese to confer strength and courage.)

In India tigers are now protected animals and it is forbidden under any circumstances to export their hides or bones. This protection may well have come too late. As recently as the mid-1940's, it was estimated that tigers were sufficiently numerous on Sumatra and in Indonesia, as to be in no danger. Today, however, after twenty-five years of uncontrolled hunting, the Sumatran tiger has practically disappeared even from the preserves on that island.

It happens occasionally that animals benefit, rather than suffer, from human folly. Thus it was during the Vietnam War. "The tigers are fat," a doctor in Saigon told me. He was referring to the fact that during the war the tigers prudently withdrew from the combat zone. At night, however, they would return to the battlefield to eat the bodies of the dead soldiers—and sometimes even those of the wounded. Thus, tigers are relatively numerous and "fat" in Vietnam. There are probably some 2,000 specimens living in the thickest part of the jungle, and it is likely that they have developed a taste for human flesh.

This brings us to the question of whether the tiger should be saved. People who live in tiger country are terrified of these animals, and their terror is not without foundation. Meeting a tiger is like meeting a shark. One never knows whether it will turn and flee or attack. A friend of mine, an ethnographer, was following a jungle trail on his bicycle, about eighty miles from Delhi, when he suddenly came face to face with a tiger. "I don't know which of us was more afraid," my friend said. My own feeling is that he was very lucky. Not all tigers are timid in the presence of man. The World Fund for the Preservation of Nature hopes to donate one million dollars toward the establishment of eleven Asiatic preserves where tigers could both be protected from human infringements and also cease being a threat to man.

At the delta of the Ganges and the Brahmaputra, there is a vast area consisting of a semiaquatic jungle extending along the edge of the Gulf of Bengal. This is Sunderband, in the new state of Bangladesh. And here, in this wild region, there are some 250 or 300 specimens of the Bengal tiger, known as the royal tiger for its magnificence and beauty. It has a white throat and its body is marked with approximately twenty black stripes. It is the largest of the tigers except for the Manchurian tiger; and it has the reputation of being a man-eater which feeds on the dead as well as on the living.

The natives of Sunderband, like many other groups in India, burn their dead, but they are too poor to buy all the necessary wood. They often place half-burned cadavers in the water, and the tigers—they are excellent swimmers and in that region of lagoons and streams they spend as much time in the water as on land—feed on these bodies. The Bengal tiger is therefore assured of a steady supply of food, and this is the reason why the Bengal tiger is the only variety not in danger of extinction.

The tigers of Bengal feed on the dead not only because they are lazy, or even because their usual prey (the boar, especially) is becoming scarce, but also because the tiger is not nearly so well equipped for hunting as is generally believed. Most of its intended victims are much faster than the tiger and they must be taken by surprise. Naturalists estimate that the mighty tiger must attack twenty or thirty animals before bringing one of them down.

The state of Bangladesh has chosen the tiger as its emblem, and an image of the animal appears on the paper money of that country. There is an appropriate symbolism here. Bangladesh hopes to make its fortune from the tiger, and it has made a determined effort to attract tourists to Sunderband by converting the area into a natural park.* The area is, in fact, unique. It is utterly wild, and the tropical vegetation, the mangrove marshes, and the sea constitute an extraordinary ecological whole. The star attraction on this preserve is the Bengal tiger itself. There are also other species in the delta which merit protection, such as deer, boars, and wild buffalo.

The situation hoped for in Bangladesh has already been realized in Ceylon, where there has been an extraordinary tourist boom. There are already three bird sanctuaries and three national preserves for large mammals: Ruhunu, Wilpattu, and Gal-Oya.

The Wilpattu preserve is in the heart of the jungle and contains a great abundance of wildlife. Elephants are rare at Wilpattu, but there are numerous deer, boars, black bear, wild buffalo, crocodiles, and noisy, multicolored birds. The Ruhunu preserve, on the other hand, has numerous elephants.

Ceylon has a unique problem with elephants. There are too many wild ones. In the center of the island it is estimated that there are some 2,000 specimens, completely wild. Every year ten or twelve human beings are killed by wild elephants, and the damage to

*In 1960 the Pakistanis had declared some 27,000 acres of Sunderband to be a protected area, or game sanctuary. This step, however, seems to have been a purely administrative undertaking, with no perceptible effect in practice.

plantations is considerable. The same problem obtains with respect to crocodiles. There are so many of them on the shores of the lakes that many animals are afraid to go to the water to drink. There is also an overpopulation of wild pigs and wild buffalo in the jungle; and especially a superabundance of crows. Even at Colombo, Ceylon's capital, the deafening screeches and the audacity of these birds are difficult to bear.

Ceylon's problem is exceptional at a time when everywhere else in the world wild animals are disappearing. The overpopulation of animals is not difficult to explain. Human civilization has disappeared in certain areas of the island and the land occupied by ancient cultures has been repossessed by the jungle and by animal life. In the twelfth century A.D. there were some 12,000 dams which were used to irrigate the fields of Ceylon, and the resulting crops were able to support a large population. But in the thirteenth century foreign invaders destroyed both the agricultural system and the political organization which had made that system possible. At the same time a large part of the population was wiped out by malaria. It did not take very long for the fields of Ceylon to be reclaimed by the jungle.

CHAPTER TWELVE

At the Service of the Heart

Like poetry, the animal represents deliverance.
—Edmond Jaloux

We no longer have bulls to domesticate or horses to train. Wolves are becoming more and more rare. The wild animals are all in zoos or on preserves. What will happen now? What sort of relationship will there be between man and animal? Man can no longer gamble on the friendship of the large animals: the lion, the horse, the chimpanzee. Indeed, he no longer knows how to do so. We are left with our dogs and cats; and we are unhappy because our dogs grow old and feeble too soon and because our cats die long before we do.

Even dogs, once our guards and our shepherds, have for the most part become city dwellers like ourselves; and even hunting dogs now live in houses. Inevitably the dog has paid the price of civilization. It is smothered with human affection, affected by human anguish, and infected by the psychological instability of its master.

Cats, once valued as killers of rats and retained for that purpose, now share our houses like poor relatives —unemployed, but attempting to repay human affection by allowing themselves to be petted and admired.

If we allow dogs and cats to multiply at a rate faster than that of the human race, it is because they are the privileged victims of our projections and transferrals;

that is, because they relieve us, at least in part, of our psychological burdens. They meet certain needs of our inner lives. They fill certain voids. But now that the earth itself seems incapable of providing sufficient food merely for its growing human population, what will be the future of that enormous population of pets and of the social and therapeutic role which they now fill?

Today there is one particular place where one is in the most advantageous position to observe the real relationship between man and animal, and that place is the waiting room of a veterinarian's office. I have had occasion to spend time there, while researching an earlier book, and also in the consultation room of the Veterinary School at Alfort. The hours spent in those places were doubly valuable. They taught me as much, if not more, about human beings as about animals. I learned that both the master (or mistress) and the animal go to the veterinarian for help. The animal is there for medical help; but the human is there for reassurance, and therefore he exhibits his weaknesses.

One of the most touching things I saw was a fox. Its eyes were infinitely sad. No doubt it had spent its whole life in a house or an apartment, relieving itself on a terrace, being subjected to the embraces of humans, being displayed to visitors as a status symbol and a conversation piece. In its face I could read limitless grief for the freedom it had never known. (The look of an animal is the only way in which it expresses its silent protest at having been turned into a living toy or a surrogate child by persons who have no other outlet for their emotions.) I heard later that the fox's master had taken it with him into the country and that the fox had escaped from the automobile and fled into the woods. I heard this news with very mixed emotions. A fox which has spent its life in human company, in a human habitation, is not equipped to survive on its own. It had the desire for freedom, as manifested by its escape; whether it had the capacity for freedom is another matter, and perhaps the saddest aspect of this story.

I have also had the opportunity to observe cats in veterinary clinics. They are at once the most independent and the most pathetic of pets. Left to themselves, cats seem to be quite capable of warding off unwanted affection from humans. As every cat owner knows, they are independent, unpredictable creatures. After all, they are not burdened with 60,000 years of servitude as dogs are.* Yet we have found a way to banish that unwelcome attitude among cats. We neuter them and turn them into fat, fluffy, lazy balls of fur which exhibit all the initiative and independence of enuchs.

The consultation rooms at the Alfort School are full of animals more pathetic than dogs and cats because they are wild animals which have been "tamed" and forced to exist in an environment alien to them: a wide-eyed lemur; a monkey, trembling with fever, huddling against a woman's breast; a bullfrog in a jar; and especially a python named Eliodore, which belonged to a friend of mine. Eliodore was brought once a month for a hot bath. Then, when he had been bathed and massaged, he was allowed to pass a white, odorless substance which was his monthly ration of excrement.

The ways in which man manifests his affection for his animals takes on forms proportionate to the state of a man's mind. Not all of these forms are as innocent as petting a dog or stroking a cat. Both medical doctors

*There is some discussion as to the length of time which the dog has been man's servant. Some authorities put the figure at 100,000 years, or even more. It seems to me that 60,000 is a more reasonable figure. We must remember that there are degrees of servitude, and that before an animal can be domesticated in the full sense of that term, there are preliminary stages which differ among different nations and regions and religions.

and veterinarians have recorded cases of sexual contact between man and animal. Formerly, instances of bestiality occurred more commonly in the countryside and were regarded as a form of sexual deviation. The victims of these contacts were usually barnyard animals: chickens, geese, rabbits and other such animals. Nor was it unheard of in the days of cavalry regiments for amorous recruits to make advances to mares. As often as not they received a kick for their trouble.

Nowadays, bestiality has expanded its horizons both geographically and socially. The Kinsey Report has much to say on the subject. Apparently it is now the upper classes which practice bestiality. Men take female dogs as their partners; and women take male dogs. Both take an extraordinary interest in the sexual lives of their animals; and sexual contact takes place, it is claimed, when the masters and mistresses of the dogs wish to give their animals "relief." Doctors sometimes find hydatid cysts on the liver or ovaries of a female patient—an affliction which can result only from canine contact.

At Alfort it is not uncommon for women—and women of considerable social and educational background—to complain that their dogs "bother" them or bother their women friends. Such complaints are usually followed by an admission that they have had sexual contact with their dogs. They describe these experiences discreetly, of course, but quite vividly and without undue embarrassment. It is usually clear from their tone that they have no intention of giving up the practice. The reason they have chosen to consult a veterinarian is usually that they are embarrassed by their dogs' aggressiveness in public, or toward their friends, and they want to know whether there is not a way to control such conduct. Another reason is that the dog is showing signs of some behavioral peculiarity, which the woman is afraid has been induced by sexual contact. "Usually," explains one of the veterinarians at

Alfort, "these are women who live alone. Yet married women are by no means exempt. In such cases the reaction of the husband is not usually known. There was one husband, however, who arrived with the guilty dog and demanded that the animal be put to death. He explained that he wanted to see it die."*

From all of this it is clear that sexual contact with animals is not confined to the mythology of the ancients. It is the manifestation of a very old maternal and sexual attachment to animals—an attachment which was probably an important factor in the early stages of animal training.

The dog, alone with the bee, is the most ancient example of a domesticated animal. With such a long history of contact with man, it is strange that we do not know whence the dog came. For a long time it was regarded as being without ancestors. It was said to be a product of human civilization, and to have appeared on earth at about the same time as man himself. It is even suggested that there might be some link between the apparition of man and that of the dog.

We now know a little more about the dog's past, though the entire complex truth still eludes us. We know that the dog has demonstrated a surprising plasticity, a tendency to evolve and to take on very different appearances. There has therefore been an extreme variability among dogs through the ages. Man, in caring for his dogs, has allowed certain aberrant varieties to escape the process of natural selection and to survive.

The polymorphic nature of the dog, indeed, is what has made it possible for the animal to render such a widy range of services to man. "In the Calmette cave,"

*M. Fontaine, V. Gachkel, and C. L. Dell, "Les Propriétaires d'animaux," in *Psychiatrie animale.*

Dr. Méry notes, "Bourguignat has discovered a complete collection of dogs, including a basset-hound, a beagle, a pointer, an Alsatian, two greyhounds, a wolf-dog, and several bulldogs."

The history of the dog runs parallel to the history of man, for the dog is the social animal par excellence; the animal whose association with the human race has endured much longer than that of any other animal.

The millennia during which the dog has been man's friend and servant have left their mark. Every civilization, from the Near East to the far North, has modified the dog and bred a variety suited to its own needs. That work of modification continues today. In that sense, the breeding of dogs is like the cultivation of roses: There is apparently no limit to what can be accomplished. The dog, therefore, is the most humanized animal in existence.

It is highly significant that the dog has been man's companion from the tombs of prehistory; that it was a god in Egypt, a fighter at the Battle of Marathon, a mummy in pre-Columbian cemeteries. It is possible that the dog has no past other than that which it shares with man; and, in that light, it is understandable that the dog is not equipped to survive on its own. V. B. Dröscher draws a logical conclusion from this premise when he points out: "Owners of dogs should realize that they are the only thing that their four-footed friend has on earth; that they are, quite literally, the whole universe to their dogs. It would be more kind to beat one's dog every day than to leave it alone for hours while one is at work, or to abandon it while one goes off on a trip."

In view of the intimate bond which exists between man and dog, and especially because of the flexibility which allows the dog to adapt rapidly to all the exigencies of human civilization, it is inconceivable that there will ever be a loosening of that bond, let alone a separation between human beings and canines. When man no longer required that his dog be ferocious, the dog was immediately content to be nothing more than an object of human affection, and in that role it has taken on qualities which it lacked earlier.

This does not mean, however, that it has forgotten its past, any more than man is capable of forgetting his. There are many dogs which cannot resist the temptation to chase chickens or to mark a fire hydrant with their odor so as to establish the boundaries of an ill-defined territory. These dogs are not throwbacks; they are doing nothing more than obeying the ancient laws of their tribe.

Despite its tens of thousands of years of domestication, the twentieth-century dog defends its territory with the same vigor and the same violence as a wild animal. The territorial instinct survives, most likely, because man has respected, and even developed, that instinct which was so valuable in protecting human habitations. What is less easy to understand is that the dog has extended its territory to include such newfangled things as the automobile. The explanation may be that even when its master does not train it to do so, it regards the automobile as an extension of the house. It is not always safe, therefore, to try to pet a dog left alone in "its" automobile. It is on guard, and it may well bark or even bite—or at least pretend that it is going to bite—for the automobile in the twentieth century is a territory.

The life of the dog is organized around a very complex system of values so far as its domain is concerned. Not every area has the same value or warrants the same behavior. First, the animal has its lair, which may be a particular chair, or a corner of a room, or a basket. This is its indispensable, sacred refuge. To attempt to deprive a dog of this spot or to dislodge it may provoke a violent reaction or a fit of despair and fear.

Around the dog's lair extends a zone which it feels it must guard, and any intrusion into that space causes the animal to bark. This area is usually the house, the yard, or sometimes a staircase or sidewalk. It is more or less marked. When a dog raises its leg,* it is in order to mark the boundaries of the space which it must defend, to warn other dogs that the area is protected and therefore forbidden to intruders.†

There are many other aspects of canine behavior which appear mysterious to humans, but which have their roots in the dog's early history. Although it is not certain, as we have noted, that the descendants of jackals were originally used for hunting, it is quite likely that they were highly regarded as a means of disposing of garbage and leftovers. When we see a dog today acting as though it were a garbage-disposal unit, we should remind ourselves that it is merely acting in accordance with a habit which goes back to the origins of its domestication. In fact, it is not unlikely that the age-old affection between a man and his dog began through the intermediary of garbage. Likewise, when a dog buries a bone, it obeys an ancient memory which requires it to store up food against hard times. And when a dog circles endlessly before lying down to sleep, we should recall that wolves do the same.

All dogs are fetishists in the strict sense of that term. That is, they are sensually and sexually attached to any object impregnated with the scent of their master. This is the reason why when one leaves a dog at a kennel it is usually suggested that a used article of the master's clothing be left with the dog.

In these and many other aspects of its behavior, the dog harkens back to an incredibly long association with

*The dog is the only quadruped to do so. No one knows why.

†Given the conditions in which city dogs live today, it is obvious that their life-style is in direct contradiction to the property instinct of an animal whose prehistoric role was to stand guard around a human encampment.

man; an association which is the occasion for constant friction between the primitive behavior of the animal and the law imposed by man. This conflict results in reactions on the part of the dog which are unintelligible to its master. And the situation is not eased by the fact that both dog and man are slaves to what Jung terms their "archaic unconscious," and that the animal from which man seeks reassurance is itself insecure. The dog, after all, is as old as man. Its psychological balance is as precarious as man's own; and the pressures of modern life have the same effect on that balance.

It is not surprising, therefore, that dogs are subject to mental illness, and that many such illnesses go completely unnoticed by man. The fact is that dogs are prey to nervous disorders. Some of them are neurotic and some are psychopathic. I once had a very nervous fox terrier which, through excitement, completely lost consciousness whenever I came home at night. She used to wait for me the whole day, with her muzzle under the door. It is easy to allow animals to develop such intense, exclusive passions, as we see from the frequency with which they do so. It is easy—but unreasonable. These sentimental adventures are not unlike human love in its most romantic form; and, as in the latter case, neither of the parties is happy. The one at fault is usually the master, who allowed this excessive affection to develop. Since that time I have been constantly on guard against allowing either myself or my animals to become involved in these intense friendships. To do otherwise, it seems to me, is to inflict unnecessary hardship both on the animal and on myself.

It is often said and written that it is an act of cruelty to keep a dog in a city apartment. What a dog needs most, however, is neither space nor exercise. Their needs in these areas are similar to those of man himself. What it needs most is the presence of its master or at least the presence of a human being with whom the dog can "communicate"—even if it is only a child. Another dog does not fill this need, and it is often a mistake to acquire a second dog to keep the first one company when the master is away. A friend of mine was the proud owner of a handsome, affectionate, obedient, and peaceful Doberman. One day this friend brought home with her a small white dog of a breed known for its nervousness. In fact, this new dog, named La Loubette, was constantly running about, barking, howling, and nipping. It was not La Loubette's fault, of course, since she belonged to a breed of postilion dogs—dogs which were bred especially to bark at and nip coach horses so as to make them run faster. The effect on the Doberman was predictable. First it became ill, but with one of those indefinable illnesses to which dogs are even more subject than humans, and which we might describe as a nostalgia for lost happiness, or simply as despair. Then the Doberman became truly insane and began to bite—not the little bundle of fluff which was its tormentor, but visitors to the house and, finally, its mistress. At that point there was nothing to do but have the Doberman put away.

Dogs, therefore, despite the extraordinary plasticity which we have noted, are not infinitely adaptable. There are limits to what they can bear. When those limits are passed, sometimes their primeval aggressivity and ferocity reawakens; and then the dog attacks and occasionally even kills. Such tragedies are, most often, crimes of passion. We are pleased at the animal's capacity for love, at its devotion and loyalty to its master; but often we forget the depth and cruelty of the dog's jealousy.

Occasionally there are articles in newspapers and magazines which serve to remind us of the dangers which lie buried in an animal which has shared man's life since the dawn of time. We read of a dog devouring a child, for example; and the dog is usually one which was always thought to be gentle and harmless. Animal lovers are astonished and shocked; other people are outraged. Yet such tragedies are quite understandable when we remember that the dog is descended from the jackal and the wolf. This double heritage can always assert itself by means of a strong emotion, a stress, a psychological shock, or even a physiological ailment. We must also keep in mind that the dog is a flesh-eater. It has become omnivorous, like man himself, only by training. For thousands of years man used the dog for sanguinary purposes: hunting lions, waging war, protecting flocks against wolves, guarding man's home. For these ends, man cultivated an aggressivity which was innate, but not overly strong, in the dog. Thus, a sheep dog is able quickly to revert to its combative instincts; for originally its job was not to guard the flock, but to protect it against wolves and even, in the Pyrenees, against bears.

For these reasons it is not always wise to advise a couple or a single man or woman—as we so often do—to "get a dog." Not every dog is suited to every man or woman; and, ideally, to match a dog to a human one must know not only the whole history of the dog, but that of the human as well. It often happens that a dog, rather than alleviating the problems of a household, aggravates them by aggravating the irritability, instability, or insecurity of the master. And, of course, the converse is also true. Animals, like children, are quite capable of giving rise to absurd or conflictual situations within a family.

The fact that "breed" dogs are costly has also contributed to the mental and physical instability of these animals. Because they are so valuable, the people who breed such dogs are unwilling to sacrifice one or two puppies from a litter as was the practice twenty or thirty years ago. The result is that these too numerous offspring suffer from diminished resistance and from all the marks of consanguinity. There are numerous instances of this neuropsychological fragility among dogs, animals which we tend to think are healthier and sturdier than man. Actually, the dog is even more vulnerable than man, especially the most fashionable dogs—such as poodles and boxers.

A disease which is common among dogs, and especially among nervous breeds such as German shepherds and Poms, is epilepsy. At the Alfort clinic, 20 percent of the dogs examined are found to suffer from this affliction. The first seizure often follows a violent emotion, or a punishment, and this seizure takes the form of spasms and convulsions. There is even a kind of epilepsy which is peculiar to pack dogs.

The emotional life of a dog, like that of a human, often has external effects. It is not uncommon for an emotional shock—for example, an automobile accident —to cause a dog to suffer hair loss over a more or less large area of its body. The most striking example of such sensitivity in recent times, however, took place in Belfast, where thousands of dogs had to be killed because they could not bear the insurrectional atmosphere of the conflict between Catholics and Protestants. Some of the animals went mad; others refused to eat; and others were afflicted with continuous trembling.

As a journalist I had the misfortune on two occasions to assist at the mass execution of dogs abandoned by their masters. The first time was during the Spanish Civil War; the second, in the former Belgian Congo. The fact that dogs are killed when abandoned is extremely significant. It is based on the assumption that the dog is not a domestic animal in the same sense as, say, chickens and cows. It is killed because of its privileged situation with respect to man. The tacit contract between man and dog is more imperative than in other instances of domestication, because love forms part of that contract. The implied meaning is clear: The dog was given to man not only so that man might feed it and protect it, but also so that man might give it happiness. The killing of abandoned dogs is therefore a recognition of the fact that without man, the dog, even if it survived, would no longer be happy. This is the only instance of domestication in which affection plays a greater part than self-interest. If the contract is not honored, if the dog is unhappy, it not only dies like any other domestic animal; but it also goes mad—much as human beings do in the same situation.*

Anyone who has ever owned a dog knows what man gains from the association between man and dog. But what does the animal gain? The constant display of emotion and sentiment with which we inundate our pets has very little to do with the true, deep, and sometimes dramatic affection which a dog is capable of feeling for its master. The trouble is that we no longer look for such affection. Today, people want their dogs above all to wag their tails constantly and to lick the hand of the first human to come along. They want their dogs to be a certain color, to have ears or paws of a certain shape and size. Accordingly, over the past fifty years, breeders have given much attention to the development of such characteristics. I know of no breeder, on the other hand, who has made a concerted effort to develop the intelligence of dogs. The reason, obviously, is that we do not ask for intelligent dogs. We want "nice" dogs; dogs which cuddle; dogs which like to be petted, or at least allow us to pet them.

*A conference of veterinarians was held at Lyons in 1972, and one of the conclusions which came out of the conference was that instances of mental illness and nervous depression among household animals was on the upsurge. There was a state of "general moroseness" prevailing among man's companions, the veterinarians noted. This, one may believe, is one of the effects of civilization. For example, 80 percent of male dogs nowadays die without ever having had intercourse with a female dog.

There are today some 500 million dogs in the world, and the canine population, like the human population, is growing constantly. Moreover, dogs, like human beings, over the past fifty years have seen their life span increase because of advances in hygiene and medicine and also because of the comfortable circumstances in which their masters allow them to live. The number of dogs and cats in any given country, interestingly enough, corresponds to that country's economic standing. There are more household pets in the United States than in any other country; and, in China, there are the fewest. The reason is that only a wealthy country can afford to feed large numbers of animals. Countries constantly on the brink of famine have other, more important uses for food. Thus, the Chinese government has ordered all dogs to be destroyed, except for a few which are kept in zoos.

We are therefore faced with a situation in which, while the number of wild animals is growing steadily smaller* because of the inroads of civilization, the number of household animals—dogs and cats—is rising at the same rate as the human standard of living rises through a technical and industrial development. Dogs and cats, since they are regarded as external symbols of affluence and also as antidotes to the ills of contemporary life, will apparently prosper as mankind prospers. It has been estimated that there will be approximately 1 billion dogs on the planet by the year 2000, compared to a human population of 7 or 8 billion. It is not impossible, therefore, that the age-old association between man and dog will end in tragic overpopulation. In such a case, is it conceivable that man's best and most constant friend will become an undesirable creature?

The two animals to which man has given a place in his home are very different from each other. Moreover,

*The only exception is the rat, which is increasing in numbers.

one appeared much later than the other. The dog has had 60,000 years of common life with man; the cat, only 5,000 years. It is only natural, therefore, that the cat has been able to preserve its dignity and something of its independence.

It is generally believed that cats are relatively indifferent to their masters; that they are more attached to the home than to the humans in it. The truth is that sociability varies from one cat to another. As a genus, however, it is accurate to say that the cat is not a group animal. It is essentially solitary and seems only rarely to experience affection, even for another cat. Indeed, it is more inclined to show affection for an animal of a different species—a dog, say; or sometimes even a chicken or a duck.

Some zoologists, basing themselves upon the cat's independence, refuse to classify it as a truly domesticated animal. Certainly, since the cat has been spared the dog's prehistoric state of subjection to man, it has been much less modified in its mind. In any event, the domestic cat is the only member of its family which can be regarded as other than a wild animal.

In vain do we look for a painting of the cat on the walls of the prehistoric caves of southern France or in the Sahara. It figures prominently, however, in the frescoes of Egypt, where it first appeared during the fifth Dynasty (*c.* 2600 B.C.). This cat is thought to have descended from an animal common in Libya, the gloved Abyssinian cat, which is more easily tamed than the wildcat known in Europe and America.

Surprisingly, the purpose of the Egyptians in domesticating the cat was not to deploy it as a rat-catcher in their granaries. They had already an excellent rat-catcher at their disposal, the genet, which also was more or less domesticated. The cat was initially incorporated into Egyptian life for religious reasons. Therefore, like many other domestic animals, as we have seen, it had a religious character before assuming a utilitarian role.

The cat was associated to Bacht, or Bastet, goddess of the moon and of love; and this association was manifest in images of the goddess which show her with the head of a lion and later of a cat. Bacht's temple was at Bubastis, and there her priests were charged with predicting the future by interpreting the positions of the hundreds of sacred cats which inhabited the temple. Archaeologists found the mummies of some 300,000 cats at Bubastis. (These mummies were later shipped to Liverpool, where they were sold as fertilizer.) Later the male cat became the sign of the sun and of Osiris while the female cat was associated with the moon and Isis.

Cat-lovers will no doubt point out that the elegance and dignity of cats are the consequence of their sojourn in the temples of the gods, where their attitudes and movements were regarded as divine prognostications. Be that as it may, it is obvious that the cat's wealth of expressions makes it an ideal candidate for such a role. Unlike the dog, which either wags its tail or does not wag its tail, the cat possesses a wide range of means to convey its emotions: It arches its back, makes its fur stand on end, meows, rubs itself against furniture and against humans, purrs, lashes its tail, spits, and hisses. The priests of Bacht, therefore, had ample material for interpretation.

The cat had an honored place in the Egyptian household, and to kill a cat was a crime sometimes punishable by death. If a cat died, the head of the household shaved his eyebrows and went into mourning. At the same time the cat was more or less expected to earn its keep, and beginning with the Middle Empire (2100 B.C.), the Egyptians, who were adept animal-trainers, developed many specialized varieties of cats. There were hunting cats, fishing cats, snake-killing cats, and (naturally) rat-catching cats.

The Egyptian word for cat was *myou*—obviously an onomatopeic noun. The English word *cat* probably of Nubiant (Kodis) of Celtic origin, as are the equivalent nouns in most modern European languages: the French *chat,* the Itallian *gatto,* the German *Katxe,* etc. Caesar had been introduced to the cat family during his conquest of Gaul, to which region the cat had been probably brought by the Phoenicians.*

Western Europe did not rediscover the domestic cat until the ninth century, and its introduction at that time was of considerable historical importance. It served to keep down the rat population which, throughout the Middle Ages and until the nineteenth century, was responsible for the recurrent plagues which periodically decimated the human population of Europe. It is fair to say that without the cat, the hordes of rats which invaded Europe several times following the development of maritime relations between East and West might well have put an end to Western civilization.

During the Middle Ages the ships of the Crusaders returning from the Holy Land brought back with them a veritable army of black rats infested with fleas; and these spread the plague. Europe had had mice since Neolithic times, but the black rat had been unknown until the Middle Ages. Their coming spread a reign of terror across the Continent, from East to West, from city to city. The intelligence of these animals, and especially their capacity for reproduction,† made them a formidable and potentially fatal enemy of man. Germany was the country most affected, and the catastrophe is commemorated in the legend of the Pied

*It is fairly well established that the present-day domestic cat is not a descendant of the wildcat which is still found at large in Europe, a variety with which the domestic cat does not crossbreed.

†A pair of rats begins reproducing at the age of three months, and each year they may produce five to seven litters of from five to fifteen young. At that rate, one pair of rats in three years may produce several million descendants.

Piper of Hamelin—Hamelin being a town the name of which will forever be associated with rats. Then, in 1647, gray rats overran Europe and contended with the black rats for supremacy. A hundred years later, both gray rats and black rats were wiped out by a new conqueror, the terrible brown rat which, following an earthquake, left the shores of the Caspian and invaded Europe.

Some idea of the devastation wrought by these successive invasions of rats may be gained from the fact that during the plague which raged between 1346 and 1350, 48 million people died—25 million in Europe and 23 million in Asia. Such cataclysms were periodic. In 1665 there was a great plague in London; in 1720, at Marseilles, etc.

Without the cat, the value of which was finally understood by the peoples of Europe, and which also arrived by ship from the Near East, it is not inconceivable that the entire human species would have been wiped out by the plague-bearing rats, and that today the dominant life form on earth would be—the rat.*

The relationship between man and cat is quite different from that which obtains between man and dog. The basis of that difference is perhaps that the cat is much less dependent than the dog on man for its material well-being.

In the relationship between cat and man, it is man who is in the position of soliciting the attention and affection of an animal which is wary and prudent, and which still maintains intact the flight-distance of a wild animal when it comes to dealing with persons unknown.

*India, where cats are regarded as impure animals because, like the dog, the cat is a carnivore, the plague is still rampant. As recently as 1920, for example, no less than 11 million people were its victims. Apparently, no mere utilitarian consideration can overcome the discredit in which the cat is held in that country. In India there is a whole plan of civilization in the opposition between herbivorous animals (such as the cow) and carnivorous animals; and the fact that the cat would be extremely useful in combatting the plague seems to have little bearing on the matter.

Some cats, in fact, either by a quirk of temperament, or because of some unfortunate past experience, or simply because of their way of life, never allow themselves to be picked up or petted.

The relationship between cats and humans is archetypal of a privileged relationship between man and animal. By its air of independence and disdain, the cat holds itself aloof and treats with man as an equal. Its solemn immobility, its mysterious eyes, all make of it an animal that we can only dream of conciliating and that we must recognize is impossible to constrain. Man can force a horse or a dog to do what he wishes; but no one has ever been able to compel a cat in any respect.

The cat, even more than the dog, is capable of meeting man's tactile needs. It is able to respond, if it wishes to do so, by arching its back, stretching, and above all by purring—the signs of gratification which its master expects of it. Yet not all cats are willing to exhibit these signs. There are cats, as there are dogs, which allow anyone to pet them; but there are many which are very reserved and distant—and are loved for precisely that reason.

The cat, a wild animal in miniature, a bundle of nerves, is regarded by many people as the ideal house pet. They prize its cleanliness, its silence, and above all its reserve and the fact that it does not offer its friendship to the first person to ask for it. The more difficult it is to win the affection of a cat, the more that affection is treasured. Such relationships, as may well be imagined, are not only complicated and mysterious, but charged with an intriguing uncertainty. "When I play with my cat," Montaigne wrote, "I never know if she is playing in order to please herself, or to please me."

Since the cat is not far removed from its wild past, it remains very attached to a living space divided into various zones. According to author and researcher Jacques Goldberg, a cat living in complete freedom requires a territory of about 125 acres. But all cats divide their territories into four zones. There is a forbidden area within which no other being is allowed; there is the area of refuge where they hide in case of danger; there is the hunting area; and, finally, there is an independent area where they live their love lives, or wander, or do battle. These territorial needs represent an aspect of the independence which cats have retained. Territory is essential to them, and every cat, no matter how illustrious its pedigree, must periodically escape to roam the alleyways and yards of its neighborhood.*

The fascination which cats exercise upon humans seems to be growing. In the United States today there are more cats than dogs as household pets. The same holds true in France. Sometimes, however, that fascination can be carried to excess. The *Société Protectrice des Animaux* (the French equivalent of the ASPCA) cites the case of a lady who kept approximately a hundred cats in her small apartment in Paris. "When my mother died seven years ago," the woman explained tearfully, "I felt so lonely that I adopted one cat. Then I got a female cat to keep him company. They started having kittens. . . ."

What could have been a fairy tale turned instead into something of a drama. The neighbors protested the presence of so many pets, claiming that there was an offensive odor emanating from the lady's apartment. They called the police and finally they circulated a petition demanding that the lady get rid of her cats.

"I could never do that," the lady replied. "I'd die first. I've saved other animals—lost dogs, sick pigeons. I love animals. Why do people want to be so mean? The love of animals should be a way for people to understand one another."

*High-bred cats are similarly democratic in their sexual contacts, and similarly unpredictable. The female cat over which one hears nocturnal battles being fought does not necessarily choose the victor as her paramour; and the pedigreed female is as likely as not to bestow her favors upon a disreputable tom with torn ears.

The *Société Protectrice des Animaux* deplores such situations as being opposed to the well-being of the animals themselves. They advise, as a preventive means, that males be castrated and that females be sterilized. They even suggest a painless way of killing kittens. . . .

Not everyone can bring himself to have cats "put to sleep" in order to be rid of them. An unexpected case in point is that of Pope Paul VI, who was informed in June, 1972, that the Vatican housed more cats than it did people. The reason for this overpopulation may have been that the cats were living, so to speak, under the protection of the Lateran Treaty, since they had occupied the Papal gardens, which are protected by the privilege of extraterritoriality. In any event, the Pope was put into the somewhat awkward position of having to ask the Socialist government of Italy to remove the cats. However, he could not bring himself to have them put away. They were taken out of the city and released in the Roman countryside.

What was Pope Paul's motive in sparing the lives of the Vatican cats? Was it fear that public opinion would condemn such a massacre? Was it perhaps Jung's "archaic unconscious" at work, inspiring the Pope with respect "for that breath of life accorded by Genesis to fishes and reptiles, to the birds of the air and the beasts of the field?" Or was it perhaps an indication of a sentimental phenomenon unexpected in the life of the Catholic Church? Hitherto, the Church, in order to emphasize the primacy of man and to assure him of an undisputed place in the order of creation, has refused to recognize that animals possess intelligence, thought, or—especially—a "soul." Whatever the reason, it cannot be said that Pope Paul, in his laudable act of mercy, set a precedent.

The story of the Pope's cats is all the more significant in view of the fact that in past centuries Catholic Europe regarded cats as satanic and as creatures to be feared and hated. There was no trial for witchcraft without a black cat accused of having participated in the witches' sabbath and in a pact with the devil. There were many wholesale massacres of cats in which the animals were burned by the dozens for being "limbs of Satan." The element of passion in the relationship between men and cats is especially pronounced. The cat has been deified, loved, hated, tortured, and put to death. Even today there are as many people who dislike cats as love them.*

In the past twenty years dogs and cats have come to occupy a disproportionately large place in contemporary life. Their increasing numbers are already creating new problems, and their future presents even more difficulties.

The reasons for which a man or woman, or a family, will choose to adopt a cat or dog are often of a selfish nature and have nothing to do with the good of the animal itself. People want company, contact with a living being, or merely entertainment. Thus, when a stronger and conflicting desire makes itself felt, a need for other pleasures, the animal is promptly sacrificed. The pet has become merely one more product of the consumer society: a toy.

The animal's place in modern society, therefore, is both prominent and precarious because of the ambiguity of man's feelings toward animals. Since the household pet has no real role to play, it may always be displaced by another object which is more flattering, more docile, or less trouble. We often see the results of this ambiguity when the presence of the animal becomes inconvenient; for example, when it appears that a hitherto prized animal may interfere with a trip, or a vacation, or with the renting of a new apartment. It is not unusual in such cases for the animal's master to try to drown the dog or cat, or to lose it in a strange part

*Cats of a particular color have a long history of being regarded as unlucky. There is disagreement, however, over the color. In France and the United States a black cat is an omen of bad luck; in Britain it is a white cat.

of the city, or even to throw it from the window of an automobile.*

Perhaps the time has come for man to recognize his responsibilities toward the animals which he has invited to share his life. Of all domestic animals, dogs and cats are those which man has most thoroughly "de-natured"; that is, they are the ones which he has removed from nature in order to modify them in accordance with his own whims and preferences. He has made exceptional creatures of them and only he is in a position to assure their survival. It would seem simple justice for man, having thus created these animals, to accord them a minimum of dignity and respect.

The essential expression of this sense of justice must be the elaboration of an ethical code regarding the treatment of dogs and cats; and the only way in which such a code may be developed and promulgated is through a process of public education by which man is made aware of the extent of his responsibilities.

The concept of the animal-object which man can, according to his mood, either allow to live or condemn to death, is wholly inadmissible both morally and juridically. So many people own animals that their mass insensitivity, their negligence, or perhaps their indifference, causes thousands upon thousands of beings to die every year. Experience teaches us that the solution lies in prevention rather than in correction. It would be better to limit the number of household pets rather than to punish cruel or careless masters, especially since the latter step would be neither easy nor popular. Above all we must bear in mind the first law of kindness to animals: Never adopt, accept, or buy an animal unless you have made yourself aware of precisely what responsibilities are entailed in sharing your life with an animal.

*Cats are apparently easier to dispose of than dogs. Their absence is not as quickly apparent and is less heartrending.

CHAPTER THIRTEEN

The Prehistoric Era Is Still with Us

Contrary to what is generally believed,
nature did not expend all her ingenuity and energy
on the vertebrates and on man.
—Rémy Chauvin

THE process of domestication begun during the Neolithic age is not over. Since the nineteenth century man has turned his attention to beings infinitely smaller than horses and dogs and cats to bacteria and microbes. To some extent he has succeeded in controlling and enlisting these creatures in his service. There are two areas, however, in which man has only begun to make inroads: the sea and the world of insects. In the sea, for instance, there are some 60,000 varieties of mollusks, of which man has been able to domesticate only the oyster and the mussel. And among the insects, only the bee and the silkworm do man's bidding.

Man's very recent success in penetrating beneath the surface of the sea has opened up to him a whole new world of fishes and marine mammals. We have barely crossed the threshhold of that world, for we have really had access to it only for some thirty years—compared to man's millions of years of common history with land animals. Until very recently, therefore, the world of the sea was closed to man; but it was not closed to man's depredations. The diver exploring beneath the surface today discovers not a virgin world untouched by man, but one already depopulated, polluted, and moribund. Uncontrolled fishing has compromised life in the sea, and the waste of our technological civilization is in the process of poisoning what life remains. The sea, in a word, is as ill as man himself.

If our sins with respect to the sea have been ones of commission, then so far as the insect world is concerned, we are guilty by reason of omission. Human civilization has committed the most incredible act of negligence: We have forgotten to make use of insects. Our reaction to them has been one of revulsion and disgust rather than of interest, and we have mobilized all our chemical resources to exterminate them. Even in that we have failed; and we can hardly point with pride to the fact that, in failing, we have succeeded only in poisoning our prairies, our fish, and our mollusks. Thus, in a demonstration of ironic justice, man has ended by poisoning himself.

Below me I saw nothing but a few round rocks and white sand. I floated quietly, suspended in the clear water, watching the fish around me unhurriedly going about their accustomed affairs. This was in 1945, and for the first time I had strapped heavy bottles of compressed air onto my shoulders, buckled on a weighted belt, and allowed myself to sink into the limpid waters of the Mediterranean. I recall that I felt no trepidation, no fear at being in this strange new world. I moved, and the water sustained my weight. What I had hitherto regarded as a fluid had now become a substance.

The rays of the sun illuminated the water around me by its oblique rays. I looked up and I saw above me the frontier separating the world of water from that of air, a glittering expanse extending as far as I could see: the surface of the sea, viewed from beneath. From the beginnings of his existence, man had been unable to cross that frontier and remain beyond it as I was doing for any length of time without dying.

There was not the slightest doubt in my mind that I was living the most important day of my life, and that the development of the apparatus I was wearing marked the beginning of a new stage in the human adventure. I know, certainly, that in the twenty-eight years between that time and this, I have not been quite the same man as before. My view of the world has changed. On that day I discovered an extension of the earth; an extension which remained to be explored and inventoried. In retrospect, I am astonished at my naïveté. Man's imagination seems incapable of carrying him as far as the reality of nature. My diving friends and I had no way of knowing that marine exploration would revolutionize the relationship between man and animal, and that after doing the same for technology, geography, biology, and geology, it would open a new chapter in human awareness.

For the first time man was able to see marine animals face to face, to exist in the same space with them, to draw near to them, even to touch them. Yet his first concern was not to observe and to learn, but to kill. Divers did not pride themselves on exploration and discovery. Instead they collected trophies in an exercise of absurd vanity, and had themselves photographed alongside an unfortunate grouper or loach. It had taken decades for these victims to reach the size at which the hunter, in one second, put an end to their lives. And the hunter did not have even the excuse of prehistoric man: that he needed to kill for food. The day of the marine hunter is not yet over. There are still those for whom the sea is nothing more than a vast preserve of animals fit only to be killed.

But man is learning, just as he learned to live on dry land. He learned to conserve the soil, to breed animals and plants, and to turn nature into a source of nourishment and life. He created the horse, the dog, the ox, and the sugarbeet. But it took thousands of years for man to attain these goals. We have just learned to exist in the sea without dying; and now we must learn to live there without killing the sea itself. This is not the work of a day or even of a decade. The land, after all, is man's work. What grows in our fields is to a large extent our own creation. The sea, however, is as yet unchanged. Man has not yet had the opportunity to intervene. Its plants and its valleys are intact, as are the "wild" animals. The sea has not yet been subjected to the massive effort, spread out over seven or eight thousand years, which succeeded in transforming dry land into one enormous food factory.

Today, therefore, the diver finds himself in a situation which is literally prehistoric. He is in the same position as his ancestor was some 10,000 years ago, at the beginning of the Neolithic age, as he was making his first attempts at the breeding and cultivation of animals.

These attempts are the same as those which man must now make in the sea, and they consist primarily in learning to approach marine animals. This is no easier in the water than it was on land. The flight-instinct is basic to animal behavior. It not only enables the animal to preserve its own life, but it also assures the continuation of the species; and this holds true for marine animals as well as land animals. The secret of domestication consists in depriving the animal of this instinctive impulse to flee when it is approached more or less closely. The other side of the coin, however, is that animals not endowed with that instinct have either become extinct or are on the road to extinction: *e.g.*, the giant penguin and the dodo of Maurice Island, among land animals; and the manatee and the dugong in the sea, both of which could have become veritable cows of the sea.

Even though we have not been able to create marine

domestic animals in the few years that we have had access to the sea, there is really nothing to prevent us from trying to tame such animals. Fish are more susceptible to this process than is generally believed. In the Red Sea, for instance, there was Jojo, the famous grouper which used to wait for divers so that he could swim with them. Also in the Red Sea, there was a certain triggerfish which circled constantly around an experimental undersea house which had been constructed there, and as soon as a diver signaled by tapping on a porthole, it would immediately present itself at the airlock.

One of the problems in approaching animals, obviously, is that of overcoming our own prejudices and misconceptions. The killer whale long had the reputation of being the most ferocious of all marine animals—until a group of divers at Vancouver succeeded in striking up a friendship with these formidable animals. Similarly, the giant octopus was once thought to have a taste for attacking ships and dragging them down into the depths. Today, at Seattle, a woman diver plays games with them.

On the whole, it is encouraging to note that in the past thirty years divers generally have gone from slaughtering animals to petting them. Today it seems more praiseworthy to strike up an acquaintance with animals than to harpoon them. It is more difficult to do so now than it was when we first began to dive, for in our three decades of marine exploration, we have succeeded in putting the fear of man into the animals of the sea. I recall vividly that in the early days of diving these animals showed no signs of fear or timidity in the presence of man. They do however regain that earlier confidence rather easily; and in some remote areas where they have never been hunted, they have never lost it. In the Indian Ocean, for example, Yves Omer, a member of the Cousteau team, was able not only to approach a moray eel, but to pet it. (The moray has always had a particularly bad reputation because it exhibits a set of terrible teeth; and, in the water as on land, animals are judged good or bad according to their appearance, the form of their heads, or the size of their jaws.)

A diver from Brittany, Serge Courseaux, spent eight years making a marine film at Dakar and the Cape Verde Islands. Moray eels play an important part in the film, and Courseaux, when he wanted to get a particular shot of a moray, simply took hold of it and moved it to the proper spot. Naturally, he was careful to use only those animals which appeared to tolerate such behavior. "When you've tried to approach them several times," Courseaux explains, "you quickly learn something about their individual temperaments. These animals all have different characters. For all we know, there might be certain factors—digestion, or their love life—which, as in human beings, make them extroverts or introverts. I do know this, however, that no one was ever bitten by a moray while we were making our film."

It would be misleading not to mention that such friendships are based upon gifts of bits of meat, or, in the case of octopuses, of crabs and lobsters.*

Obviously, not everyone has the opportunity or the patience to strike up an acquaintance with a grouper by spending hours at sixty or seventy feet beneath the surface of the sea. However, I would suggest an experiment to the many practitioners of scuba diving. Break open a sea urchin and offer bits of it, at arm's length, to nearby fishes. You will soon have them eating out of your hand, literally. By using this method, my wife, who is an expert diver, made some fast friends among the fish living in a cove at Ibiza.

*See *Soft Intelligence: The End of a Misunderstanding*, by Jacques-Yves Cousteau and Philippe Diolé.

For the past eight years, a friend of mine on Corsica, in a small bay near Calvi, has been taming two species which are reputed to be very difficult to approach. Every day he distributes several pounds of cheese (gruyère), and as the years go by he is able to get more and more difficult performances from his fish. They now allow him to touch them, and they have become bold enough to swim into his hands. As soon as a diver goes into the water in my friend's bay, he is immediately surrounded by several dozen fish, all swimming around and brushing against him.

Obviously, the behavior of these tamed fish presents a temptation that line fishermen are unable to resist. Moreover, these men are unable to understand the indignation of my friend and his associates when they try to protect the fish. I have witnessed these encounters, and I must say that the attitude of the fishermen seemed to me to be one of total incomprehension. Fish, they feel, are fish. And how can one persuade a fisherman not to fish when he has no understanding of fish?

In the process of taming as carried out at Ibiza and Corsica, and no doubt elsewhere, there is a small enigma which I have never been able satisfactorily to resolve. The results of this process endure from one summer to the next. As soon as the water is warm enough for my wife or my friend on Corsica to begin diving again, their fish friends begin eating out of their hands almost immediately, whereas the first year they showed considerable hesitancy. On Corsica, it has been eight years since my friend began his experiments, and there have been eight generations of fish. Yet the young fish are no more timid than the older fish. The latter, one might say, know from experience that they are in no danger. But how do the young ones know it?

It would be easy to attach too much importance to these modest experiments so far as scientific worth is concerned. Their real importance, I think, is that they are able to inspire man with both curiosity about and respect for marine life. To explore beneath the surface, to try to see and to recognize the beings that live there, is in fact to react against the burden of ignorance under which man has labored for centuries with respect to the sea; it is to take the first steps toward correcting his misconceptions concerning that mass of water into which he has hitherto been incapable of penetrating.

What I have called man's underwater adventure,* which may well be one of the most beautiful chapters in the human story, is far from being complete. It is a question not only of conquering the mineral (oil) and biological resources of the sea, but also of enriching human awareness and arriving at a new understanding of marine animals, of attaining a renewed respect for all forms of life. The new accessibility of the marine world has presented us with an opportunity to discover that intuition, that sympathy and that affection toward animals which was so necessary to our ancestors in preserving the human species in the midst of a world of animals.

In some important respects, however, the human confrontation of life in the sea presents problems which are not quite the same as those of prehistoric man when he contended with animal life on dry land. In the latter case, and for tens of thousands of years, the power of animals and the relative perfection of their senses gave them a great advantage over the prehistoric human hunter, at least so far as physical capability was concerned. In the sea, man is at an even greater disadvantage in that he finds himself in an environment which is alien to him. One has only to note the disproportion between a diver and a fifteen- or twenty-foot shark. The shark was the first denizen of

***L'Aventure sous-marine*, Paris, 1949.

the high seas and appeared in the Mesozoic age, some 250 million years ago. It has highly developed teeth and seems to have invented hydrodynamics. It is the most fearsomely equipped animal of the sea, and its innumerable nervous cells provide it with an awareness of its surroundings so precise and thorough that we can hardly conceive of it.

Twenty years ago, Captain Jacques Cousteau and *Calypso*'s team of divers first encountered the sharks of the Red Sea in open water. They were the first to demonstrate that men, so long as they did not panic, and so long as they knew how to use a shark stick properly—could share the water with sharks, if not in absolute safety, then at least with no more than an acceptable level of risk.

Cousteau and his men went even farther. They attempted to provoke the sharks to a state which zoologists know as "frenzy"—a veritable murderous frenzy which possesses sharks when they attack a victim and taste its flesh and blood. For this purpose, *Calypso*'s divers offered pieces of meat to the sharks, sometimes at arm's length. The result was a nightmare. The sharks tore the meat to shreds. The men were surrounded by the gaping maws of the animals on all sides and had to fight for their lives. The first sharks that were wounded were immediately devoured by the others, and the water turned red with blood. Some sharks, so severely wounded that their entrails were floating in the water behind them, seemed oblivious to their own condition and continued to tear at other wounded animals until even the rear deck of *Calypso* was awash with blood. The entire scene was recorded on film, and constitutes the most dramatic scene of Captain Cousteau's classic *The Silent World,* which was shown for the first time in 1955.

It is interesting to note that the shark scene, though full of blood and violence, evoked nothing but praise. There was not a word of criticism, not even among the British, who are particularly sensitive to the well-being of animals. In 1955, evidently, sharks were the enemies of man. A single shark was enough to spread a reign of terror in the water. Therefore, to kill as many sharks as possible was an enterprise as praiseworthy as that of Hercules when he cleared the land of monsters.

In 1972, however, *The Silent World* was shown again on French television, and during the debate which followed, a deluge of complaints was received from French viewers, all protesting against the shark scene, and particularly against the killing of sharks by *Calypso*'s divers.

What had happened was that in seventeen years everyone's attitude toward animals had changed. There was a new feeling of respect for life, even for the lives of the great predatory animals. The death of the shark, a ferocious killer, now shocks and alarms television viewers. And they are perfectly right. The function of the predator in the order of the universe is to bring death. It is illogical for us to hate or to kill a predator for doing what it is supposed to do, for performing the essential role in maintaining the biological equilibrium of the planet. Instead, we must understand. Life in the sea, like life on dry land, is a chain of murders. We must accept that.

Generally speaking we have great difficulty in understanding land animals because their modes of expression are strange to us. Even so, people who know animals are able to interpret at least some of those expressions. They know that when a horse lays back its ears it is about to rebel; that when an elephant raises its trunk it is about to charge. This knowledge is the result of long experience and is shared only by a few. In the sea, we have not even that esoteric knowledge. There is no man who can tell us when a whale is angry, or when a cachalot is going to dive, or when a killer whale is going to attack.

This absence of intelligible communication has wide

applications, the most common of which is the popular belief that fish do not feel pain. This is a convenient conviction, and one which excuses anything that we may choose to do to a marine animal. (We used to say the same thing about land animals.) It is most likely based upon the absence of a sign from a suffering animal—or at least a sign that we can understand as denoting pain. A wounded fish does not scream. Even when we see an animal in agony, its mouth open, we tell ourselves that it feels no pain because its nervous system is "rudimentary" and its brain is "primitive." Our attitude, in fact, is that anything that comes from the sea is devoid of feeling and intelligence, and therefore does not deserve our sympathy. We do not hesitate to boil a live lobster, nor do we think of putting a wounded grouper out of its misery. Yet would we boil a dog alive? And what hunter could be so cruel as to leave a wounded deer, or a rabbit, in agony?

In prehistoric times, the jackal and the wolf had to make the first steps toward an understanding with man; today dolphins and animals such as Jojo the grouper are taking the initiative. Despite our newfound aversion to the killing of sharks, we have a long way to go before arriving at a covenant with marine life.

For me personally, the discovery of the sea has taken place in two stages. First there was the astonishment of exploring the Mediterranean. In those rather somber waters I learned to know the fish and the fixed animals alien to land: the clumps of sea fans, the lacelike bryozoans, the sponges, and the Botryllidae. I was able to observe forms of life until then unknown to me, creatures which resembled nothing that exists on dry land. Then, second, came the revelation of the abundance of life in the sea, the wealth of forms which surpassed anything found on land even in the most beautiful and undeveloped lands.

As abundant and as unexpected as all this was, it was less striking than the feeling which it awakened in those who had the opportunity to observe it. In going down into the water, man's awareness was opened to new images; he was able to witness those edifices of living flesh, that pluralistic cellular life which is the great secret of the sea. Thus, the opening up of the oceans and seas established a new relationship for man; a relationship with living creatures which had not yet played a role in man's history. We have yet to discover all the consequences which man's invasion of the world of water may have on his future, his mind, and his behavior. Perhaps not the least of these consequences will be that the enormous treasure of life which is now open to man, the availability of the uncounted forms of life which man can now observe and touch, will serve to awaken his curiosity and his sympathy. Perhaps it will distract him from his obsession with things mechanical and restore to him respect and admiration for life itself.

In the vast world of marine life, man has only to select his friends. All, or almost all, forms of that life are capable of showing curiosity about divers, and a certain attachment to those who give them food. Groupers, octopuses, and morays are more approachable than many wild animals on dry land. In many cases, especially when dealing with marine mammals, it is not even necessary to offer food. The mere presence of man and the offer of his company often serve to tame. Perhaps the most important thing we must learn in this respect is that it is possible to establish a relationship with a marine animal and that such a relationship is pleasurable. Skeptics and introverts ignore one of life's greatest possibilities. The first Palaeolithic man who stretched out his hand to pet a dog did more for mankind than the man who threw the first stone.

However, petting is not always what is called for. The diver, like prehistoric man, must never forget that there are predatory animals which present a threat to his safety. The shark is the equivalent of the cave bear of Palaeolithic times, or of the woolly rhinoceros. Before such an animal, in the sea as well as on land, man is able to dominate, to make the animal respect him; and he is able to do so because of his mind. We can record that fact, but we cannot explain it. The ability to control animals, to dominate them, does not lie in man's technological or scientific accomplishments. The divers of Captain Cousteau's team are neither technicians nor scientists, but they have rediscovered man's prehistoric gift of intuition; an intuition by means of which man lords it over the animals, over sharks as well as lions, and over dolphins as well as horses.

I am not referring to domestication of any kind. Before an animal can be domesticated, or even tamed, it must be approached in such a way that it does not flee. It is in that approach that human magnetism—for want of a better term—comes into play. It is an act of the will to which the animal, whether it consents or not, must submit, and from which it cannot flee. There is no reason why that magnetism, which has worked so long and so well on land, cannot work equally well in the sea.

The present-day relationship between man and marine animals undoubtedly sheds light on what must have been the feelings of prehistoric man toward the fearsome animals around him. These ambiguous feelings, ranging from love to slaughter, from carnage to protection, are in the twentieth century precisely what they were among our ancestors. I will give a single example: the reactions of my wife the very first time that she was surrounded by sharks. It was in the Red Sea, off the island of Shadwan. By stretching out my hand, I could hear her screaming into her mouthpiece; but they were screams of utter admiration rather than of fear. The spectacle around us was worthy of her emotion. A huge Carcharhinus was moving to our left, accompanied by two other sharks the species of which I was not able to identify. They swam past, staring at us with their small round eyes, crushing us with their sovereign disdain, filling our field of vision with an image of total power and total control before disappearing behind a rock. I cannot believe that there has ever been a lion or an elephant capable of evoking such wonder in man.

It would be inexcusable, in a chapter about marine life, not to speak of dolphins. I know them well. I have dived with them; and I have even invented games with them. But they were games for us alone, without an audience. There were four of us in the water: three dolphins and I. That, I am afraid to say, is the only way that one can truly appreciate the qualities of this remarkable animal—its intelligence, its gentleness, and its patience. It has everything to become the associate of man in the exploration of the sea, which is the great work of our time. Moreover, if ever there has been an animal eager to become man's friend, to be understood, to show its affection, that animal is the dolphin.

In our own efforts to know the dolphin and even to familiarize ourselves with their language, we are following a very ancient tradition established by the Cretans and the Aegeans. Both those civilizations regarded the dolphin as a sacred animal, as the animal which guided ships into port. And since they were both seafaring peoples they never killed dolphins. But we are not certain how far they went in their efforts to approach the dolphin, or even if they succeeded in domesticating it.

In recent years, dolphins, killer whales, and other marine mammals on display in the marinelands of America and Europe have served to awaken great public interest in the extraordinary qualities of these animals. From that standpoint it cannot be denied that our marine zoos have accomplished a useful purpose. Still, it remains true that a zoo is a zoo, and that captivity is particularly difficult for animals which, until their encounter with man, had the entire sea at their disposal.

Some of the keepers in these institutions affirm, in all good faith, that their dolphins are "happy." They point out that the animals eat and play and that they show every sign of pleasure in performing the stunts that they have been taught. They mention a sick dolphin which, despite its indisposition, performed all its tricks perfectly. The only indication of its illness, they explain, was that the dolphin refused to eat the fish which it usually was given as its reward.

These things are all true, of course. By the same token, animal trainers in circuses can argue that their animals are happy. And prison wardens can argue that their prisoners are content because they play baseball and make license plates. The fact remains that for animals as much as for man, there is nothing more precious than freedom. It is quite conceivable that it amuses dolphins and killer whales to entertain us. But it is not conceivable that they find a few cubic yards of water a satisfactory substitute for the immensity of the sea.

It may be that the only solution possible is that presented by the apparent willingness of free dolphins to "visit" bathers and divers in the waters off our beaches. There are many instances of such contact; and there could well be many more if man were willing to take advantage of them.

Albert Falco, chief diver of *Calypso*'s team, recalls with horror his experience with a recently captured dolphin in a marineland. Falco was "walking" the dolphin in its tank, petting it, when it broke away and smashed its head against the side of the tank repeatedly until it died. It is debatable whether an animal can deliberately commit suicide; but it may certainly, in a fit of despair, smash itself against the concrete wall of the prison which has reduced its living space and deprived it of freedom.*

The attraction of the dolphin and the octopus toward man is established beyond doubt.† If we wish to take advantage of that attraction, we must not do so by making prisoners of these animals and compelling them to perform tricks for the amusement of the public. In so doing, we subject them to a situation at least as degrading, if not more degrading, than that to which we subject lions and tigers in a circus. How much more generous it would be on our part if we would consent to meet them in total freedom, in the sea.

The great mammals of the sea, the whales, are perhaps the most social of marine animals. Despite all our laws and regulations they are threatened with extinction. If we should somehow manage to save them, it remains unclear how we will ever be able to approach them, to understand them, and to continue to protect them. It is a situation marked by pathos, for whales have

*Similarly, a captive octopus has been known to gnaw at its arms until it seriously mutilated itself.

†The attraction is not always purely platonic. Both male and female dolphins often show an embarrassing sexual interest in divers; an interest which, in the male dolphin, is manifested unequivocally by an erection. This is one of the reasons why keepers rarely go into the dolphins' tanks to groom them. One can only imagine what it must be like to be sexually assaulted by a creature seven feet long and weighing almost 200 pounds.

A friend of mine, Jerry Brown, who trains killer whales in Seattle, had a female fall in love with him. On one occasion, when he was swimming with her, the whale forced him against a wall of the tank and began rubbing against him in unmistakable passion. It took the other divers ninety minutes to pry him out of the embrace of the amorous killer whale. Her name was Shamoo; she was twenty feet long and weighed a ton.

The sexual peculiarities of marine mammals are not limited to an attraction for humans. Paul Budker, my friend, has observed pronounced homosexual tendencies among dolphins. This is not an infrequent occurrence among captive mammals, but in the case of the dolphins in seems the result of a natural penchant rather than of the lack of females. On one occasion, after two male dolphins had been living together for several months on terms of the greatest intimacy, their keepers placed a female in the tank. The two males attacked her so violently that she had to be removed in great haste.

a strange affinity for human beings. Some of them "talk," and we do not understand. They allow divers to approach them, and even to touch them, and they do not exhibit the slightest hostility. It may be that it would only require a small clue for us to be able to cross the barrier which separates us. To tame a whale? Such is the stuff of which dreams are made.

As long as marine animals were regarded as belonging to another world, to the forbidden world of the sea, there was no cruelty toward them that did not seem justified. Calumny was mingled with man's natural indifference, and whalers spread stories about the ferocity of the animals which they slaughtered. *Moby Dick,* the whaling novel par excellence, is an encomium to human courage in the face of the murderous, diabolical cachalot or sperm whale.

But today, when we read accounts of whaling expeditions, we are moved to sympathy by the giant, transfixed by twenty harpoons, pierced to the heart by a lance, its eyes gouged out, crazed by pain. . . . In its agony, we wonder, how could it not overturn the whaling boat? Indeed, why did it not do so more often? And what do we say today about whalers who kill a whale calf because they know that the mother will rush to its aid and therefore come within easy striking distance of their harpoon?

Nowadays, whaling has practically no economic interest and has been abandoned by almost all nations. An international organization—the International Whaling Commission—has been established to protect the lives, and above all the biological equilibrium, of the great whales. We may ask whether we are giving up whaling on the one hand in order, on the other, to intensify our attacks on other mammals such as the dolphin, the killer whale, and the blackfish, and to increase the population of our marine zoos. It sometimes seems that we intend to save the wild animals of the earth by making prisoners of them. If we succumb to that temptation, what will happen when the sea has become a fishbowl in which man's intervention is a constant necessity if anything at all is to survive? If we wish to save the sea otter we must begin by protecting its food supply—which consists of abalone and urchins. Then we must also protect the algae on which the sea urchins feed—and soon we are caught up in an endless alimentary chain each link of which we are compelled to protect.

Not very long ago there was much talk of the sea's ability to provide food for the world. The truth is that the resources of the sea are already almost exhausted. Every ten years we double the amount of fish that we take from the sea. It was 20 million tons in 1950; 30 million tons in 1958; 64 million tons in 1968. Our giant trawlers are able to take on 150 tons of fish in a single stroke.

Crustaceans and shellfish are becoming more and more rare. A fisherman from Brittany recently told a French journalist that "Ten years ago we made enormous catches, but in the last few years we seem to have exhausted our fields. We now go after scallops, but in the last four years our catch has been half of what it was before. Make no mistake about it: In a few years fishing will no longer be a profitable occupation. I don't think there will even be any fish, because we will have ruined our waters."*

Man had high hopes when he first was able to dive into the sea. He had been quite justified in thinking that he could not attain his full development until he had conquered that mass of water which covers two-thirds of the surface of the earth. Until then he had ignored the sea in order to devote his energies to developing plants and animals on dry land. Then, in our lifetimes,

*Jean-Pierre Sergent in *La Vie des bêtes*, November, 1972.

the sea and all its resources were thrown open to man—only for us to discover that it was mortally ill, wasted, polluted even before we had been able to explore it thoroughly, and before we had learned to use it with wisdom and love.

There is another kingdom in which man is still in a prehistoric situation, and that is the world of insects. It is an ancient world, one which existed some 300 million years before man appeared on earth. There were insects flying 50 million years before the first bird. And today insects constitute four-fifths of all living species. "There are more species of the fly in France," Rémy Chauvin tells us, "than there are species of mammals in the entire world."

For this great and ever-increasing world of small creatures, man has found no use other than as victims for his pesticides. We send spacecraft to the moon and submarines to the depths of the sea, but we have not yet been willing to make the intellectual effort necessary to take advantage of this limitless animal-power.

It is not that we have made no beginnings. Fifteen or twenty thousand years ago man discovered honey and knew how to gather it from hives. Several prehistoric paintings in Spain, at Peña, show a man at the top of a tree, surrounded by a swarm of bees, collecting wild honey. I have seen that prehistoric scene reenacted in the Ubangi jungle, while I was living with the Babinga Pygmies.* I was offered wild honey as a gift of friendship, after the Pygmies had gathered it from the giant trees. I shall never forget its extraordinary fragrance as it lay there in the leaves in which it had been wrapped, combining all the fragrances of the

*The Babinga Pygmies are not to be confused with the Ituri Pygmies. The Babinga hunt small antelope, gather fruit, and collect honey. They are at the mercy of their black "bosses," who provide them with weapons and tools in exchange for game, and give them Indian hemp to smoke to make them more docile. The Babinga are a nomadic people, but they build round huts out of branches and leaves, like the Bambuti.

rarest flowers of the jungle.

In Paraguay there is a civilization based on honey, among a people called the Guayakis who live deep in the jungle.* The Guayakis are perhaps the most deprived people on the face of the earth. They live in a hostile and impenetrable environment, in constant fear of all other humans. They are totally ignorant of agriculture and what they obtain by hunting and fishing is insufficient to sustain life, since they have nothing more than primitive bows and arrows and stone axes. Fortunately, the honey of wasps and wild bees abounds in the jungles of Paraguay, where no edible fruits or plants are found; and thus honey is the salvation of the Guayakis.

The people of the tribe are familiar with every kind of honey, including that which is deadly. They make most frequent use of the honey and wax of the Melipona bee—tiny black bees the stings of which are atrophied. "They cannot sting," Dr. Vellard explains, "but when they are disturbed they pour out of their hive, get into one's clothing, ears, eyes and hair. Some of them bite, and their toxic saliva leaves a small red mark which lasts for several days."

Honey, therefore, is an indispensable resource to the Guayakis people, more important than the game they kill or the fish they catch. Beeswax, which is black and rich in resin, is also of importance and serves many uses.

The Guayakis know much more than we do about the different kinds of honey and also about the insects which produce honey. Some varieties of honey, as Dr. Vellard learned from the Guayakis, are intoxicating and induce a stupor. Others are extremely poisonous. "A single spoonful of the honey of a certain wasp, the Lechiguana colorada, is sufficient to send an adult male into a deep coma, and sometimes to bring about his death. . . . Saint Hilaire, the botanist, in the course of

*The Guayakis have been described by Dr. Jehan Vellard in his fascinating *Une Civilisation du miel.*

his expeditions to the heart of Brazil, was poisoned, along with several of his associates, by honey. He attributed part of his sufferings, which eventually led to death, to that experience.

Bees may well be considered animals which are susceptible to training. Beekeepers are able to accustom their charges to building a blue hive, to preferring the scent of the rose to any other, and even to collecting honey three times daily at certain hours. (It has been demonstrated that bees have an extraordinary sense of time.)

Dr. Karl von Frisch, the eminent expert on bees who discovered that bees communicate among themselves by dancing, points out that contrary to popular opinion bees are not strict conformists. In fact, the bees most valuable to the hive are those worker bees which ignore orders and fly off on their own in a direction different from that taken by their coworkers. These are the bees that discover new sources of booty; and it may be said that the society of bees owes much of its prosperity to these individualistic, and perhaps even anarchistic, workers.

It appears that the ancients were more aware of the world of insects than we. I know of at least one Creto-Mycenian bowl decorated with grasshoppers. But it was in Asia, especially, that man seemed to live in familiarity with the insect. The feast of the cricket, which is celebrated everywhere in China, and during which a tiny cage containing a cricket is hung before every door, is of very ancient origin. Cricket-fights, in fact, are still quite popular in China; and crickets and grasshoppers are not only fried and eaten, but bred for the sake of their singing.*

*Male grasshoppers "sing" by moving the left elytron back and forth against the right elytron. The latter has a membrane which vibrates and produces the singing. Male crickets sing by rubbing their anterior wings against their posterior paws.

Our debt to the Chinese, however, is not for crickets and grasshoppers, but for breeding the silkworm which is associated with the culture of the white mulberry tree. We do not know when that breeding began, but it has been established that by the eighth century B.C. the Chinese had already done much research in the production of silk.* It is also known that, until the third century B.C., the Chinese would allow no information on the production of silk, or even the silk itself, to leave their country.

The methods of breeding silkworms remained unknown in the West until the heyday of the Byzantine Empire, in the middle of the sixth century A.D., when the Emperor Justinian dispatched two monks into Asia to discover the secret of silk. The monks had no need to go all the way to China. They discovered a silk factory in full operation at Bukhara, in Central Asia, and they were able to bring some of the precious worms back to Constantinople with them, hidden inside their bamboo canes.

Despite such exposure to the potential uses of insects, the interest of the West in these animals remained negligible. The world of insects has been as poorly exploited as that of marine animals. It is significant that our modern languages are as poor in the names of insects as they are in those of marine animals. There are some 750,000 species of insects—the vast majority of which have no name in either English or French.† We must therefore have recourse to scientific names taken from Latin or Greek.

Man has had no better luck in understanding insects than in understanding fish. To him, they are only creatures to be killed; and the insect, unlike the fish, is

*See Henri Algoud, *La Soie;* Rene Grousset, *Histoire de la Chine.*

†There are approximately 1 million known species of animals. It is estimated that there are another 5 or 6 million species that are as yet unknown—most of which are insects.

not even eaten once it has been killed. The notable exception is the grasshopper, which is considered (quite justly) a delicacy in the Sahara. Otherwise, the insect has never been regarded as a source of food, except in Africa, where many people live on the larvae of certain species.

Man has not only neglected to attempt any domestication of the insect, but he has also developed the habit of regarding the insect with fear and disgust, and has marshaled all his resources in order to exterminate it. We have ignored the fact that, if controlled, insects may present unlimited possibilities.

With insects and with marine animals, the only course worthy of man is that of domestication. Insects are presently unemployed in our civilization, but they are not indifferent to us. They must be either friends or enemies. We have barely begun to scratch the surface in that respect. Alfalfa, for example, is incapable of fertilizing itself, and that operation is left to the bee. This peculiarity has given rise to a veritable industry in the United States, where there are vast fields of alfalfa. Bee-raisers load hundreds of beehives onto their trucks and then take them around and rent them to planters of alfalfa.

Specialists have tried to make a more effective use of insects by pitting one species against another in a true war of the insects. The most celebrated example of this technique occurred in California, and consisted originally in importing bugs to rid the grapevines of an aphis plague. Then, in 1868, a large species of ladybug, *Icerya purchasi,* wreaked havoc in California's orange and lemon orchards. An American entomologist conceived the idea of finding the ladybug's natural enemy in its native country, Australia. The enemy turned out to be another species of ladybug, the *Novius cardinalis,* which was then imported into California and quickly put an end to the *Icerya purchasi.* This was the first example of biological warfare. The same method was adopted, with similar success, in France in 1912.

Later, another and more dramatic invasion of ladybugs took place in California, and immediately the experts recalled their earlier experiment. They imported another Australian variety of ladybug, *Cryptolaemus montrouzieri,* which, it was discovered, could not survive the California winter. At that point, it was decided to breed the necessary ladybugs in the United States, and a "factory" was built for that purpose. (Another was constructed later, in Spain.) In 1928, the Riverside factory in the United States sold 48 million ladybugs, bred on potato sprouts in constant-temperature chambers.

"Is the insect really our enemy?" asks Rémy Chauvin. "Or can we make use of it? It seems that we can. If we have not done so until now, it is because we are the slaves of our prejudices." Chauvin cites the case of the red ant, which is "in the process of becoming a domestic insect and the protector of our forests because of its formidable appetite. An anthill requires over two pounds of insect meat every day." Chauvin suggests the use of mobile anthills, which could be installed wherever the services of the red ants are needed to destory other insects—just as beehives are carried from place to place in order to pollinate fields of alfalfa.

A. S. Balachowsky, who has devoted a fascinating book to the utilization of insects, cites a dozen cases in which insects have been used to destroy unwanted vegetation. One such instance took place in Australia, where Saint-John's-wort had taken over some half-million acres of land in Victoria and had grown to a height of almost four feet. Imported insects put an end to the wort. The same method has been used successfully in Hawaii, in Madagascar, and in the Fiji Islands.

Too often man has made use of chemicals rather than insects to fight his battles for him against other insects.

Then he discovers that after a few months the species evolves a strain which is resistant to man's synthetic toxins. It has even been discovered that in some cases these toxins favor the multiplication of insects. And, as everyone knows, they also attack animals, compromise the pollination of plants, poison the rivers, and threaten man himself.

Perhaps we are ready to learn from our past experiences. There is more than sufficient evidence to indicate that we are waging a losing battle against insects. The alternative to killing them is to utilize them; and for this, domestication offers infinitely more possibilities than does chemistry.

CHAPTER FOURTEEN

A Meaning to One's Life

Organisms are not machines; they are subjects.
—J. von Uexküll

In the nineteenth century, faith in progress was the order of the day, and a concomitant conviction was that man's situation in the world would become more and more comfortable and that man, therefore, must necessarily become happier and happier.

Today we are by no means so certain. Science, technology, and industry have indeed ameliorated man's material situation, but it is becoming obvious that we may well have paid too high a price for our comforts. We have all the luxuries, but in order to attain them we may have sacrificed the necessities: air, water, and earth. For the first time in our history, our planetary capital is in danger.

It is possible that some brilliant discovery, social or philosophical or scientific in nature, may be able to assure us of a future supply of space, water, and oxygen. If so, who can tell what will then become of our animals? It will not be possible for some Noah of the twentieth century to embark alone on his ark, for man is not solely a creature of the forests, the rivers, and the land. His life is bound up with the lives of other beings, with skins and hides and furs. Behind him man has a million years of common existence with animals. A hundred years of sidewalks and streetlights, fifty years of automobiles, twenty years of nylon, ten years of plastics—these are not spans of time in which man's mind and soul can be formed.

We have discarded our age-old relationship with animals almost as carelessly as we discard a serviceable but "outdated" automobile. But it would be foolish to pretend that we are able to resume that relationship as casually as we purchase a new vehicle. Animals, as our ancestors knew them—even as our fathers and grandfathers knew them—no longer exist. We have only caricatures of those creatures which our forebears feared and loved, and sometimes deified.

However, not everything has been lost. We may have degraded and deformed our animals but somehow we still feel affection and respect for them. These sentiments serve to bind us to them, just as we were bound when man was young and his very life, in this world and in the next, depended on the life and death of animals. The animal, more than ever before, is loaded with taboos. Moreover, to a greater degree than ever before, it imposes on man a heavy burden of guilt.

Of all the mysteries which man has confronted, that of the animal will prove to be the most enduring.

It is strange for a man to be able to say honestly that if he had his life to live over again he would change nothing in it. Yet I can say it. It is not that I have always been happy, or fortunate, or even wise in my choices; but rather that in retrospect I see that my life, through no design of my own, has been filled with images of things and places which no longer exist except in my memory. From Djanet to Chichicastenango, from the Cape of Good Hope to Mandalay, from Timbuctu to Bali, from Tananarive to Mossâmedes, I have stored up civilizations, countries, peoples, and animals. There was a time when I half believed that my mania for seeing, observing, and knowing was the passion of a disordered mind. Now I can say that it was all for the best, and that I would change nothing of what I have done.

When I say that what I have seen no longer exists, I mean it quite literally. There has always been change, but until now it has been man who changed, or society, or fashion. The fields and the rivers, and the animals themselves, either remained the same or changed so slowly that the span of a man's life was insufficient to note that evolution. Man's surroundings appeared stable. Today it takes only a decade, or perhaps only a year, for the exterior world to change to the point of being unrecognizable. Our environment is changing faster than we are.

It would be impossible to count the number of times when, as I walked the streets of a city, I have been overcome with longing for the sounds of the jungle, for the gray lizards and the bullfrogs which were my fireside companions in the evening, for the unexpected and ever-marvelous sights which Africa, as I knew it, offered indifferently to both blacks and whites. Memories crowd into my conscious mind, like that of a bearer waking me early one morning to show me a family of crocodiles which had begun hatching only minutes before—fourteen perfectly formed babies, their bodies only half out of their shells. I see them today as vividly as I did then, and their evocation is accompanied by an acute sense of loss for that wild Africa, gone today, where I felt so much at home and at peace. It was inevitable, I know, that a continent so rich in manpower and resources would be developed. I loved it as it was, in all its grandeur and its primitive charm; but there is more than a grain of truth in the saying that primitive charm consists in the misery of other people. I know that the world cannot remain stationary, and I have resigned myself to the fact that the Africa I knew exists no more. Still, no other place that I have traveled, no matter how strange—and many of them were stranger than Africa—has ever equaled the Dark Continent in its abundance of life, its all-pervasive animal scent, in the feeling of blood and smoke which suffused the jungle.

Friends die, families scatter, couples separate, but animals go on. They replace themselves in such a way that one cannot even say that they grow old. Not long ago I returned to Tahoua to see the lions. They were there, as they had been many years ago, filling the delicate substance of the night with their cavernous voices.

Sentimentality? Of course. But how significant that in the final analysis the animal is the one most stable of our sentimental values. That is as it should be, for the animal is a stabilizing factor in human life. Although we often try to do so, we cannot separate the animal from its history or from its changing environment. If there is one truth that I have observed in my long experience with life, it is that life is not only a whole, but a continuity: There is not human life on the one hand and animal life on the other.

The vital current which unites man and animal flows in both directions. In our interior lives we are dependent on them; and they, in theirs, are equally dependent on us. Man is largely responsible for this solidarity among living things. Animals, especially young animals, become attached to humans—and I am not referring only to domestic animals. They seem to enjoy, or at least to seek, the company of man.

Zoologists employ a highly descriptive term to designate this phenomenon. They call it "impregnation." One impregnates an animal with a sense of dependence, and perhaps even of love. Man is not the only being capable of such a phenomenon. An animal of one species can also inspire the same sentiments in an animal of another species.

The significance of impregnation appears to be that a

living being has a need to be close to another living being. It is a manifestation of the ancient, deep-rooted solidarity of creation—as well as of the emotions observed in the waiting room of any veterinarian: A man loves a horse which loves a dog which may love a duck or a cat or an old shoe. . . .

In the encampments of certain Amazonian tribes (the Choroti and the Ashluslay, for example), one finds not only the usual domestic animals, but also a large number of tamed wild animals: wild pigs, nandu, otters, cranes, and, above all, wild ducks, which are the playmates of the children. Most often, the Amazonian Indians do not deliberately set out to tame these animals. The animals themselves seek out the humans and make the first advances. This is by no means an unusual occurrence. In Siberia the reindeer is said to be attracted by human urine, and this is the explanation offered for the presence of these animals around the camps of the Tchouktches and the Samoyeds. In Africa I have seen similar manifestations of the infinite curiosity of animals with respect to man among jackals and antelope; and in the Caribbean I have seen it among agoutis. This attraction, however, should not be construed as the first step toward domestication. As we have already noted, domestication does not consist in the taming of a wild animal, but in modifying it—that is, in an act of zoological creation. Many species of animal live cheek by jowl with humans while preserving their freedom intact. Some of them—birds and rats, notably—have adapted to the world of man and have learned to take advantage of what it offers. They eat from man's table, so to speak, just as the boar, the deer and the ox ate from that of our ancestors in the primeval jungle. Often they exercise astonishing ingenuity in so doing. There is a species of bird, the great tit, which in several British cities has learned to peck holes in the cardboard milk containers left on doorsteps; and they have even learned to distinguish, by color, the containers of cream from those of milk.*

It is evident that some animals have not only accustomed themselves to man, but have also adapted very well to man's own environment. In such circumstances it is difficult even to know of which animal one is speaking. When we speak of the great tit, for example, do we mean the great tit before its introduction to milk containers, or after?

Such questions are not merely imaginative exercises. They are indicative of a situation in which animal life now appears zoologically confused. What has happened is that we have allowed some species of animals to evolve, to adapt, to incorporate themselves into our lives and to become attached to us, but without ever considering anything other than our own pleasure and advantage. We have allowed other species to disappear or to be spoiled without even taking notice. We are just beginning to awaken after a period of indifference—an indifference based on our conviction that as humans we are infinitely superior to the animal kingdom. That conviction is rather recent in origin; it is, in fact, part of our heritage from the eighteenth century, and it had its roots in the seventeenth, in the systems of Descartes and of Malebranche (who used to beat his dog in order to prove that the animal felt no pain), in the mechanistic explanations of Buffon, and in the sterile quarrel concerning the respective roles of intelligence and instinct.

It is anomalous that man, who for so many thousands of years considered himself as the inferior and the servant of the animal, ended up believing himself to be entirely different and infinitely higher in the hierarchy of living beings. Only our stubbornness in demonstrat-

*W. Kühnelt, *Ecologie générale.*

ing our superiority to our own satisfaction could account for such a conviction; and only that stubbornness can explain the fact that in the ancient world as in the Middle Ages, among both civilized races and "primitive" cultures, the animal was treated with greater esteem than in modern times. Even the seventeenth and eighteenth centuries were too preoccupied with man to worry much about animals. The romantics—the poets and the painters—were the only ones who were interested in them, not as reflections of man's glory, but in themselves.

It has only been a little more than a century since the attitude of civilized man began to take a turn for the better, a beginning which was marked in Europe in 1860, when at the request of General-Count de Gramont, founder of the Animal Protective Society, a law was passed in France which for the first time prohibited cruelty to animals. To be sure, the animals covered by this law were domestic animals, and especially the horse, which was the foundation of the economic system of the nineteenth century as well as the mainstay of its *beau monde.*

It was this same nineteenth century, however, which gave birth to extraordinary cruelty toward troublesome wild animals both in Africa, where lions were slaughtered, and even in Europe: the wild boars of the Ardennes, the bears of the Pyrenees, and the last wolves on the Continent. Hercules and Theseus were still public heroes worthy of emulation in their efforts to free the earth of the monsters who were man's enemies, and one never tired of praising those massacres aimed at the extermination of "vermin"—the vermin, in this case, being lions in Kenya, kangaroos in Australia, and screech owls in France.

The truth was that the animal in general had been devalued in the name of science and of religion. Domestic animals were regarded as worthy of protection, but the wild animal was hated and condemned and was hunted relentlessly. This unreasoning attitude persisted in full vigor until the middle of the twentieth century. Then, suddenly, in the past twenty years, an about-face has taken place. The wild animal has now been rehabilitated. It is widely admired and defended, sometimes passionately. For the second time, civilized man's attitude toward animals has changed radically. It seems unlikely that even that most fashionable of new sciences, ecology,* would have been sufficient to unleash such a widespread movement. But commitment to ecological effort both private and public, along with the creation of preserves and parks, with a vast increase in tourism, and with the constant exposure of animals on television and in publications, have all combined to awaken a new spirit of respect and affection for animals.

This is not an illogical development. Respect for animal life, as we have repeated throughout this book, is a sentiment which goes back to our most remote past—a sentiment which has now been brought to the fore once again by the pressure of circumstances. As we have already remarked, the more man is cut off from nature, the more he longs for the life of nature. Thus, while the animal kingdom is an integral part of the human experience, today it has been rendered totally dependent on that experience. There has always been a dominant species on the earth. Today it is man's turn; it is up to him to decide what to do with the animals now that they have lost their strictly utilitarian value for him. In his heart, from an emotional standpoint, man has already reached a decision. He is opposed to the killing of animals and to the extinction of species. What concerns him is the search for the means to implement this ill-defined conviction. He is aware that it is not enough simply to desire the well-being of animals, but that he must also make it possible for them to live in

*The word is less recent than the phenomenon. It was coined by Haeckel in 1870.

conditions which conform to their physiological, climatic, and—especially—psychological needs.

More and more, man appears to be obsessed with life—a bizarre affirmation when one considers the wars, massacres, and genocides of the twentieth century. Yet man is always able to find a social, political, or demographic justification for his crimes. It may well be that the people responsible for such atrocities make use of their affection for animals as a form of self-justification.

It may also be, however, that the apparent contradiction between contempt for human life and respect for animal life goes deeper than that. Georges Gurvitch says: "The inviolability of human life was not originally a matter which fell under the protection of penal law. Human life was not considered sacred, and murder was not a sacrilege."* What was a sacrilege was the desecration of objects and beings which fell under the public taboo—such as animals. In a very real sense, therefore, animals were once regarded as more worthy of respect than man himself.

We speak of protecting our natural resources and we shed tears over the fate of baby seals and giant penguins. Yet when we go out into the country for a weekend or into the mountains or woods for a vacation we hardly ever leave our automobiles. We never stroll among the trees or look up at the sky or peer down into a lake. Even at twenty miles per hour, how can we see the kinglet wren, which is the lightest of the birds; or the roe, as she nibbles at the first buds of spring; or the fox, as it leaves its lair at dusk for an evening of hunting?

The French and the Americans have at least this in common: We both believe that there are no more animals except in zoos and preserves. And we both act as though we can approach animals only by means of a

* *Vocation actuelle de la sociologie.*

mighty vehicular procession, bumper to bumper, encased in a chassis of steel and enveloped in a cloud of gasoline fumes. Yet we have persuaded ourselves that on weekends we are able to return to nature and to plunge into the world of animals. We are not ill-intentioned; it is just that we have been misled. For between nature and us, between the life of animals and our life, a solid wall of commercial duplicity, trickery, and confusion has been erected. In two or three generations the distance between the animal and man has been increased to the point where we have forgotten completely what we once knew of the animal's role, and of its behavior and psychology. Animal life, which surrounded our ancestors and the presence of which they perceived instinctively, no longer has meaning for us. It does not touch us. Its sounds have been drowned out by the clamor of our automobiles, television sets, and stereophonic equipment. The roar of our machines has stifled all that our environment once had to say to us.

There are many people alive today who remember when camping meant hiking out into the countryside, into the woods, or up into the mountains, pitching one's tent on a grassy knoll or on the slope of a hill, and going to sleep while listening to the sound of the nocturnal animals. It meant being separated from a sudden shower only by a fragile shelter, and rising at dawn. It meant, in a word, living in conditions which approximated those of man when he truly lived "in nature." Camping today means automobiles and house-trailers and blaring radios and television sets in those "campgrounds" which are the cultural concentration camps of our time.

The fact is that although we flock to films about animals and buy books about them in unprecedented numbers, we continue to work against nature and against the balance established by nature. It is as though we were compelled to destroy nature in order to assure ourselves of man's grandeur and of mankind's continued progress. Outdated as such concepts may be, they are still everywhere with us. We still take outrageous pride in "reclaiming" land, in draining marshland, in destroying forests so as to build highways. All these things are regarded, as the killing of animals once was, as victories of man over nature, of mind over matter, of courage over untamed ferocity.

"Since the nineteenth century," Jean Dorst remarks, "we have been persuaded that man is able to transform any natural habitat on the face of the earth, and that this transformation will automatically result in a substantial benefit to man. This postulate, which is still accepted in many otherwise well-informed circles, is grossly erroneous, as is demonstrated by the series of recent financial and technical failures all over the world. . . ." The phenomenon described by Jean Dorst is precisely the attitude which has led to a pernicious practice common in the twentieth century: the casual, arbitrary destruction of the vegetational cover of the earth. We are not the first to do so. The Greeks did it; and our immediate forebears did it in Black Africa. It was and is what the experts in an egregious misuse of the term call "reclaiming" land. It was by virtue of this process of reclaiming that a part of the American continent has been condemned to aridity,* and that today in Nigeria almost a million acres of land are lost every year through erosion. Apparently we have learned nothing from such disastrous mistakes. Even now, devotees of progress are congratulating themselves, and one another, on the inroads being made into the Amazonian jungles.

One of the most deeply rooted and harmful of

*I am referring to the American dust bowl, from which the wind, every year, removes some 200 million tons of soil, with the result that millions upon millions of acres have been ruined. The creation of a federal soil-conservation service has not prevented several reenactments of this catastrophe. In Texas, for example, several hundred thousand acres of wheat were lost in 1965.

contemporary dogmas is that which maintains that human interference in nature, in addition to being infallibly beneficial, is always inspired by rational, prudent, and worthwhile considerations. Nothing could be farther from the truth. The principal motives for such intervention have always been greed, an appetite for wanton destruction, superstition, ignorance, laziness, lack of reflection, and a penchant for violence.

Destruction, when it is accomplished by means of bulldozers, has an element of candid violence about it. It is a demonstration of man's willingness to overcome all obstacles so that his will may be done. Within that context the destruction of a forest, let us say, may be explained as an unabashed and exuberant show of power on man's part. That is bad enough; but we are not content with our bulldozers. We now make use of a more insidious weapon. The most frightening thing about this new weapon is that it is seldom brought into play solely for the purpose of killing. Its popular name is pollution, though its proper name is poison. It plays a major role in the ecological crisis of the late twentieth century by reducing still further the habitable area of animals as well as of man. The oxygen which is necessary to support life in the water has now virtually disappeared, for example, in the Baltic. In the past two decades, the lead fallout generated by American automobiles has doubled over Greenland. Cases of the pollution of cow's milk by various insecticides are reported frequently, and in concentrated milk the poisons are also present. An investigation which followed an epidemic of digestive disorders among wet-nurses in New York disclosed that 80 percent of the mothers breast-feeding their children had DDT in their milk.*

Man is defined as a social being. What makes man social, however, is the fact not only that he lives in

*W. Kühnelt, *Ecologie générale.*

groups, but also that human groups combine with other species to form communities of mutual aid and mutual service. This is a truth which we have not forgotten. We no longer recognize that human society is not exclusively human. Nonetheless, it is not, and never has been, so. From the time that he appeared on earth, long before the domestication of animals, man has lived in a mixed society; that is, a society composed of men and animals. "If it is true that we exist spontaneously with other men," writes Dr. Lanteri-Laura, "then it is equally true that we exist just as spontaneously with an entourage of animals."*

Yet, as the human element in this community increases in size, the number of species comprising the animal element is decreasing. We may describe this situation as being the result of a "conquest"—a much abused term—as part of man's program to conquer the earth, space, and the animal kingdom. It, too, is part of our nineteenth-century heritage, when the concept of conquest (as in "the conquest of science") was part of the notion of infinite progress. So thoroughly have we conquered the animal kingdom, in fact, that we hardly know today what to do with those of our "enemies" which survive. Only now does it occur to us that it might have been better to develop a method of coexistence than to indulge our taste for domination.

We are reaping the fruits of that indulgence today. In order to remain in contact with animals one must lead an extraordinary life. Yet a large part of what I might call our interior capital depends on animals. It is certain that a hunter of mammoths or a trapper of rhinoceroses had more opportunity to accumulate a store of rewarding experiences and to resolve difficult problems

*In *Psychiatrie animale et troubles du comportement,* Lanteri-Laura continues: "During childhood we take cognizance of the existence of other humans, but also of the existence of forms of life less individualized than that of humans but quite different from that of mere objects. Thus, we must certainly include the experience of the existence of animals among the essential categories of human experience."

than, say, a rider of subways. It is hard to doubt that life 20,000 years ago required more ingenuity and more attention from man than it does today. We complain that people are cold-hearted, jaded. Is it possible that our dissatisfaction has something to do with our isolation from life even in the midst of life? Is it perhaps because our animal horizon is now so circumscribed?

If there is any merit in this book it is that it may compel the reader to realize that the relationship between man and animal has changed drastically in the second half of the twentieth century. We are living through a social and biological revolution, and we have arrived at the moment of truth. We must either condemn the animal irredeemably, or we must find a new place for it at our sides, a place in which the animal will play a new role.

The cause of this revolution is essentially that space for wild animals has become increasingly scarce, and that it will become even more scarce. By the year 2000 there will be 7 to 8 billion humans on earth, and by 2020, 14 billion. Within ten years the urban population will have doubled. In Europe, one farmer out of two will have to leave the land. The population growth, the multiplication of means of transportation, the development of urban and suburban centers at the expense of open spaces, will leave less and less space for nature and for the animal at liberty. This is the biological dead end toward which we are heading.

It must be admitted that man's presence on the planet has been an unending source of destruction. Our very existence ravages the earth and causes the disappearance of interdependent vegetable and animal species. In the fifth and fourth millennia B.C. the Hercynian forests were destroyed. In the third millennium the Mediterranean forests disappeared. It took only a hundred years to destroy the forests of America; and the African jungle has been nibbled away in the past decade. Now we are starting on the Amazonian jungle.

All the formulas that we have developed in order to provide a substitute for wildlife are nothing more than stopgap remedies; and all of them are to be condemned to a greater or lesser degree. Our zoos, preserves, and circuses are only pretexts for exhibiting animals, and criticism of them will increase in severity until, finally, the growth of human population and industrial development will reduce them to virtual nonexistence.

The saddest and most recent animal story to be made public illustrates strikingly what we have said concerning the present-day relationship between man and animal. The story begins near Paris, in the famous zoological park of Thoiry. The lions of the park are so well cared for that they bear many young. By the spring of 1972 there were sixty-five lion cubs at Thoiry. The owners decided that sixty-five was too many and proposed sending the healthiest of them to Africa, where lions apparently were becoming more scarce than in France. A home was quickly found for the cubs. The national park at Niokolo Koba, in Senegal, had no lions of its own and declared that it would be delighted to take in the animals. The cubs were therefore put into boxes and shipped by air. (They appeared on television, balls of downy fur, not yet old enough to be sure of their footing. . . .) They arrived safely in Africa and after a brief stay in an enclosure were turned loose in the brush. These, however, were not African lions. They were French. They had nothing in them of fear, or violence. They did not flee from humans. In other words they were totally unequipped for life in the jungle. They did not even know how to hunt, for Thoiry is no place for a cub to acquire such skills. Therefore when they grew hungry in Africa they did what they could: They killed a donkey and mauled three rangers—before the eyes of a group of terrified tourists.

But that is not the end of the story, or of human folly.

Since the lion cubs were too "dangerous" to be left at liberty, they were deported to the Hann Zoo at Dakar. Having tested freedom, the animals—by now they were full-grown lions—had developed a taste for it. One night there was a report that lions were loose in the streets of Dakar. The police, the fire department, and the army (in full battle dress, with helmets and automatic rifles) were called out. By dawn there was nothing left of the lions. Their bloody carcasses lay on the sidewalks of the city, their eyes closed forever on the cruelty of a world in which there was no place for them. Senegalese commandos had their pictures taken, standing next to the dead lions like so many Hemingways.

The tragedy of the lion cubs of Thoiry is a perfect summary of all we believe about animals. We still think of them not as living beings, but as objects. We still believe that we can move them from place to place, transplant them from one environment to another, and force them to live lives for which they are wholly unprepared. We are astonished and horrified when a wild animal in such a situation becomes man's enemy once more, when it escapes, and perhaps kills. Then, those who hunt down such an animal are regarded as laudable.

We take great pride nowadays in our love of animals. Yet this is how we show that love.

This is not to say that there are not many perfectly sincere animal lovers and protectors of animals in our time. The young, particularly, have taken the cause of the animals to heart. We hear a great deal about baby seals, and screech owls, and storks; and the new generation is at the head of these conservation crusades.

The case of the storks deserves particular mention. These birds are part of the folklore of Alsace, in France, where they go every spring to build their nests. In the past few years the number of storks has decreased alarmingly. In 1960 there were 145 nesting couples. In

1971 there were only eighteen. There is much debate concerning the reasons for this disappearance. Some say that the television antennas on the roofs keep the storks from building their nests. Others maintain that it is the birds' long migratory voyage—they cross the Sahara, migrating to Senegal—which kills them; not the distance, but the high-tension cables encountered en route, the hunters and trappers in Tchad, and the machine gun-happy soldiers of the Republic of Mali.

The Alsatians, subscribing mostly to the last explanation, decided to keep the storks from migrating. The method adopted was to cut a few feathers. The stork, once these feathers are removed, seems to lose its migratory urge, perhaps forever. In any event, by this method a variety of sedentary storks was created and they are being bred like geese. They are fed vitamin-impregnated chopped meat.

Such solutions to particular problems are always possible, especially when in our efforts to preserve a species we turn its members into objects with which we may do as we wish. But what will happen if this method is applied on a universal scale? Will entire nations set themselves up as defenders of predatory animals and others as protectors of their prey? Will we eventually go to war to protect our frogs from the aggressions of some stork-loving country? Will there by bloody battles between monkey-lovers and leopard-lovers?

Such questions are absurd on the face of them, but no more absurd than the premise on which they are logically based, which is the belief that we can save screech owls or elephants or tigers or storks as individual species. This conviction, from which we are apparently unable to free ourselves, has its roots in the doctrine of fixed species as set forth in Genesis: God created the animals one after the other, ending with man. Each species then exists in isolation from the others, never evolving, never being affected by other species, or by climate, or by its living conditions. Such was the pre-Darwinian view of life, a concept which we reject intellectually but to which we still adhere emotionally. Life, in that sense, does not exist in reality. In nature there are only biological communities, aggregates of vegetable and animal life which belong to a certain habitat and which are in continual interaction.

Thus, when man destroys the flora or the fauna in an area, or changes the proportions of the species living there, or destroys one species and introduces a new species, he is really destroying the habitat by plunging it into disorder.

We may form a thousand leagues dedicated to saving owls and cheetahs and we will have accomplished nothing. What we must save is the totality of nature: those complex ecological systems of checks and balances which have been developed through the evolution of centuries. For all living species, far from being isolated in the pre-Darwinian sense, are actually members of alimentary chains* and form well-defined biocenoses or ecosystems.†

If there were not such solidarity among plants and among animals, and between plants and animals, human interference would not have such far-reaching consequences. The fact is, however, that the living world is a chain of individual lives which may be broken at any of its links.

Quite recently naturalists have decided to rush to the defense of the American alligator and the African crocodile, both of which are predatory animals and neither of which have enjoyed a particularly good reputation.

I have seen many crocodiles in Africa and on

*The term alimentary chain designates a series of associated species, each of which lives at the expense of that which precedes it in the series.

†A biocenosis is an ecological unit comprising the animal and vegetable population of a certain habitat. An ecosystem is the structural complex which envelops, in a single functional unit, the biotope and the totality of the animal or vegetable organism which exists within it.

Madagascar, and there has never been one that I found particularly attractive. Yet my wife and I have often bathed in rivers infested with these animals and we have never had an unhappy experience with them. There are, however, many stories of women and children being cut in two by the snap of their great saurian jaws, and I tend to believe that at least some of those stories must be ture. Certainly, the African crocodile is a formidable animal, sometimes reaching twenty feet in length.*

The American alligator is somewhat smaller and its snout is flatter and more square at the tip than that of its African relative. The American variety is also comparatively inoffensive, at least in my opinion. In the Florida Everglades they are great attractions for tourists, who come for many miles to "feed the alligators." This sympathy between man and alligator is quite new. Until very recently crocodiles and alligators were being hunted mercilessly wherever they could be found, so that ladies and gentlemen of fashion might exhibit purses, briefcases, wallets, and shoes of "genuine alligator." The high price fetched by alligator skins even induced poachers to invade parks and preserves in search of the animals. It was difficult to muster public opinion against such a slaughter, for the crocodile and the alligator were "disgusting" animals; while the shoes made from their hides were greatly esteemed. It was not until twelve of the twenty-one species were listed in the Red Book† of the International Union for the Conservation of Nature that we became aware, belatedly, that even crocodiles and alligators play an important part in the biological equilibrium and constitute one of the links in the alimentary chain. In the Everglades, for example, the alligator creates pools by digging in the damp soil. These pools become the lairs of fish which

*Their ancestors, some 170 million years ago, were even more fearsome, and attained a length of over fifty feet.

†The Union's list of endangered species.

eat mosquito larvae. The alligator, therefore, has been revealed as one of the animals which we must keep from extinction if we wish to preserve a certain natural aggregate of animals beneficial to us.

If we were really as isolated in creation as we believe ourselves to be, then paradoxically there would be no solution to the problem of our relationship with animals. The conflict between the "progressives" and the conservationists would fizzle out in polemics, campaigns, and crusades, with one side doing battle on behalf of industry, technology, and progress and the other on behalf of nature. What saves man, as it does the animal, is the fact that for better or for worse he is a being who lives in groups. In the preceding chapters I have perhaps too often referred to man as an isolated being or as an immutable prototype. Man, in that sense, does not exist in zoology any more than he exists in politics or economics. He is a fleshless ghost. What we have always had are human associations—societies which developed customs, fashioned life-styles, and promulgated laws; societies which, above all else, developed and *changed.*

Again, we are living in an age of change. One area of that change is in our attitude toward animals. We are seeking to define a new relationship with them, and it is within ourselves and within them that we must search for that definition. But we are creating enormous problems in this search when we decide artificially to prolong a system of coexistence which we can justify only in terms of sentimental attachment to animals. That attachment must, at the very least, be genuine, be contained within proper limits, and be translated into institutions and laws inspired by the needs of the animals themselves rather than by human emotion or by vestiges of magico-religious systems.

We expend our energy to protect animals against slaughter and extinction. That is as it should be. But we must also struggle to free ourselves from the spirit of awe, superstition, and adoration with which for uncounted millennia man has regarded animals—a spirit of which we are not even conscious, but which nonetheless dictates our attitudes. We must demythologize and desacralize the animal and thus free ourselves of a sense of guilt in its regard. Only then will we succeed in finding a reasonable place for the animal in contemporary society.

From time immemorial, animals have been linked to human anguish. They have been divinized, turned into caricatures of man, made to bear the burden of our sexuality and our frustrations, transformed into surrogate mothers and fathers. How can the animal in the twentieth century escape from its own past or from ours? How can even the death of an animal not serve to remind us of our own mortality? We cannot save the animal from death any more than we can save ourselves. What we can do, however, is to exorcise the phantoms by means of which we hope to escape our own destiny, either by substituting animals for ourselves or by sparing them in the hope that we ourselves will be spared.

I said in the beginning that a book on animals must necessarily be a book on death. Some domestic animals are raised to die; that is, to be slaughtered for food. Wild animals, likewise, have a right to death, which is the great regulator of life—especially on the preserves. It is not death from which we must save the animal, but needless suffering. Death is part of the animal's environment as it is part of our own.

But not any death. There was a time when death came as the blood of the animal flowed in sacrifice. Today it is in danger of flowing in man's wars. Do we have the right to recruit dolphins and seals to fight our battles for us, as the U.S. Navy is doing? Do we have even the right to multiply our zoos, circuses, and marinelands? I think not. We must recognize the fact of death; but this does not allow us to regard death with indifference or to inflict it with cruelty. On the contrary, sensitivity is the foundation upon which a new understanding between man and animal must be built. It is what men and animals have in common, and the means through which they may approach one another. It is sensitivity which dictates that not all animals are alike and that they must not all be treated alike. Some species—once more numerous than they are today—are able to live in understanding with man. Some species are able to bear life in zoos, while others suffer even in the semicaptivity of preserves. These latter animals must be isolated and protected in inaccessible sanctuaries—as long as we can do so. But here again there are some necessary distinctions. When man offers protection at any cost, when he intervenes constantly in the parks and preserves, he is not necessarily making the lot of the animals more bearable. Curiosity, the offer of food, even the process of taming, are not proofs of affection and interest. We find it difficult not to become overly emotional over animals such as bears, elephants, dogs, and cats. With respect to these animals we have become overprotective masters just as we sometimes become overprotective parents. In dealing with animals, sensitivity is essential; but it must be kept within the bounds imposed by reason.

One could go on indefinitely debating the question of why man remains emotionally involved with animals even when the latter have lost all utilitarian value. One consideration, however, underlies all such discussion: Man is unable to be content in a totally artificial environment. Our ancestors lived in forests, even in trees. They were hunters, shepherds, breeders, planters. Man cannot hope to forget, in twenty years, what he spent so many thousands of years in learning. He cannot rid himself of the behavioral patterns acquired of necessity in those various situations. In vain does he lull himself with synthetic substitutes: a tiny plaza at the entry of a skyscraper, squares, "green spaces" which do not even qualify as gardens, lapdogs, riding-school horses, or even home-bred lions.

It is true that our situation has changed enormously. Once, we fought to win space from the animals. Today we must fight to leave a little space for them. Once, we experimented with animals to develop speed, strength, and docility. Today we exercise our ingenuity to preserve their wildness, their nobility, their pride—everything that makes of an animal a being so singular that it is irreplaceable by any technological creation.

Daniel Rops once said that "In every study of animals, there must be a humanistic intention." If contemporary man believes that he can escape from his anxieties by reawakening his affection for animals, if he believes that he can suppress his own taste for violence by enclosing wild animals in zoos and preserves, then he has been seriously misinformed. He has confused a love of nature and animals with tyranny.

Here, obviously, we are far from a discussion of the material means of solving the problem of our relationship with animals. Yet any solution to that problem must ultimately be a spiritual one. Jean Plaquevent, a theologian, has put it very nicely: "Man can be truly complete, wholly aware of himself, only when he plunges his roots as deeply as possible into the whole extent of the animal world. It is only there that his soul will finally be joined to the rest of nature, from which he is inseparable."*

It is my own opinion that we will never succeed in solving the problem of animal space, life, and liberty at a purely material level. Nor do I believe that we can look to a "return to nature" as a new Golden Age for mankind. (To which nature would we return? To that of the Magdalenian era? The medieval period? The first few years of the twentieth century?) We can no more

**Le Mystère animal, de la bête à l'homme.*

restore the forests of the Mediterranean than we can bring the aurochs back to life or turn Florida over to the jaguars. But there are some things that we can do. We can, for instance, dismantle the wall of incomprehension that has separated man and animal since the seventeenth century.

We have already made the first step in that work. We have begun to realize that man is not independent of nature. We have sensed that we have need of all forms of life in order to preserve the quality of our own lives. We have begun, in other words, to do what we must do. Threatened by our own technological civilization, we can save ourselves only by rediscovering our animal nature, by accepting ourselves for what we were in our most distant past, and by building a community, one composed of both humans and animals. It must be a new community, different from that which existed 20,000 years ago, or even two centuries ago.

How can we go about this work? Must we develop a new philosophy, a new religion, new doctrines, a new way of life? Certainly, all these things are necessary. It will not be the first time in his history that man has undertaken such a task. It would be no more difficult, let us say, than the creation of the religious art of Lascaux, of the mythology of the Greeks, of the Sevenfold Way of the Buddhists, or the Sermon on the Mount of the Christians.

Indeed, what we propose has much in common with these examples. Our observations and suggestions on man and animal are nothing more than an attempt to define a rational and generous attitude by means of which man may accommodate his own behavior to that of others—the others in this instance being animals as well as other human beings. After all, we have no reason to believe that we now stand at the summit of human development, at the pinnacle of evolution. Human life is something which we must invent with each new day.